ANCESTORS OF THE CRAFT

The Lives and Lessons of Our Magickal Elders

Edited by
Christopher Penczak

COPPER CAULDRON
PUBLISHING

Credits

Editing: Christopher Penczak
Proofreading: Karen Ainsworth, Michael Cantone, Antonella Ercolani, James St. Onge, Tina Marie Van Orden
Cover Art: Kala Trobe
Cover Design: Jonny LaTrobe-Lewis
Layout & Publishing: Steve Kenson

A Note on the Text

Due to the mix of submissions from authors from both America and Britain, we have chosen to keep the authors' native spellings intact, to reflect their own preferences, culture, and style, rather than standardize the entire book to match U.S. or U.K. norms.

A Note on the Cover

Cover painting graciously provided by author and artist Kala Trobe, with cover design by Jonny LaTrobe-Lewis.

Copyright ©2013 Temple of Witchcraft, All Rights Reserved. Individual contributions are Copyright ©2013 (or earlier) of their respective authors. *Ancestors of the Craft* is a trademark of Copper Cauldron Publishing, LLC, in the United States and/or other countries. No part of this work may be reproduced, stored in a retrieval system, or transmitted in any form or by any means, without the prior permission in writing of the Copyright Owner, nor be otherwise circulated in any form other than that in which it is published.

For more information visit:
www.templeofwitchcraft.org
www.coppercauldronpublishing.com

ISBN 978-0-9827743-9-7, First Printing

Printed in the U.S.A.

I am the key.
I am the gate.
I am the tree,
watcher of fate.
I am the root.
I am the stone.
Secrets of ages,
scriven on bone.
I am the crown.
I am the art.
Jewels of the Mysteries,
Bones of the Art.
I am the path.
I am the way.
Keeper of crossroads,
forever this day.

On this sacred crossroads,
in the center of the worlds,
we call to the world between.
We call to all the spirits of the living,
and we call to the spirits of the dead.
We call to the Hidden Company of our Timeless Tradition,
Brothers and Sisters of the Eternal Sabbat.
You who gather close around the edges of our circle.
You who have danced within this circle,
be present here with us.
We seek your wisdom.
We are your descendants
and followers in your ways.
Hail and welcome.

— Steve Kenson, Temple founder, at Stonehenge, August 2011

TABLE OF CONTENTS

Introduction 1

Part One: Lightbearers of a New Age
Helena Petrovna Blavatsky (1831-1891) 8
Alice Bailey ("AAB") (1880-1949) 19
Mother Shipton: Visionary or Witch? 30

Part Two: Founders of Modern Magick
Aleister Crowley and the New Aeon: Beyond the Legend of Infamy
    (1875-1947) 34
Dion Fortune (1890-1946) 45
The Alphabet of Desire: Austin Osman Spare (1886-1956) 55
Yeats' Stolen Children: William Butler Yeats (1865-1939) 61
Franz Bardon: 20th Century Magus (1909-1958) 65
Kenneth Grant (1924-2011) 76

Part Three: Crafters of the New Witch
Gerald Gardner (1884-1964) 89
Doreen Valiente: Mother of Modern Wicca (1922-1999) 99
Alex Sanders (1926-1988) 119
Charles Godfrey Leland (1824-1903) 124
A Pellar's Fate: Robert Cochrane (1931-1966) 128
Sybil Leek (1917-1982) 139
Daughter of the Night: Rosaleen (Roie) Norton (1917-1979) .. 142
Felicity Bumgardner 156
Searching for Pearls: Dorothy Clutterbuck (1880-1951) 168
Stewart Farrar (1916-2000) 181
The Roebuck Within: Evan John Jones (1937-2003) 186
The First Family of Feri: Victor Anderson (1917-2001), Cora Anderson
    (1915-2008) & Gwydion Pendderwen (1946-1982) 198
Gwen Thompson (1928-1986) 210
Elizabeth Pepper Da Costa (1923-2005) 221
Lady Sheba (Jessie Wicker Bell): Witch Queen (1920-2002) 227
Hans Holzer (1920-2009) 230
Scott Cunningham (1956-1993) 238
Edmund "Eddie" Buczynski, Jr. (1947-1989) 248

Herman Slater (1938-1992) 251
Philip Emmons Isaac Bonewits (1949-2010) 253
Ted Andrews (1952-2009) 257
Andrew Chumbley (1967-2004) 262
Passing the Rattle: The Goddess Magic of Shekhinah Mountainwater (1939-2007) 267
Shawn Poirier (1967-2007) 272

Part Four: Personal Guides on the Path

Bragi and the Dead 276
Elders of the Coven of the Catta: Lady Phoebe and Lord Merlin 282
The Lady Circe 295
George "Pat" Patterson 302
Pattalee Glass-Koentop "Lady Phoenix" (1943-2002) 306
Ted Mills (Lord Theo Mills) 308
Margaret Maher Hoffman Hickman 311
In Memoriam: Fuensanta Arismendi Plaza (1950-2010) 315
Denessa Smith (1965-2008) & Tempest Smith (1988-2001) 319
Jane Y. Rojek (1947-2011) 323
Deborah King 328
Rosalie Penczak (1944-2011) 330
Epilogue: What is Remembered, Lives 341
Contributor Biographies 353

INTRODUCTION

The origin of this book is found in the fact that many intelligent and well educated modern Witches don't know their own history. The modern Witchcraft and Wicca movement doesn't have a very long history, and even at this point, many key figures are unknown and forgotten, let alone the historic yet enigmatic figures whose work supported the rebirth of Witchcraft but whose writings you won't find stocked on the shelves of your local bookstore.

To remedy this, in the seminary training of the Temple of Witchcraft, each student must complete a report on a craft elder, living or dead, as assigned by the instructor, and then share that report with the rest of their classmates. As we continue, the list grows and grows, and the number of students in any given class is too small and does not cover the entire list. And as the years go by, the list continues to grow, including some obscure, but important figures. And sadly as the years go by, many who were in the category of the living, are now standing with the dead, making it even more important to remember their contributions.

While we focus on our teachings as a Temple, we are broad based, drawing from a wide variety of sources in Witchcraft, folklore, occultism and cultures. Our understanding of history should reflect that wide based approach, but not sacrifice depths for breadth. We need to go both wide and deep in our understanding of the Craft. We are at a crossroads at the dawn of the new century and the New Aeon, like the early Christian Church in its most Gnostic and personal forms. The more free form Christians became a dogmatic institution that typified the Age of Pisces. We could have a tendency to do that as well, as some strains of Neopaganism become more conservative and seek recognition by the mainstream. We must find a way to go deeper in our work, scholarship and mystery without becoming crystallized and frozen, an unevolving tradition. That which ceases to grow and develop must die. We must keep our freedom without becoming shallow or trite. Many expressions for many people are needed. Who shall guide us on this path? Those who have pioneered and come before us. Their lessons, what they have and have not done, shall guide us.

Recently, while attending a class by one of the authors in this anthology, Gardnerian elder Rich Wandel, I was struck by his unconventional wisdom. While sharing information and insights on Gerald Gardner gleaned in his research for the contributing article, he discussed how the gods choose those who have the correct flaws, not necessarily the correct virtues, to get their work in the world done. And good old Gerald has the perfect combination of flaws and idiosyncrasies to get Wicca popularized and herald the rebirth of the Craft. If many of his more sober minded and better respected peers' wishes were followed, such as the beloved Doreen Valiente, many of us might never have found the Craft. It would have remained too secret and too hidden. His freedom in initiating, his desire for publicity and his global background made the perfect mix to get the word out and make it more accessible to the mainstream who sought out magick and Witchcraft. His flaws worked in our favor. Makes you wonder which of your flaws the gods are currently using, doesn't it?

Gardner was but one magickal current that added to the mix to make our own work possible in the world. The author Kenneth Grant, devotee of Aleister Crowley, makes an interesting observation in his book, *The Magical Revival*. While an advocate for Aleister Crowley's Thelema as being the rectifying force amongst all magickal traditions for the New Age, he cites that the three major currents of magick were held by three of the most influential and innovative occultists of the early twentieth century, all peers of each other. While he described these currents differently, I immediately recognized the Three Soul model found in various forms of Witchcraft. Although most likely coming to us in the popular current through Victor Anderson and his Feri tradition of Craft, and popularized by Starhawk in her classic *Spiral Dance*, many other traditions, including the Temple of Witchcraft, use the concept of three selves, most simply a higher self, middle self and lower self. And these three currents corresponded to them.

Crowley's current of Thelema focused on the higher self, what he called the Holy Guardian Angel or Bornless One. His invocation to the Bornless One, *Liber Samekh*, is a core practice to Thelema. One must not only have Knowledge of Conversation of the Holy Guardian

Angel as described in Qabalistic attainment, but union with it to proceed further up the tree in the stages of initiation.

Dion Fortune, on the other hand, focused on the development of the balanced personality, what Grant called the lower self, but what we call the Middle Self, the personal self. Her interest in psychology, and focus on polarity workings and balance tends to focus on being the most functional in day to day life, and the use of magick to make one a better, more whole person in society and relationships. She was an advocate of assuming and dismissing the magickal personality, as evidenced in her novels such as *Sea Priestess* and *Moon Magic*. In many ways the main character was her magickal personality, but she did not enter delusion and was able to function quite effectively in her life, running an organization of occultists not just from the astral, but in day-to-day affairs. She has been described by Alan Richardson as the Shakti, or priestess of the New Aeon, to Crowley's prophet, but there is a third, connecting element often overlooked due to the obscurity of his work.

Austin Osman Spare never really started an order for magicians, though his work eventually led others to name him the "grandfather" of the Chaos Magick movement started by Peter Carrol with his methods of sigilization and the Alphabet of Desire. Grant links him with the "voodoo" traditions of trance, sex, and art working through the subconscious or unconscious. While Voodoo has much to do with these topics, Austin Spare had little to do with the religion of Voodoo, and while a patron saint to Chaos magicians everywhere, he apparently identified as a Witch due to his training, albeit a non-traditional one. His work would best be embodied by the magick of the Lower Self, the intuitive, instinctive and primal self that one could equate with the unconscious.

The same triad of current impulses can be found in three different traditions that formed the underpinning of the occult movement where Crowley, Fortune, and Spare could form their influential ideas, namely in Theosophy, Spiritualism, and Ceremonial Magick. They form the foundation of what we think of as modern metaphysics, or New Age, today.

Spiritualism formed a core of psychic exploration with the realms of the dead, and sometimes those of higher spirits. It formed in a

Christian framework, but essentially worked with the skills of the lower self, the intuitive or psychic ones. In essence, the practice of Spiritualism was very simple and many participated in it, even simply by attending séances if not being a medium proper. It provided a new challenge to mainstream ideas of religion and communication with the spirit world, hearkening back to a tribal ideal. All the tribal traditions from Africa to Asia, from North America to South, considered primitive by Victorian England, also had great reverence and communication with the ancestors.

Theosophy, as started by Madame Blavatsky, used the mediumship techniques of Spiritualism and much of its flash and show, but ultimately was focused on higher worlds of ideals and information. Their dead were the Mahatmas, the Masters, who had merged with their Higher Self in enlightenment and escaped the Wheel of Rebirth. The lore was high minded, focused on the transcendental forces of the cosmos rather than the everyday. She brought eastern lore of India and Tibet to the west and its focus not on salvation, but enlightenment. The tradition continued on with a variety of personalities, not always staying in the same name as Theosophy, but spiritually holding true to the original impulse. Alice Bailey and Rudolph Steiner carried onin Blavatsky's footsteps.

Ceremonial Magick was the third piece. Though seemingly focused on the Higher Self, it stressed the intellect and was best pursued by those with wealth and means in society. Follwoing the occult manuscript traditions of philosophers such as Cornelius Agrippa and Francis Barrett, along with a healthy dose of Rosicrucianism and Masonic lodge traditions, it flowered with the Hermetic Order of the Golden Dawn, of which both Crowley and Fortune were members.

A third manifestation of this triad comes about with the rebirth of Witchcraft and ties us to those whom we identify with as our spiritual ancestors in Witchcraft. The two priests most often credited with the revival, Gerald Gardner and Alex Sanders, were the most influenced by the traditions of Ceremonial Magick. Gardner padded his book of shadows with passages from the Key of Solomon and spent time with Crowley, creating the legend that Crowley was actually the creator of Gardnerian Wicca, not Gardner. Sanders has profound experience with the Magic of Abramelin the Mage, the source material for Crowley's *Liber Samekh*, which altered the course of his life and put him on the path of the public Witch. If you felt Gardnerian Wicca was peppered with ceremonial references, then Alexandrian Wicca was even more filled with Qabalstic rituals and symbolism. These two tended to serve the gods, knowingly and unknowingly through virtues and flaws, but all in a love and service to a higher power. They embody the current of the higher self.

The mother of Wicca, Doreen Valiente, on the other hand, best embodies the balanced impulse of the Middle Self. Profoundly influenced by Dion Fortune and her refurbished feminine archetype of the Witch as priestess, she removed much of the Crowley inspired material from the Gardnerian Book of Shadows when Gardner's High Priestess, with his permission, and replaced it with beautiful liturgical poetry that it still used today by Wiccans. One need only read the novels of Dion Fortune to see her influence in Doreen's own work. They were two powerful women of magick in times when that was even harder than it is today. Doreen kept the most balanced relationship with people, and those still alive today who knew her speak of her with great affection and kindness. She went back to folklore, kept grounded and looked for real world, practical solutions to problems at hand. That brought her into conflict with Gerald at the end, as well as with the keeper of the third impulse, Robert Cochrane.

Born Roy Bowers, and writing under the pen name of Robert Cochrane, he was the magister of the Clan of Tubal Cain, a hereditary tradition of Witches in what is called today Traditional Craft, to distinguish it from the ceremonially and now New Age influenced Wicca and initiatory formal British Traditional Wicca. It is claimed that he coined the term Gardnerian as an insult, to separate Gardner's brand of Witches from more traditional ones. There were no books to his rituals. The tools were simple. The gatherings occurred outdoors in nature, and involved more ecstatic techniques, in tune with our Lower Self. While decidedly different from Austin Spare, one can look at Spare's art, and see the sabbat of the Traditional Witch.

Here through three generations we see three basic currents of magick manifest, illustrating a chain of history from the ancestors to us, if we only take the time to look, to listen, to experience the larger pattern and ask ourselves where we fit into it. The Temple, and many other traditions, seeks to bring the three currents together into one system of magick, with each practitioner finding their own balance. Through knowing our past and our ancestors we can better participate consciously in our future. Through our magick we can contact them directly for blessing and guidance, and many of us do. Hopefully we do not repeat their mistakes and use our virtues and our flaws to advance our Craft.

I've asked many honored elders, peers, friends and students to write about those they feel passionate about remembering. Some have direct personal connections or lineage connections. Others just share a spiritual kinship. Many of the essays are very formal and academic. Others are anecdotal remembrances. But each has a passion for their subject, their ancestor, to be remembered. We've divided the anthology into different themes and eras, keeping those bio-sketches of those of a similar type together, to keep a thread of continuity rather than organize it haphazardly or simply by chronology. Beyond the modern era elders, we shall also explore some personal guides and teachers who might not earn a place in the history books of the Craft, or even be directly connected to Witchcraft, magick or metaphysics, but through love and devotion, wisdom and teaching, have earned a place with one of our authors, and, ultimately, in this little book of history.

All of the funds generated from this anthology go directly to the Temple of Witchcraft, a 501(c)3 nonprofit religious organization, to further its work in education and community. None of our authors make a royalty, nor does the publisher keep a profit. We thank you for supporting the Temple of Witchcraft in its mission of Love, Power, and Wisdom for the Great Work.

Blessed Be,
Christopher Penczak
Samhain 2011

Part One: Lightbearers of a New Age

Helena Petrovna Blavatsky
(1831-1891)

By Kala Trobe

Alone, the One form of existence stretched boundless, infinite, causeless, in dreamless sleep; and life pulsated unconscious in universal space, throughout that All-Presence which is sensed by the 'Opened Eye' of the Dangma.

This description of the cosmic state of 'unbeing' is taken from *The Book of Dyzan* (allegedly of ancient origin) which provided the lynchpin for Helena Blavatsky's *The Secret Doctrine*, and which she claimed was scribed by 'a people unknown to ethnology...written in a tongue absent from the nomenclature of languages and dialects with which philology is acquainted'. Ancient, possibly Tibetan, most certainly replete with semiotics designed to aid mankind's evolution and remind the spirit of its Akashic origin; her proclamations varied. Whatever her truth of the moment, Blavatsky's followers came to believe that the literature she produced was of arcane spiritual origin, maybe the work of an ancient people of Atlantis, perchance from another star...while skeptics claim that she 'cribbed' the manuscript from the Rig-Veda and lateral religious texts. Certainly the 'opened eye of the Dangma' reflects the Eye of Siva, and is symbolic of the searing insight of the ascetic whose sole focus is Spirit: devotees who eschew social mores, wearing *vibhuti* instead of clothes, begging for alms in the quest for yogic union with Godhead...who, like the lady herself, throw their all into dissolving the Veil between the worlds.

The authenticity of Blavatsky's work is, in my opinion, a moot point. She wrote in great waves of history, philosophy and cosmic evolution: the 'forest of symbols' is easily obscured by focussing on the species of tree it contains, and the type of bark there-on. Her semiotic woodland spreads from the steppes of a pioneering spirit and expansive mind across the nineteenth century into which she was incarnated, and we are still finding new routes through those trees, and new flowers amongst its infrastructure.

Born in 1831 to the noble family von Hahn in the wilds of Eurasia, Helena Blavatsky was a fearless equestrienne, a Russian warrior-princess, from girlhood almost living on horseback, riding up to the Tibetan borders which surrounded her family's land, where she would talk with Tartar nomads in their own tongue. She also spoke English and French, and received the comprehensive education bestowed upon 'ladies of means' at that time. Because of her proximity to Tibet, she had an early knowledge of Buddhism combined with the Russian Orthodox Christianity of her social class and caste. By the time she wrote her first opus, *The Secret Doctrine* (1888), she had travelled widely in Russia, Tibet, India, France, Egypt, Greece, and England, thereby acquiring a comprehensive understanding of a formidable range of religious beliefs. Small wonder, then, that her 'received' stanzas contain a variety of sources. She already understood the principles of Collective Unconscious and Archetype later to be clarified and immortalised by Jung. Indeed, all rays of manifestation emanate from the same Akashic source, and contain the Essence of the Divine, and their similarities should surely be embraced as a return to spiritual truth, rather than vilified as 'plagiarism'. Hair-splitting scholars were a major irritation to this Binah-wave of a woman, herself the expression of a collective experience pertaining to the Asiatic Ama, infinite Soul of the Creatrix.

On a microcosmic level, Blavatsky was an independent Leonine lady upon whom the gods of Karma had smiled, and a natural Feminist. At seventeen she was married to a wealthy older man, General Nikifor Blavatsky, but after a mere three weeks, she abandoned 'old whistlebreeches' as she dubbed him, opting to make her own way in the world. All she maintained of her marriage was the name, which was soon to become famous and infamous by turns. Continuing her childhood passion, she worked on horseback as an acrobat in a travelling Circus, making a ducat or a dime wherever she landed. She craved visceral experience and adventure. She wrote constantly, and meditated where and when she could. It is said that she smoked (tobacco and marijuana) like a chimney, and drank and swore like a trooper; facts impossible to verify, but the passionate image certainly fits.

Barely surprising that it should be such an intrepid woman who is largely responsible for the return of the Goddess to consensual reality in the Western world. Blavatsky lived, and wrote about, the Cosmic Reawakening. Her writings incorporate much more than sexual politics and religious outlook, however; like any comprehensive Scripture, they span the range of human experience.

One cannot summarise such a vast body of work in a short essay, but let us briefly look at some of the major Trees of Life in her literary and magickal forests, and at the most relevant branches thereof.

A cornerstone of Blavatsky's Theosophy is belief in 'the Hidden Masters' who preside on the Astral/Causal levels and who are devoted to aiding mankind's spiritual, social and material evolution. The sudden popularity of Theosophy in the early 1900s ushered forth some rather strange 'Masters', such as British Lords Erskine and Eldon, and other characters whose socio-political status seems by far to outshine their spiritual import, at least during the personal life specified. Others are more easy to recognise as potential guides, such as the Master Jesus, Melchizedek, and Djwal Kuhl. These beings tended to appear in person to major Theosophists: Blavatsky for example first ran into the Master Morya in London in 1851.

Apparently by moonlight near the Serpentine, Hyde Park, young Helena was approached by 'a tall Hindu' in the company of 'some Indian Princes'. He asked her 'to do certain work' for him. Only a woman with a sense of humour and fearless spirit would take this encounter with such equanimity: a group of dusky men by a city river at night, a demand for services...she seems only to have perceived it all as mystically encouraging.

He appeared again later in her life, apparently going so far as to write letters to her family, as did Kuthumi. The latter purportedly contacted her aunt, Lady Nadejka Andriewna Fadeeff, who in 1870 was concerned that Helena may have died as it was so long since the family had heard from her. The aunt reports: 'I received a letter from the Being whom you call, I think, Koot-Hoomi, which was brought to me in the most incomprehensible and mysterious way, in my own house, by a messenger with an Asiatic face, who vanished before my eyes...(it)...begged me not to be anxious and assured me that she was safe.' Similar letters, purportedly from Kuthumi and Morya, are now housed in the British Library.

Alice Bailey claims to have had almost identical experiences to HPB's; likewise with 'a man in a turban' who materialised in 1895 in her grandparent's library, eventually requesting her co-operation as his 'psychic secretary'. Annie Besant and C.W. Leadbeater, disciples of Blavatsky's who later caused the schism famously associated with deification of Krishnamurti as Metraiya, attested to numerous such encounters: 'I have on many occasions seen the Masters appear in materialised form at the Headquarters at Adyar', Leadbeater conveniently reports, for example. This particular person seems to have been a pederast and deeply corrupt character, so how genuine these experiences were is open to debate. It is possible that imagination has again provided 'the ass that carries the Ark' – but, the occasional weirdo aside, if the volumes of work produced by Bailey, Besant and Blavatsky reflect the depth of their belief in the sanity and authenticity of their experiences, then the 'Ascended Masters' may convince.

With each of the masters is associated an 'Ashram', a native Ray of Being. These may be summarised as follows:

- The First is led by Morya, Helena's personal guru. The themes of the First Ray Ashram are Willpower, Politics, and universal Occult matters. Clearly Blavatsky saw power, wealth and global decision-making as positive, rather than as a superficial quest for personal glory. If the 'leaders' of her heyday weren't conscientious, then the powers that guided their hands must have been, in her opinion, due to their ineffability. The colour of this Ray is electric blue, its Theosophical 'residence' on the material plane is Darjeeling in India, and it relates to the Throat Chakra. Its planetary ruler is Pluto/Vulcan. In Qabalistic terms this corresponds with the diamond-white light of Kether.

- The Second Ray Ashram is that of Love combined with Wisdom, which manifests as Education. Its Masters include Kuthumi (Koot-humi) and the Tibetan Master, Djwhal Khul. The colour here is indigo, which personally I relate to the Ajna Chakra: but the Theosophists ascribe the Crown Chakra. Its location in terrestrial terms is Shigatse in Tibet, ruled by the illumination of the Sun and the expansive generosity of Jupiter.

- The Third Ray Ashram is the province of 'Paul the Venetian'. Philosophy, active Intelligence and the Rise and Fall of Nations are his major preoccupations. The history of civilisation is choreographed here in the Green Ray, which pertains to the Heart Chakra, parts of the South of France, and purportedly New York, and to Earth and Saturn. It is understood in the greater Western Mystery Tradition as a Pagan Ray sacred to

Netzach on the Tree of Life, to nature Devas as well as the themes already mentioned.

- The Fourth Ray Ashram is focussed on the Arts and Humanities, and on achieving Harmony through conflict. Drama is therefore pertinent to it. The Masters specific to this Ray are Serapis, Jupiter, and 'the Master P'. Its colour is yellow, its geographical location Luxor in Egypt, and it relates to the Base Chakra and to the Moon.

- The Fifth Ray Ashram is the part of the spectrum in which Science abides. Hilarion rules it; the Master said to have dictated The Voice of Silence to Helena Blavatsky and The Light on the Path to Mabel Collins. Its colour is orange, its place Crete in Egypt, and it relates to Venus and, we are told, the Ajna Chakra.

- The Sixth Ray, which is red, is sacred to all of the world's religions. Here, the essential tenets and Truths of each are formulated: the rhetoric and corruption that exists in every religion is created by men, not Masters. Jesus is one of the latter who abides here. Mount Lebanon is its Theosophical attribute on the terrestrial plane, and Mars, Neptune, and the Solar Plexus Chakra are also ascribed.

- The Seventh Ray Ashram is concerned with the translation of material consciousness into a spiritual format, such as ritual. This is dominated by the Master Rakoczi, who reputedly included in his former lives those of Roger Bacon, Christian Rosencreuz, and the Comte de St Germain. Its colour is violet, its geographical location Transylvania, where Blavatsky roamed in early life, and its Chakric correspondence is the second, or Sacral. Its planet is Uranus.

In the same way that the individual Rays are facets of a larger Ray before it is passes into the Spectrum, Blavatsky's teachings, in her own words, 'belong neither to the Hindu, the Zoroastrian, the Chaldean, nor the Egyptian religion; neither to Buddhism, Islam, Judaism nor Christianity exclusively. The Secret Doctrine is the essence of all these.' The intent behind her teaching is to remind mankind of the force behind the form. She aimed to reignite the fire of Spirit in humanity: 'to show that Nature is not simply 'a fortuitous concurrence of atoms', and to assign to man his rightful place in the scheme of the Universe; to rescue from degradation the archaic truths which are the basis of all religions; and to uncover the fundamental unity from which they all spring; finally, to show that sacred Nature has never been appreciated by the Science of modern civilization.' 'Modern' at this point was 1888, and Blavatsky's tracts follow in the wake of the Industrial Revolution, Darwinism and the Great Exhibition in London, featuring the latest scientific discoveries and 'fruits of the Humanities' in the Western world. Christianity felt the threat of Science, and Science was turning its nose up at 'Mystical Truth'. It was Blavatsky's mission to do what Blake and Whitman were attempting through poetry; what Dickens and Hardy hoped to achieve through their novels; and what Disraeli was defending in his political stance: to prevent the loss of 'angelic' sentience via the depletion of magical, mythological and religious impulses of atheistic skepticism, the new sidekick of Science. Blavatsky hoped to bring the Alchemist back into the scientific laboratory to work alongside the Logistician, as did Carl Jung in later years.

Perhaps Helena Blavatsky's personal life ought not to concern us: certainly it is the work of such luminaries that endures and speaks for itself; yet the subject is alluringly open for debate. Her work is deeply original – she is the person first responsible for weaving Eastern spiritual philosophies in with Western; and her influence has been so vast in the world of esoteric study, that it's natural to be curious as to where it all came from, exactly, and what the vessel might have been as a person. Blavatsky says 'Ascended Masters': an analyst would read this as 'Collective Unconscious' or 'Ghost-Gurus of the Mythopoeic Imagination'. The ramblings of a stoned lunatic is the usual judgement of the cynical educated, while 'satanic' is the general verdict of the Fundamentalist Christian.

We can only judge by our personal reaction to her works. How Blavatsky reached this prolific state is a point of curiosity merely. I have always assumed that she did indeed use marijuana and alcoholic spirits to aid her work – not a technique that would prove effectual for most people, but Blavatsky was not 'most people'. The reason for this belief is prevalent reports that she always had 'a roll-up cigarette' burning between her fingers, was perpetually surrounded by a fog of aromatic smoke and a tipple or three, and that she wrote in such a visionary, erratic manner that ordinary consciousness is definitely in question. Additionally, almost every biography mentions her fondness of joints. Conversely, in the biography Blavatsky and her Teachers (1995), Jean Overton Fuller states: 'Nobody even saw Madame Blavatsky take hashish, and it is in the highest degree improbable that she ever did so'. Yet she admits of Blavatsky's extraordinary visions: 'she could not have attributed it to her recollection of past incarnations, for she did not at that time believe in reincarnation. It would be thirty years before she accepted that doctrine, and then, not as the result of spontaneous recall'. Blavatsky talks of 'the images of the symbols of all religion and creation moving before my inner eye in impossibly quick succession.' Additionally, Fuller is the sole biographer to claim directly that Blavatsky did not 'take hashish'.

Helena Blavatsky's ardent student Alice Bailey says of *The Secret Doctrine:* 'I was intrigued by it but completely bewildered. I couldn't make head or tail of it. It is a difficult book for beginners for it is badly put together and lacks continuity. HPB starts with one subject, wanders off to another, takes up a third at length and – if you search – you find her returning to her original theme sixty or seventy pages further on. HPB would write page after page, never numbering the pages, and simply throw them on the floor beside herself when she had finished them. When she was through writing for the day, Mr Wright and her other helpers would collect the sheets and endeavour to get them into some kind of order and, as he said, it is a wonder that the book is as clear as it is'. This slothful attitude certainly suggests the intervention of drugs. With a team of eager helpers, however, the Vision found a Voice. The publication of *The Secret Doctrine* in 1888 became a major event in global esoteric history.

Blavatsky's other 'magnum opus' is *Isis Unveiled*, originally published in 1877. On the title page, Helena Blavatsky calls the book 'A Master-Key to the Mysteries of Ancient and Modern Science and Theology'; it is arranged into two concomitant sections: Science and Theology. The essential thesis is to demonstrate the unity between the two, decades before Quantum Physics corroborated the facts. Indeed, it might be said that atomic theorist Susskind and his 'microscope gang' were merely continuing and affirming the work of this Russian visionary, by making it all the more obvious to the public that the Hindu scriptures predict Science. Relativity and Time are major themes of both. Physicist Richard Feynman once remarked: 'I think I can safely say that nobody understands Quantum Mechanics' – and certainly the same may be said the minutiae of Helena Blavatsky's teachings.

'Matter is Spirit at its lowest point of manifestation, and Spirit is Matter at its highest', Blavatsky remarks of the Law of Synthesis, echoing the Hermetic tenet 'As Above, So Below'. In 1875 she decided to form a group promoting esoteric research and 'the Universal Brotherhood of Humanity' – this was the Theosophical Society. It pledged 'to be without distinction of race, creed, sex, caste and colour'; quite revolutionary in the time when racial segregation was more common than not in the Hindu, American and British cultures of which Theosophy was mainly comprised. The society was intended 'to encourage the study of Comparative Religion, Philosophy and Science', and 'to investigate unexplained laws of Nature and the powers latent in man'.

Colonel H.S. Olcott, one of the founding members, declared alongside HPB that they were inspired to start the Society by the Hidden Masters, also referred to as Adepts, Mahatmas and Masters of the Wisdom. Ironically, this stance quickly became popular amongst the social and educated elite, satisfying the intellectual curiosity and need for tenable spirituality and 'manifestation' which many schools of Christianity actively prohibited. Theosophy was 'full of Eastern promise', and with its beliefs based on global events such as the arcane drowning of Atlantis and the upcoming Age of Aquarius, it offered both excitement and a sense of purpose, along with a comprehensive discipleship. Its adherents were primarily well-to-do, educated, and ready to throw mind, body and soul into such an absorbing and original religion: and so they did.

It was not long before Helena Blavatsky was the main luminary of the Theosophical Society, the greatest Prophetess of 'the New Era'. Her work has inspired and infiltrated numerous areas of esoteric study and development across the world, but especially in Europe, the UK, India and the USA. Without her, metaphysical researchers and exponents such as Annie Besant, Dion Fortune, Alice Bailey, the modern Freemasons and the Golden Dawn would have operated in an entirely different manner. There would have been less mythic scope, a diminished geographical perception in the work (many religions ignore the truths inherent in the world beyond their immediate vicinity, thus becoming 'cultic': someone as well-travelled as Blavatsky could never allow this), and words such as Kali Yuga, Chakra, Karma and Akasha would be a great deal less prevalent.

Most important, in my opinion, is Blavatsky's rejuvenation of the Dark Goddess in Western cosmology. She regenerated the sense of mysticism arguably abandoned by Christianity in the Mediaeval era, with such charisma that she inevitably attracted envy, and with it, virulent criticism. Sadly, what most people remember today is that she was 'proved' by the Society for Psychical Research to be faking some of the manifestations that occurred during her psychic sittings. These habitually involved her 'talking' with Masters (usually Kuthumi), which participants would perceive as a soft tone, like a low bell chiming, or as I tend to imagine it, like the deep vibration of a Tibetan singing bowl. It was originally noted that the sounds sometimes occurred when Madame Blavatsky moved her arms in a certain manner. Unfortunately she was indeed drawn – perhaps through financial necessity – into the parlour spiritualism so popular amongst the fainting classes of the Victorian era.

Because of the prevalence of fakery in such scenarios, coupled with her strong personality, Blavatsky aroused hostility and scepticism as well as awe and inspiration. In 1885 she was openly accused by the Society of Psychical Research of being a fraud: by 1886 they had recanted and published an apology, but by then the papyrus of her credentials was indelibly blotted. One can imagine that a feisty lady such as Madame Blavatsky might be tempted to play with, and possibly to, her audience: her intelligence was peerless (her aunt speaks of near-genius from an early age), and she may have decided to 'give 'em what they want' – which in those days was table-tapping, tipping, ghostly materialisations, and 'apports'.

Whatever the veracity of her 'sittings', Blavatsky's writing speaks for itself with quintessential brilliance and authenticity. She finally vanished behind her beloved Veil of Nuit-Isis in 1891. Her sixty years of life had been a cataclysm of originality, etheric and intellectual cross-reference, esoteric and religious synthesis. Without HPB, modern Magick would be a very different menagerie of thought-forms; she enriched her legacy in equal measure with the burnish of the Orient and the dark lustre of the Feminine Divine.

Contemporary witches and mystics of many paths and 'traditions' owe this Astral Ancestor a debt of gratitude, for she spoke from the heart of Original Spiritual Truth, non-denominational and available to all equally, translating its almost implausibly ancient glyphs into the active, evolutionary energy that still flows through, and spiritually vivifies us, today.

Resources

Three Remarkable Women – Harold Balyoz (Altai Press, 2000)

Isis Unveiled – Helena Blavatsky

The Secret Doctrine – Helena Blavatsky

ALICE BAILEY ("AAB")
(1880-1949)

by Kala Trobe

This 'astral elder' is of particular interest to me as she turns out to be one of my physical ancestors too. The significant thing, though, is that I had no idea we were scions of the same French Huguenot stock until, in ultra-modern style, I 'Googled' my own surname (by birth, La Trobe-Bateman) and discovered that Alice, whose books I had known for years but under Alice Bailey, had shared my own unusual appellation before she married. Having rushed to the family tree, I ascertained that she was in fact a daughter of my forebear Frederic Foster La Trobe-Bateman, and Alice Hollinshead, a descendant of 'the Chronicler' of the same name, but following their early deaths, was raised by my great-great-grandparents, John Frederic and Anne Fairbairn La Trobe-Bateman, at Moor Park, Surrey. Her spiritual 'eccentricities' had since been obscured by the somewhat embarrassed members of our otherwise mundanely illustrious family; indeed, many records acknowledge only her sister Lydia, who cut a pioneering career in science. Not only this, but as with most records of women, birth-names are obscured by those of marriage, and Alice married twice, becoming first Evans and then Bailey; the ages-old headache of those interested in female ancestry! By the time I stumbled upon this bloodline connection, I had several books of my own already in print on subjects almost identical to hers, and was on the verge of discovering other young female relatives similarly-inclined. All of us share a proclivity for Hindu-Buddhism, the elevation of Good Will in world consciousness, and the application of metaphysical principles to day-to-day life. The esoteric DNA matrix apparently manifests in perpetuity!

A spiritual seeker ill-defined by the social protocols and conventional Christianity within which she was raised, Alice Ann La Trobe-Bateman found childhood difficult. In her Unfinished Autobiography, she describes the culmination of circumstances which caused her to begin adult life as an evangelical Christian, pontificating primarily in her native UK, then in India, eventually progressing into Theosophy. Intelligent and self-critical to the point of thrice attempting suicide in early life, she was always tortured by paradoxes, particularly that of Leadership versus Ego. In due course she would create the spiritually unifying Lucis Trust with her second husband, Foster Bailey, in the USA. Her best-known contributions to modern spirituality are the phrase New Age, which she was one of the first to employ in its current 'esoteric' sense, and the popular prayer for the ascension of humanity's consciousness, The Great Invocation (received in 1937), a 'Mantram for the New Age and for all Humanity':

From the point of Light within the Mind of God
　Let light stream forth into the minds of men.
　Let Light descend on Earth.

From the point of Love within the Heart of God
　Let love stream forth into the hearts of men.
　May Christ return to Earth.

From the centre where the Will of God is known
  Let purpose guide the little wills of men –
  The purpose which the Masters know and serve.

From the centre which we call the race of men
  Let the Plan of Love and Light work out
  And may it seal the door where evil dwells.

Let Light and Love and Power restore the Plan on Earth.

The 'Christ' mentioned here is not so much an individual as a current: it is Christos energy, as represented by Tiphareth in the Qabalistic Tree of Life. Most religions yearn for a World Teacher or Saviour, identifying this Sublime Being under such names as the Christ, the Lord Maitreya, the Kalki Avatara, the Bodhisattva, and the Messiah, terms which are used in Christian, Hindu, Muslim, Buddhist and Jewish versions of the Great Invocation; Alice latterly perceived these to be one and the same. This Unitarian concept follows in the footsteps of Theosophy by bridging Eastern Philosophies with those of the West. Participants need only to be 'bastions of Good Will' and engaged with the elevation of the entire species unhindered by nationality, class, gender, level of spiritual advancement, or native religion. In these senses she strongly resembles Wellesley Tudor Pole (founder of Chalice Well Gardens in Glastonbury), Sir George Trevelyan, and other great thinkers of 'Aquarian' philosophy.

Alice was born in 1880 in Manchester, England. The men of the family were highly skilled water engineers and architects, primarily – an interesting physical parallel to her own 'spiritual hydraulics' and 'Astral temple-building'. One of her great-uncles, Charles La Trobe, was the first governor of Victoria, Australia, who instantly defined his stance by banning the shooting Aboriginals for sport – astonishingly, this was hitherto considered a gentleman's pastime. Another was Benjamin La Trobe, architect of the USA Capitol building, an illustrious traveller and polymath. Her aristocratic birth provided the mixed blessing of a disciplined, well-educated childhood blighted by social protocol and religious expectation. Alice spent many of her younger days with a piece of holly attached beneath her chin, devised to keep her manner 'dignified'. Charity was supposed to flow from such 'noblesse', as were natural modesty and conformity.

Although other members of the family had included Christian mystics and artists (such as Pre-Raphaelite Edward La Trobe), in some cases visibly inspired by subjects as 'outré' as Greek mythology, and connections with visionary artist/poet William Blake are traceable via the Moravian Church of Fetter Lane, London, young Alice was given no access to the less conventional forms of inspiration, and mistakenly considered her forebears very dull indeed. When she became the prominent esotericist we know of today, mutual repudiation ensued. I have spoken with other living relatives of Alice's who consider her at best eccentric, at worst completely insane; the La Trobe/La Trobe-Bateman family lineage has long been plagued by the dichotomy of conventional versus innovative, religiously dutiful versus divinely inspired, and as Alice's great uncle Benjamin La Trobe might have put it: "Apolline versus Dionysiac". (This illustrious astral ancestor, Benjamin La Trobe or "BHL", also installed the first Lousiana Waterworks, designed the spires of St. Louis Cathedral, New Orleans, and was architect of Hammerwood House in East Grinstead, recently owned by the band Led Zeppelin... amongst many other endeavours.)

Her upbringing did however set Alice in good stead when it came to writing the twenty-five "AAB" books still in print today. The stifling orthodoxy of her native religion: High Church Anglican and Scottish Presbyterian by turns; and the social tedium of her class made her desperately seek something greater, something spiritually 'real'. From an early age she was tortured by her own 'bad temper' – which I personally translate as a rebellious streak perfectly natural under the circumstances, but in England the 'thinking classes' specialise in virulent self-criticism, and the belief that she was fundamentally 'deeply unpleasant' hounded Alice throughout her life. Her ongoing urge to sacrifice herself echoes this belief: starting with the attempted conversion to Christianity of the 'condemned masses', then moving to a physically abusive relationship with her first husband, Episcopalian priest and preacher Walter Evans, with whom she lived in America. Perhaps she would never had left him had it not been for the safety of their three young daughters; but this ranting, violent husband and father was thankfully abandoned by his womenfolk before he could maim them permanently.

Alice underwent further humbling experiences due to the poverty that inevitably followed separation from her husband, having to work in a fish factory for very little pay, for example. This was quite a come-down for a member of the British aristocracy, but she took it with humility. She became friends with many of the factory-women, and very swiftly shed any snobbery that may have lingered in her outlook.

It had been at the age of fifteen that Alice had her first full-on esoteric experience. On June 30th, 1895, she was sitting in the family library with nobody but the servants at home, when in walked – a man in a turban! She was more alarmed by his headwear, the likes of which she had never seen before, than by his sudden appearance before her. He said: "I am the Master, and I have work for you to do, young lady. But in order to serve me and the other members of the Cosmic Hierarchy, you must first improve yourself and make yourself into a suitable secretary for us."

Such apparitions were rather in vogue at the time, and one wonders how much of this alleged experience was actually the retrospectively imaginative 'ass that carries the Ark' – either way, Alice certainly determined at this point to make herself useful to Spirit. She first became a Christian missionary and preached to soldiers in Ireland (not exactly a heathen country however) and then she decided to head to India – possibly on the trail of her mysterious visitor, who had not reappeared since.

On her way to India, our little English lady learned another important lesson in humility. As she explains in her Unfinished Autobiography, there was a man on the ship who epitomised all that she felt she ought to take a stand against. He drank heavily, he smoked, he was raucously jovial, and worse still; he gambled! Scandalised, Alice did her utmost to give him a wide berth, praying in the privacy of her own cabin for the Angels to keep him far away from her, and, if they could see their way to it, to save him too. He was clearly a Lost Soul, an inferior creature mired in hedonism and gluttony. The fact that he was widely liked by her fellow travellers did not sway her judgement in the least. He was to be avoided at all costs. And, when she was able, she made her disapproval of him clear to all, with disparaging looks and thin-lipped mutterings of disdain.

They arrived in Bombay. For some reason Alice had not made arrangements to be met here – possibly because the chaos and sheer volume of people were unimaginable to her – and she found herself having to make her own way from the filthy, terrifyingly hectic capital city railway station to the Missionary project in Quetta. Nothing could be further from the calm green suburbs of Surrey to which Alice was accustomed: suddenly she was all alone with her luggage, surrounded by beggars screaming for baksheesh (alms), by warped and disabled peasants crawling in the dirt with goats and dogs, horned bulls wondering willy-nilly with painted bhindis on their brows, and a rabble of stinking, breeding, brooding and staring humanity such as she had never before beheld. Not to mention the heat, so stifling to her in her thick, prim coat and long Victorian-style skirts! Alice was overwhelmed, and believed that she would faint and be attacked at any moment. Trembling and sweating, she cast around for somebody to give her guidance and protect her from the dark, threatening-seeming crowds all around her.

"May I help you, my dear?"

Who should she turn around to behold but that 'lost soul' from the ship, smiling kindly at her and offering his arm in support? Despite the sanctimony she had inflicted on him throughout the voyage, and the measures she had wished to impose between this man and his pleasures, he was the sole person who had thought to ensure that the tense young lady was not abandoned. She accepted his offer with indescribable gratitude, and for the rest of her life, was never again judgemental about other people's 'bad habits'. This 'dissipated' gentleman had, in fact, redefined her sensibilities, thus enabling her to better serve the 'Hidden Masters' when the time finally came.

Alice spent several years in India, preaching, helping the sick, teaching children, and developing into a compassionate tour-de-force. Eventually she departed due to the dilapidation of her physical health. Once recovered in England's green and pleasant lands, she set out for the USA to continue her missionary work. In 1907 she met and married Walter Evans, the man who was to drive the final shreds of pride out of her, and with whom she had her three adored daughters, Dorothy, Ellison and Mildred.

It was not until 1919 that she was visited again by 'the Master of the Second Ray'. This time he announced that he wished to write books through her. Alice balked. Was she worthy yet? Worse, was she completely delusional? The mystically-minded reader will appreciate the dilemma of an apparition known to bear no relation to life as ordinarily perceived, which emanates intelligence indubitably singular, but which, as the conscientious visionary acknowledges, might be a delusion of Ego. How could Alice verify this vision, she asked? The Master told her he would give her time to intuit: Alice pondered, then decided that what she had here was, in fact, the purpose of her present incarnation. Being a fully functional mother, employee and member of society, she was clearly far from insane or narcissistic. Though some 'mystical' experiences are clearly self-obsessed fantasies in disguise, Alice concluded that she was too busy and too self-critical for this to be the current case. There was actual work to be done here, and surely the results would be the best gauge of the situation.

Thus began her career as 'psychic secretary' to Kuthumi and The Tibetan Master Djwal Khul; one which was to prove highly prolific and to last for the rest of her life. With the exception of the Unfinished Autobiography, Alice claimed to have authored none of her books. She was merely the 'pen pusher' receiving dictation from the Inner Planes, she maintained. It is certainly true that *A Treatise on White Magic*, *A Treatise on the Seven Rays*, *The Light of the Soul* and other of their 'collaborations' are highly technical and quite different to the freer flow of Alice's own prose, when she occasionally allowed herself to write it.

The teachings Alice thus received have provided an important contribution both to Theosophy and to World Spirituality. They can perhaps be summed up by the final line of the Great Invocation: 'Let Light, and Love, and Power restore the Plan on Earth'.

What, however, is this 'Plan'? Here, the cosmology becomes rather complex. The key points may be summed up as follows:

1. The approach of the Hierarchy – that is, the ten Masters of Wisdom who aim to help humanity in its spiritual evolution.

2. The return of the Avatar – usually referred to by Alice as 'the Christ', but the term is generic and means the spirit of positive redemption. The phrase has occasionally been updated to 'the Coming One', as this is not religiously specific, and is as pertinent to Jew, Muslim, Buddhist or Wiccan as it is to Christian.

3. The Science of the Seven Rays, in which human and spiritual consciousness are categorised according to seven different (but equally important) levels, each represented by a colour, position in the 'Cosmic Spectrum' and various other specifics. These are energy levels on which we operate as 'ensouling entities' and by which 'we shall find ourselves able to co-operate more wisely with The Plan as it is seeking expression at any particular time'. This system is seen by some as the psychology of the future.

4. The importance of Good Will and Right Human Relations. Though Alice Bailey has at times been vilified as anti-Semitic, such an attitude would clash completely with her belief that humanity is One, that all are striving towards the Light, and that every soul on earth ought to be free to ascend by its chosen means. All religious paths and impulses are respected within her cosmology.

5. A system of prayer and channelling of positive energies through the use of Triangles. This involves three people, not necessarily in the same location simultaneously, building an *Antahkarana* or 'Rainbow Bridge' from the mundane realms to the spiritual. The colours of the Seven Rays compound this imagery. It is facilitated by the meditative activation of the Great Invocation and by the beliefs outlined above.

Many of these principles will be familiar to those involved with Aquarian consciousness. Through the Tibetan Master, Alice Bailey pinpointed this era as the most relevant of all to the ascension of humanity, particularly in the West. The spiritual energies manifesting here will be climaxing, according to Djwhal Khul, 'between the years 1965 and 2025' – which of course tallies perfectly with the perceptions of most other 'New Age' philosophies, from the Mayan concept of 2012, to the post-1960s perception that now is the start of the Age of Aquarius.

In 1919, at the Theosophical Society's Krotona branch in Hollywood, Alice met Foster Bailey, whom she married as soon as her divorce from the abusive 'man of God' Walter Evans came through. Like her, Foster was spiritually-minded and devoted to the evolution of human consciousness. Both of them found the competitive nature of the Theosophical Society members and leaders to be a drain: as with many 'spiritual' groups, there were some within its ranks whose primary interest was merely their own place in the pecking order. For example, when Alice recognized one of the Masters mentioned at a Theosophical Society talk as the Kuthumi she had encountered in England all those years ago, and innocently remarked: "Oh then, He must be my Master, for I've talked with Him and been under His guidance ever since," the speaker's response was not encouraging or affirmative, as she had hoped, but rather, 'withering'. Alice (like Dion Fortune in her early days) was instantly perceived as an upstart. As she quickly realized:'Learning to hold one's tongue is essential in group work, and one of the first lessons which anyone affiliated with the Hierarchy has to learn.' It was experiences such as these which led Alice and Foster to set up their own Theosophy-based splinter group, the Arcane School, and its umbrella organization and publishing house, the Lucis Trust.

Bailey's writings teach meditation as a way of life, with a particular emphasis on group and moon calendar-orientated meditations. This is not to attain personal gnosis so much as to serve 'the Plan', since according to AAB, as she now became known: 'There is one Soul and one Plan for humanity, and the intention is thus to bring the human soul and the separated personality into a synchronized condition of unity and fusion.' This aim continues into the present: to quote the group's current manifesto: 'The objective of occult meditation today is the achievement of a perfect balance between the vertical life of the soul on its own plane and the horizontal life of the soul-infused personality within the world of men.' There is a direct parallel with witchcraft in that the Lucis Trust promotes a particular spiritual rapport with the Full Moon each month; a time, says AAB, when 'the will-to-good' is especially empowered. The New Moon is also deemed of particular importance, facilitating another positive wavelength to and from the Hidden Masters and the Cosmos at large. It is, in fact, modern witchcraft under another name, and it is likely that, had she been alive today, Alice would have be a great deal less oblique in her parlance and 'labelling'. After all, in the early days she wrote *A Treatise on White Magic* (1934) and *Letters on Occult Meditation* (1922) – and originally, she and Foster had named their publishing company Lucifer (the same light-bringing root as 'Lucis', obviously), so we can see that she was in fact attracted to this effective and modern vocabulary, but changed it to more innocuous phrases in order to pander to the hyper-sensitive Christian mores of the USA. One can only imagine the misunderstandings of the Christian community about such appellations as 'Lucifer'.

'The Souls of men are One' – this is a primary tenet of the Arcane School, which AAB founded in 1923 as a correspondence-based training course in 'The Science of the Soul'. The group emphasised that 'all claims to spiritual status' are defunct: we are what we produce and how we live, rather than how we perceive ourselves, and credit (as well as blame) belongs to us all, not simply to the individual.

The 'occult obedience' of man (that is, the obedience of the personality to the soul) is paramount to AAB's core ethics. Ideally, the mind will react spontaneously at the behest of the soul or 'Higher Self'. Eventually the soul and personality will become inseparable.

While a great deal of AAB's work is dense and bears the intellectual stamp of the Old Era, it has certainly served as a bridge to modern consciousness. In her lifetime alone, the Arcane School trained over 20,000 people: add to this the domino-effect of her books, and the ongoing work of the Lucis Trust. Always modest to a fault and, as her husband Foster wrote, 'All through her life, AAB shunned any statements of action which might be interpreted as claim-making, as to her own spiritual status', the quote probably most applicable to Alice Bailey comes from one of her main spiritual masters, the Master Jesus: 'By their fruits, shall ye know them'.

The fruits of Alice's labour are her books and, in turn, the many recipients whose minds and practices have been adjusted to receive this most crucial of evolutionary leaps: that of our transition from the Age of Pisces into the Age of Aquarius.

Recommended Reading

Bailey, Alice A: *A Treatise on Modern Magic, Discipleship in the New Age, A Treatise on the Seven Rays,* Unfinished Autobiography

(All Alice Bailey books are published by The Lucis Trust Publishing House, and remain in print.)

Balyoz, Harold: *Three Remarkable Women* – (Helena Blavatsky, Alice A. Bailey, Helena Roerich) – Altai Press, 2000

Schuchard, Marsha Keith: *Why Mrs Blake Cried: William Blake and the Erotic Imagination* – Random House, 2007

Mother Shipton: Visionary or Witch?

By Virginia A. Villarreal

"Very morose and big boned, her head very long, with very great goggling, but sharp and fiery Eyes, her Nose of an incredible and unproportionate length, having in it many crooks and turnings, adorned with many strange Pimples of diverse colours, as Red, Blew, [sic] and mixt, which like Vapours of Brimstone gave such a lustre of the Night, that one of them confessed several times in my hearing, that her nurse needed no other light to assist her in the performance of her duty."

These are the words that were said to describe Ursula Sontheil who was born to a 16 year old homeless prostitute in Norfolk, England in the year 1488. Her mother gave birth to Ursula in a cave in Knaresborough which is known as Mother Shipton's Cave to this day. Ursula was said to be the child of the devil and that is why she was born so hideous. She married a local carpenter named Toby Shipton when she was 24 years old. They never had any children but she was later known as "Mother Shipton" because she helped so many people. Mother Shipton was born with a gift of seeing the future and would tell the people what she saw as she saw it. She did not sugar coat the bad if bad was what she saw. She didn't believe in making things simple for the people she read for and wanted them to know what they were up against. If she saw tragedy coming she warned them so that they could prepare for the worst, but most people did not heed her warnings and regretted the consequences.

Mother Shipton lived during the time of Henry VIII and foretold England's defeat of France. She predicted the death of Cardinal Wolsey by telling him that he would see York but never enter it. He sent three men to threaten her to change what she saw and instead she told them that she saw that they would die on the pavements of York. Cardinal Wolsey traveled to York and climbed to the top of a tower where he was able to see the town of York from a distance but before he was able to go into the town a messenger from Henry VIII arrived telling him to return to London to be tried of treason. On the way back to London, Cardinal Wolsey died and the three men that he had sent to Mother Shipton died exactly the way she foresaw it.

She also saw the invention of cars, airplanes, submarines, ships made of steel, the telephone and even the Internet. She had seen the death of Henry VIII and the birth and death of his son, Edward VI who died shortly after being crowned. Mother Shipton predicted the reign of Mary and Elizabeth I and the beheading of Mary Queen of Scots. Most of her predictions did not become known until after her death in 1561. She was 72 years old when she died and had made many friends but also many enemies because of her frankness. In 1641, eighty years after her death, her prophecies were printed by an unknown editor. In 1684, Richard Head wrote about Mother Shipton's prophecies and for the first time introduced the story of her birth and her life. There are some that think that Mother Shipton was not a real person but a hoax made up to give England a soothsayer just like France's Nostradamus. What is known about Mother Shipton is that if she was a real person, she was a simple woman and was not worried about fame and fortune, she just wanted to use the gift that she was given to help other people. Some of her predictions are said to have been written by someone after the incident happened but those claims have not been proven. To this day the truth about the origins of Mother Shipton has baffled the world but one thing is true, Mother Shipton has intrigued the world and has made her cave a tourist attraction and made its location famous.

Mother Shipton's prophecies have also told of things that have not come to pass yet and that has to do with the end of times. At the time she lived she was called a soothsayer, a visionary and she was allowed to live but if she would have been called a witch who was the daughter of the devil, would she have been killed as all other witches of that era? Was she really a person or was she the invention of someone's overactive mind. This is something that we may never know but her name has carried her wisdom and sight for centuries.

Here is one of her prophecies about the future; can you tell what she is talking about?

I know I go – I know I'm free
I know that this will come to be.
Secreted this – for this will be
Found by later dynasty
A dairy maid, a bonny lass
Shall kick this tome as she does pass
And five generations she shall breed
Before one male child does learn to read.
This is then held year by year
Till an iron monster trembling fear
Eats parchment, words and quill and ink
And mankind is given time to think.
And only when this comes to be
Will mankind read this prophecy
But one man's sweets another's bane
So I shall not have burned in vain.

References

Wikipedia. Mother Shipton. Wikipedia.com. *http://en.wikipedia.org/wiki/Mother_Shipton*

Nexus Magazine: March 1995, Vol. 2, No. 24

Part Two: Founders of Modern Magick

ALEISTER CROWLEY AND THE NEW AEON: BEYOND THE LEGEND OF INFAMY (1875-1947)

By Paul Weston

I believe that Aleister Crowley was the most comprehensive prophet of the twentieth century in all of its diverse, ecstatic, terrifying glory. There are immediate problems in trying to understand why that might be the case.

Crowley has accrued around himself a remarkable legend of infamy. In the nineteen-twenties, during his lifetime, the British press described him as the "wickedest man in the world." "A man we'd like to hang." Here was the King of Depravity. A bisexual drug addict who practised the worst forms of black magic. Since his death the reputation has expanded still further until it's easy to find accounts describing him as a practitioner of human sacrifice.

One particular quote seems to represent the hardcore of the legend of infamy. It's in Crowley's 1928 book *Magick*, from a chapter entitled "On the Bloody Sacrifice." "For the highest spiritual working one must accordingly choose that victim which contains the greatest and purest force. A male child of perfect innocence and high intelligence is the most satisfactory and suitable victim." In a footnote Crowley then says "he made this particular sacrifice on an average about 150 times a year between 1912 and 1928." The quote is thrown up again and again in exposes by Christian authors and even allegedly serious occult writers. The very last sentence of Crowley's "Bloody Sacrifice" chapter says "you are likely to get into trouble over this chapter unless you truly comprehend its meaning."

So let's think about this one. We're being asked to take this passage as evidence that Crowley murdered 150 children a year from 1912 to 1928. That's over 2,400 of them. This would make him unique in the annals of crime. It's strange how he got away with it really. Rather odd that we have no record of any of the victims. No witnesses. No evidence. Although expelled from some countries and refused entry to others, he was never arrested for any offence, let alone served a jail sentence. Some of his books were banned, even burned as pornographic. He lost a libel action in Court. The little matter of those 2,400 child murders seems to have been ignored.

Perhaps there's another explanation. Crowley was a great jester and a man who loved to write in code. He put cryptic meanings into his books that only those with a certain commitment to the subject would be able to understand. Although he didn't mind being upfront and shocking in some of his poems, *Magick* was a serious work which he hoped to see remain in print and reach a wide audience. By 1928 he'd seen himself condemned in the kind of cultural climate that would make works like D.H. Lawrence's *Lady Chatterley's Lover* unavailable through their use of material related to sex. Crowley's magickal practices involved sex. The "male child of perfect innocence and high intelligence" refers to a procedure relating to sperm. It's as simple as that.

As a human being he had many failings which rendered him sometimes a sad tragic figure and often showed him as reprehensible in his relationships. He inherited a fortune that would be valued in the millions today and was able to live a superb romantic life for over a decade. A complete lack of functional intelligence, which he readily admitted to, meant that he entirely squandered his resources and was reduced to becoming in effect a ruthless beggar who thought nothing of wasting the generous gifts of friends on high living whilst those close to him starved. And he did suffer himself. Two of his young children died. The loss of his fortune and the lack of commercial success and acclaim of his literary work, along with the unprecedented vilification in the press and his prolonged slide into a wretched heroin addiction with an attendant long-term weakening of his general health, was assuredly a major test of his gigantic egotism. Through all this nonetheless, he did demonstrate a stoic determination to disseminate his ideas and this never failed him even in his last frail days in a Hastings boarding house.

Yes he did, here and there in rituals during his career, kill an animal, and I personally don't approve of that.

He didn't however, as another persistent story states, kill his "occult son," named Macaleister. The tale is that, at some point in the nineteen-twenties, Crowley had a "magickal" son who he had named Macaleister. The two of them performed a ceremony to raise Pan. Something went horribly wrong and Macaleister was found dead the next morning. Crowley, reduced to the level of a naked, gibbering idiot, ended up in an asylum in Paris.

I first came upon this tale in an introduction by Dennis Wheatley to an edition of Crowley's novel *Moonchild*. The story gets retold in many shallow surveys of the occult and variations of it continue to circulate and expand. It may seem strange that this dramatic episode is absent from the works of his principal biographers. Surely the hostile John Symonds could have created a damning chapter out of such lurid material? Basically the whole story is a complete fabrication. Macaleister never even existed.

It has often been suggested that, towards the end of his career, he was perhaps insane, at least senile, and basically a spent force. The fact that he was undeniably dependent again on heroin during his later years is usually taken to imply a complete decline. In reply to this I would simply suggest taking a long hard look at the work he produced during that time. *The Book of Thoth* remains to this day perhaps the greatest of all Tarot decks. It's creation involved six years of work with artist Lady Frieda Harris. That represents a tremendous amount of application.

It does rather seem that the legend of infamy may be some kind of smokescreen of nonsense. What lies behind it?

Crowley was a poet hailed in numerous literary journals as a genius. His work was included in the *Oxford Book of Mystical Verse* but he was also responsible for what has been considered to be some of the vilest pornography in the English language.

Crowley has also been considered to be either a monstrous degenerate or pioneer of sexual freedom for the endless lovers, both female and male, that he had throughout his life.

At one time he held some of the world mountaineering records having climbed higher in the Himalayas than anyone else.

He played chess to a standard approaching that of a Grand Master and was able to simultaneously manage two games whilst blindfolded, thus displaying extraordinary abilities of visualisation and concentration.

Crowley was one of the first westerners to immerse themselves in the study of eastern religion, having travelled extensively in Arab countries, India, and China. Beyond the studies of the many translators of the time, in the first decade of the twentieth century, he practiced physical and mental yoga with great dedication. Many works that later became famous in the West were familiar to him such as the I Ching, Tao Te Ching, Bhagavad Gita, Dhammapada and Patanjali's Yoga Sutras.

He was the first person of any note in the West to systematically experiment with the full range of consciousness expanding drugs ie, cannabis, mescaline, ether, cocaine and heroin. For better or for worse, the psychedelic revolution of the sixties was inspired more by him than anyone else.

First and foremost though, Crowley comes down to us as the magician. A member of the most famous occult group of the nineteenth century, the Hermetic Order of the Golden Dawn, he went from there to believe he had received in 1904 a communication from a non-human entity, an angel for want of better terminology, who dictated to him a scripture for a new age or Aeon. This work was *The Book of the Law* and it contains the phrase which is most strongly associated with him, "Do what thou wilt shall be the whole of the Law."

We find in the book things that seem to be fascinatingly prophetic of the Nazi era and the psychedelic sixties. There are also early indications of themes later to become increasingly visible in

New Age and pagan circles; the return of the goddess and the deities of Egypt.

A case can be made for Crowley's influence in the mid-twentieth century rebirth of witchcraft that has proved to be a crucial aspect of the ever-expanding general pagan revival.

One of the most distinctive oddities of the years since the Second World War has been the UFO phenomenon and the culture that has arisen around it. Here again, remarkably enough, his presence can be discerned.

His influence can be seen in the life of a military theorist who inspired the Nazis, a rocket scientist who had a moon crater named after him, the founder of the most controversial and powerful recent new religion, and the psychedelic psychologist who helped turn on the sixties flower children.

This was one man. And this is the enigma of Aleister Crowley. Picture the effeminate homosexual side of Crowley and Crowley the pornographer. Can we then see this man 22,000 feet up the Himalayas without oxygen? Can we see the junkie likewise? Could we picture Quentin Crisp or Sid Vicious in that context? As Thelemic writer Gerald Suster clearly stated in *The Legacy of the Beast*, "debauched degenerates don't set world mountaineering records." Contrariwise, how about Chris Bonnington? Can we see him returning from an Everest trip to write a book of mystical or pornographic verse and proclaiming himself to be Logos of the Aeon of Horus? What about some of our recent esteemed British poets such as John Betjeman or Philip Larkin? Can we imagine them performing a magical ceremony in the Great Pyramid or rites of sex magick with prostitutes or taking psychedelic drugs? As for yoga, can we imagine some of the sweetness and light types who get attracted to it composing poems such as On the Delights of Passive Pederasty, and Of Dog and Dame, or going big-game hunting?

This indeed is the enigma of Aleister Crowley. We all have different facets to ourselves but in Crowley they are written large. Very large. Any one of his different aspects would serve most people for a life's work.

The most important event of Crowley's life occurred in Cairo in the spring of 1904 when he believed that he received a holy scripture for a newly dawning epoch, the Aeon of Horus. His wife Rose began to experience altered states of consciousness and conveyed a message to Crowley that "they" were waiting for him. He always stated that, until that moment, she had shown no interest or aptitude in the magical realm. At first he was dismissive of the material but the trance like states persisted and, under his questioning, she began to reveal details that compelled his attention.

On March 18th Rose said that it was the Egyptian God Horus who was "waiting." As a result of this, Crowley performed two ceremonial invocations to him. They were interesting because the ritual details were supplied by Rose and did not conform to Golden Dawn procedures. She went on to state that the "Equinox of the Gods" had come. The old world, the epoch of Christianity, had been destroyed by fire on the inner planes. At that crucial time, Crowley was to formulate a link between the solar spiritual force and humanity.

During the whole of this process, Crowley held to a certain attitude of scepticism towards the strange behaviour of his wife. Over a period of a few days he applied twelve tests to verify the genuineness of the communication from Horus. They mainly consisted of him asking Rose to pick out various attributes of Horus, such as the planet associated with him, his weapon, enemy, and Golden Dawn colour and numerical designations. She was entirely successful in every instance. Given her complete lack of knowledge of Egyptology, Crowley considered that the statistical odds against her picking them all correctly by chance were astronomical.

The most spectacular "proof" came when, on March 21st, he took her to the Cairo Museum to see if she could identify an image of Horus. She passed by a number, which greatly pleased Crowley, as he was irritated to see his wife seeming to have a melodramatic episode like the kind of fake mediums he despised. However, she then exclaimed "There he is," pointing down the end of a corridor to an exhibit in the Boulak Collection, previously housed in another museum, that was not yet clearly in view. It turned out to be a wooden funerary stele of one Ankh-af-na-Khonsu, a Priest of Mentu, a God of War, dating from about 725 BC. On it was an image of Ra Hoor Khuit, who is a kind of amalgam of Horus and Ra. This was interesting enough but what clinched the matter for Crowley was seeing that the exhibit number was 666. This famous number, attributed to the Great Beast of the Book of Revelation, and the happy hunting ground of numerologists and crazies down through the ages, was one that Crowley had already personally adopted as his own. His parents had been members of a fanatical Christian sect and his mother had used the name of the Beast to castigate her young son. He had happily accepted this as a token of rebellion. Today educated pagans consider that it represents the energy of the sun. Some of the other tests could be interpreted as Rose somehow reading her husband's mind. This would be remarkable in itself but not as striking as the idea that an ancient Egyptian God was seeking to communicate. From that point onwards, Crowley allowed himself to go along with the strange adventure.

Eventually Rose gave Crowley instructions to enter a specially prepared room at noon on three successive days and be prepared to take dictation for an hour. On April 8th, he sat down at a desk, with Rose in attendance, and waited. At exactly noon he heard the voice of Aiwass, seeming to originate from a point over his left shoulder, behind him in the furthest corner of the room. It seemed to echo in his heart. The voice "was of deep timbre, musical and expressive, its tones solemn, voluptuous, tender, fierce or aught else as suited the moods of the message. Not bass – perhaps a rich tenor or baritone. The English was free of either native or foreign accent, perfectly pure of local or caste mannerisms, thus startling and even uncanny at first hearing. The effect was thus as if the language was "English in itself," without any background, such as exists when any one human speaks it."

In order to keep up with the pace of rapid dictation, Crowley never turned his back to look in the direction of the voice. He did experience an inner impression that Aiwass was present in a fine body, transparent like a cloud of incense smoke. "He seemed to be a tall, dark man in his thirties, well-knit, active and strong, with the face of a savage king, and eyes veiled lest their gaze should destroy what they saw. The dress was not Arab; it suggested Assyria or Persia, but very vaguely."

Over the course of the three sessions, *The Book of the Law* was dictated. Aiwass introduced himself as "minister of Hoor-paar-Kraat," elsewhere known as Hor-pa-Kred, and in Greek as Harpocrates. This is the infant Horus, usually pictured with a finger to his lips, making a gesture of silence. In a magickal sense, this represents the sealing of a formula that has been put out into the world. Each chapter contains the words of particular forces pictured on what Crowley came to call the "Stele of Revealing."

Arched over the whole scene was Nuit, the Goddess of the night sky. The first chapter is hers. It is ironic to realise, considering Crowley's reputation as misogynist and abuser of women, that the words of Nuit represent one of the first clear indications of the return of the Goddess in the magical literature of the time. If a woman had written such words they might have become a feminist scripture.

(All following quotes from *The Book of the Law* are representative selections from the respective chapters condensed together with verse numbers referenced.)

3. Every man and every woman is a star.
12. Come forth, o children, under the stars, & take your fill of love!
13. I am above you and in you. My ecstasy is in yours. My joy is to see your joy.
15. They shall gather my children into their fold: they shall bring the glory of the stars into the hearts of men.
29. I am divided for love's sake for the chance of union.
32. — the joys of my love will redeem ye from all pain.
41. The word of Sin is Restriction.
There is no bond that can unite the divided but love.
51. Also take your fill and will of love as ye will, when, where, and with whom you will! But always unto me.
53. This shall regenerate the world, the little world my sister, my heart and my tongue unto whom I send this kiss.
— ecstasy be thine and joy of earth.
57. Invoke me under my stars! Love is the law, love under will.
61. I love you, I yearn to you.

I who am all pleasure and purple and drunkenness of the innermost sense desire you.
Put on the wings and arouse the coiled splendour within you: come unto me!

A winged disc is pictured on the stele. In Egyptological terms, it depicts an aspect of an early pre-dynastic form of Horus, from a cult centre at a place called Behdet. This name was later given to the famous Horus temple at Edfu and other places of his worship. As defender of Ra he would travel the sky as a winged disc hunting Ra's enemy Set. Chapter Two is his words, but his energy is named as Hadit, which is understood as a mathematical metaphysical principle.

6. I am the flame that burns in every heart of man, and in the core of every star. I am Life, and the giver of Life, yet therefore is the knowledge of me the knowledge of death.
9. Remember all ye that existence is pure joy; that all the sorrows are but as shadows; they pass & are done; but there is that which remains.
20. Beauty and strength, leaping laughter and delicious languor, force and fire, are of us.
22. I am the Snake that giveth Knowledge & Delight and bright glory, and stir the hearts of men with drunkenness. To worship me take wine and strange drugs whereof I will tell my prophet, & be drunk thereof! They shall not harm ye at all. It is a lie, this folly against self. The exposure of innocence is a lie. Be strong, o man! Lust, enjoy all things of sense and rapture: fear not that any God shall deny thee for this.

Powerful and inspiring words but amongst them were some with a more disturbing flavour.

21. We have nothing with the outcast and the unfit: let them die in their misery. For they feel not. Compassion is the vice of kings: stamp down the wretched & the weak: this is our law and the joy of the world.

The third chapter gives full expression to such sentiments. It is the voice of Ra-Hoor-Khuit.

3. I am a god of War and of Vengeance.

11. *Thou shalt have danger & trouble.—*
Worship me with fire and blood.
18. *Mercy let be of: damn them who pity! Kill and torture, spare not, be upon them!*
51. *With my Hawk's head I peck at the eyes of Jesus as he hangs upon the cross.*
54. *I spit on your crapulous creeds.*
55. *Let Mary inviolate be torn upon wheels: for her sake let all chaste women be utterly despised among you!*

For some years Crowley rejected the work because of passages like these. He considered Chapter Three to be "gratuitously atrocious."

There have been previous Aeons, also symbolically presided over by Egyptian deities. Isis ruled the matriarchal epoch of the great mother goddess. Osiris was a dying and resurrected god, typical of the mystery cults of the Mediterranean world. Jesus and Christianity demonstrate the triumph of that form. Horus inevitably partakes of qualities of both his parents but is an individual beyond them. This individuality is perhaps the most characteristic form of what is now unfolding, for better or worse. "Do what thou wilt."

I feel that the concept of the Aeon of Horus offers, at the very least, a superb poetic metaphor to help understand the enigma of the twentieth century. It seems to me that the main players of the Nazi nightmare and the swinging sixties were rather specialised groups. They were uniquely over-qualified for the situations that they were born into. The group of characters who were available to take the whole thing to the limit and beyond, seem to have been assembled by a brilliant casting agency. The usual ways of looking at history do not satisfactorily explain to me why it all turned out to be quite so hideous, quite so ridiculously brilliant. I feel there is a deeper mystery trying to reveal itself.

There has been an explosive unleashing of knowledge and energy, symbolised by Hadit, "the flame that burns in every heart of man, and in the core of every star." Nuit's admonition to "arouse the coiled splendour within you" may have seemed obscure in 1904 to all but scholars of arcane Hindu texts, but by the sixties they seemed to sing with prophecy. LSD and the atom bomb, DNA and the space programme, were all examples of our mental horizons being expanded as never before, as the light within matter itself was unleashed.

As far as I'm concerned the twentieth century, with its Nazi and psychedelic eras, the time that Crowley has called the dawning of the Aeon of Horus is so mind shattering, heart-busting and compellingly interesting and important that at times I feel like I'm straining with every nerve to take on board every last nuance in order to maintain the altered state of gnosis necessary to comprehend it. In that comprehension is ecstasy and terror, and perhaps the most effective guide to its navigation may embody something of all its disparate qualities.

Adapted from material in *Aleister Crowley and the Aeon of Horus*. *www.aleistercrowley666.co.uk*

Dion Fortune
(1890-1946)

by Kala Trobe

'At the climax of the Mysteries of the Earth Mother all of the lights went out, and the High Priest and the chief Priestess descended into the darkness of the Crypt and there consummated a union that was a sacrament just as much as eating the Body and drinking the Blood.'

Dion Fortune is the occultist most responsible for ushering the Divine Feminine back into Western spirituality. The above words, written in an early twentieth century Britain still mired in Christianity and the patriarchal bombast of the Empire, and issuing from a woman who was born in 1890, are indubitably radical for their time. 'Hidden Masters' were becoming acceptable symbolic currency in upper class parlours and drawing rooms thanks to Helena Blavatsky and her Theosophists, but Priestesses sublimating spirituality through acts of sexual magnetism and conscious magickal circuitry certainly were not, until the alter egos of this prolific writer's novels made them so.

In her non-fiction, Dion Fortune details the mechanics behind her esoteric theories, along with the underlying principles of Tantra; but it is in her short-stories and novels that Dion's stylish and gripping mytho-poetical prose brings these principles truly to life. Themes such as reincarnation feature heavily in her works, and previously 'secret' magickal techniques such the Lesser Banishing Ritual of the Pentagram are actively employed by her characters, which along with other authentic occult techniques casually alluded to throughout her writings, indicates her active aim to bring such 'wavelengths' into popular consciousness. To help rejuvenate male sexuality and union with the God-form, she is especially keen on Pan; for women her primary deities are lunar, receptive and intuitive, ancient, and mercilessly devoted to Spiritual Evolution. The ramifications of these principles are highly visible in 'magickal' practise today.

Born Violet Mary Firth, the eventual nom-de-plume 'Dion Fortune' comes from her Golden Dawn motto, 'Deo, Non Fortuna' (by God, not chance), emphasising her perpetual aim to abide by Principle rather than to gauge success by ephemeral popularity and materialistic gain. Taking as her main influence the Western Mystery Tradition: that is to say, select religio-magickal philosophies of Qabalistic, Egyptian and Greek origin and their mediaeval and more recent derivatives, she wrote many books of occult instruction, her tap-root being: 'selfless dedication to the Highest Ideal that can be achieved'. She was of the generation mightily influenced by Theosophy, which brought into recognition Eastern terms such as 'Karma', 'Chakra' and 'Akashic Records': and importantly, the concept of Hidden Masters and parallel planes invisible to all but the psychic eye. Like Blavatsky and Alice Bailey, and even Aleister Crowley, Dion Fortune acknowledged and honoured the living presence of 'the Hierarchy' – the ten or so Masters who aid the evolution of planetary, animal and human consciousness 'from behind the Veil'. Her work is replete with references to and descriptions of the Rays of Manifestation, the Angelic forces, and other evidences of a very ordered Universe indeed. Her faith in the ultimate sanity of the Cosmos is exemplary.

Crowley is arguably the man most responsible for revolutionising modern magick; and while he apparently preferred his women dissipated for personal interaction, it was/is the prim and rather avuncular Dion Fortune who was the actual Shakti of the Aeon of Horus on the Inner Planes. Alan Richardson's biography *Priestess* is recommended for more detail on this. DNF's physical life 'in Malkuth in Assiah' was somewhat asexual and unrewarding, and highly de-feminised, but what she lacked individually on the outer planes, she coaxed and (en)chanted into being on the Inner. If she couldn't be in person the sexually alluring, independent Enchantress of myth and archetype, then her prime heroines Morgan Le Fay/ Vivien Lilith Le Fay Morgan could most certainly do it for her. And they do it in style, systematically rescuing miserable men from their isolation and cynicism, piquing their amorous interest, introducing them to 'the Goddess', and then sailing away before it all becomes too mundane. Via the figureheads she variously named Morgan le Fay, Lilith (tellingly), and Vivien le Fay Morgan, amongst others, Fortune became a spiritual glamour puss par excellence; there can be no doubt that she used her works to carve out etheric conduits which would both irrigate the souls of her readers in real life, and which would allow the author to live vicariously through her heroines.

Thus, along with Crowley, who she met in real life and with whom she allegedly exchanged a reserved respect, Dion Fortune was one of the first occultists to deliberately release the power of formerly secretive magickal lore and practise via a fictional frame. Crowley's most effective literary masterpiece is *Diary of a Drug Fiend;* a brilliant description of a personal-spiritual battle with chemically-enhanced elevation versus personal fortitude; yet it does not quite convey the technical esoteric intricacy of his non-fiction writings. Conversely, huge swathes of Dion's teachings have reached us via this most entertaining of devices, the novel. *The Sea Priestess* (1938) and its follow-up *Moon Magic* (published posthumously in 1956) are the most renowned of these, heralding through their heroine based on the legendary Morgan le Fay, the re-birth of the 'Female Mysteries' which has spilled into 'Wicca' and lateral naturo-explorative paths in our own era. Indeed, the Priestesses featured in these novels act as a template for various magickal women extant today, but when Dion Fortune was writing, the word 'Priestess' was a much rarer one.

Her 1926 collection of short-stories, *The Secrets of Dr. Taverner*, outlined her experiences as a young psychoanalyst, garnered in the days when a well-to-do person could set themselves up as a psychiatric counsellor and ply their trade on paying individuals, which she combined with her belief in and passion for esoteric lore. She worked as such a therapist at the tender age of 23, and one can humorously imagine this earnest but naive young lady trying to 'cure' neurotics of many ilks by applying her germinal esoteric theories to a hapless clientele. These interactions became the template for *The Secrets of Dr. Taverner*. In "Daughter of Pan" for example, the listless, fish-eyed psychiatric patient Diana gains her vitality through running wild and drawing, in reclaiming her inner wildness, for she is innately a 'Dark Lilith' who can hold no truck with social mores. Diana is constitutionally Pagan: 'she drew her life from the sun and the wind and the earth, and as long as she was allowed to keep in touch with them, she glowed with an inner light'. Fortune herself was increasingly drawn to the 'Green Ray' as her incarnation progressed, but never lost her Christian roots. Indeed, in the end she seemed to exemplify that healthy balance between Christianity and Paganism which is still extant in the place she most loved outside of London: Glastonbury. Having a spiritual overview, she became free of the paradoxes that blight orthodox religion, liberated from the necessity of picking one Path and eschewing all others.

In Dion Fortune's cosmology, as in Blavatsky's and Bailey's, the entirety of the spectrum was made up of seven different but complimentary Rays, each essential to the whole. The Green Ray of Paganism included rather than rejected the Yellow/Blue Ray of Hermeticism and Christianity. Despite her deep involvement in the occult and magick, Fortune's respect for and deference to the Christos never faltered, often featuring in her work via the Archangels, primarily Michael. This feature of her legacy has been of great leverage to others who do not wish to throw the baby of spiritual evolution out with the baptismal water simply because that water was sanctified in the name of Christ rather than, say, Isis. Spirit is identifiable by the illumination, healing and progress that it emanates, not by the mere name under which it operates.

Each tale in *The Secrets of Dr. Taverner* presents a psycho-spiritual solution to a social, physical and/or psychiatric complaint. An archetypal code is cracked in "The Soul That Would Not be Born", for example, in which Mona Cailey, who nowadays would be classified autistic due to her inability and unwillingness to communicate, is in fact an 'Initiate' who betrayed her lover in a past life to torture, and now plays out a Karmic debt before the very eyes of Taverner and his assistant. It's fascinating stuff, and the format of psychiatrist and assistant acts as a wonderful vehicle for Fortune's theories about the connection between psychology and the occult, a field in which she experimented in real life both alone, and under her early mentor, Theodore Moriarty. The assistant character, Rhodes, is clearly Fortune (then Miss Firth) herself. It echoes the style of fellow esotericist and spiritualist Arthur Conan Doyle, and in some senses, the darker machinations of Gothic author Edgar Allan Poe.

Of Dion Fortune's non-fiction works, the best known are probably *The Mystical Qabalah*, a thrillingly original exposition of what she called 'the Yoga of the West', and *Psychic Self-Defence*, an enthralling collection of techniques and anecdotes to aid and protect the astral explorer and general practitioner of 'occult arts'. Her didactic tone is apparently an annoyance to some readers, but, like Alice Bailey's, it is merely a product of her era and upbringing. Both inevitably wrote as the upper-middle class British ladies that, indeed, they were. Under her birth name V. M. Firth, Dion Fortune wrote two of her first works, *The Servant Problem* and *The Problem of Purity* – the former on a pressing issue of her time and class – the psychology of one's servants and interaction with these 'omnipresent spies' (she recognised the 'underlings' as conscious entities: many did not); the latter on the (possible) values of chastity and sex, and the best ways to avoid masturbation, which she considered to be psychically and psychologically polluting. According to her biographers Charles Fielding and Carr Collins (see **References**), many of the 'patients' at her clinic were compulsive masturbators, which may well explain why she felt this aversion! But, as with both Bailey and Fortune's feelings against onanism and homosexuality, these would have softened and changed in later years, and should not be seen as enduring qualities of their work, but rather as symptoms of their time. It is also true that Dion Fortune's ideals of *The Esoteric Laws of Love and Marriage* (another book and a perpetual preoccupation) fell very short in actuality within her own life, but it is only by default of her era and relatively early death that these standpoints did not develop in due course.

As she relates in *Psychic Self-Defence*, Violet's very first psychic initiation was not consciously sought, and it took her years to recover from it. In 1913 she was hired as a teacher at the Agricultural Institute, Studley College in Warwickshire, which she had attended as a pupil at the end of her 'teens. The Principal at Studley, Dr. Lilias Hamilton, was a well-travelled, idiosyncratic woman, a feminist with a darkly striking personality, a true Gothic anti-heroine indeed. She did not share Violet's scruples about garnering school funds from elderly and mentally challenged sponsors, and Violet made the mistake of warning one of these old dears that she might be manipulated into producing money for the institution. Dr Hamilton got wind of this, and what with that and Violet's day-to-day attitude, which was reportedly rather self-assured and sanctimonious, the Machiavellian mistress, we are told, decided to employ techniques of hypnotism she had learned in India, to 'destroy' the interfering young upstart.

So, the germinal Dion was confronted by her boss, alone in her study; she had already resigned in the hope of pre-empting retribution, but Dr. Hamilton was not going to let her off scot-free. "You are incompetent, and you have no confidence," she repeated, over and over. The deal was that Violet could depart as soon as she admitted to these 'facts', and not a moment before. It says much about her innate sense of protocol that she did not just get up and leave. Instead, she stayed, and fought.

Like the evil step-mother in a Grimm fairy tale, the older woman's ire rose at this earnest self-confidence, and she doubled and redoubled her efforts against the innocent young lady. Violet resisted the destructive mantra. She began to feel very unwell. Clearly her rival was attacking her etheric body. She did not at this point know how to deflect such a psychic onslaught.

Suddenly she heard a man's voice in her inner ear. "Pretend you have run out of energy," it said, "And admit defeat". She realised that this would be the only way to escape with anything intact, and admitted to the faux-lies.

The result of this episode was, she reports, a nervous break-down, a badly leaking aura, mental confusion, and a ruptured sense of Self which was not mended until her Golden Dawn initiation in 1919. This experience shocked her to the core, and she believed that, had the mysterious voice not intervened, she would never have returned to health and sanity again.

Years of occult study ensued once she was up and running once more. A major influence on her development was Theodore Moriarty, a fascinating older man who taught her a very great deal about modern esoteric practise. Her studies developed apace under his tutelage. His exact specifics remain frustratingly obscure.

In 1919 she was admitted to the Alpha et Omega Lodge of the Golden Dawn, and rose competently through its ranks, as well as forming several significant friendships there-in. However, by 1924 she had fallen out with Moina Mathers, its remaining leader, whom Fortune implies in *Psychic Self-Defence* had attacked her and her friend Netta Fornario astrally (actually causing Fornario's death, though this is highly dubious). It is likely that Mathers was indeed irritated by DNF: her book *The Esoteric Laws of Love and Marriage* was judged a contravention of Golden Dawn 'secrets'; a plagiarism, almost; and what with that, and her newly-published book *Sane Occultism,* and her numerous articles in *The Occult Review,* Mathers might certainly have found Dion challenging enough to elicit expulsion from her Alpha and Omega Lodge. Violet had also just acquired use of a property in Chalice Orchard, Glastonbury. There were many around her who would be happy to work magick independently of the formalities of the Golden Dawn.

Dion was utterly unruffled by her expulsion; indeed, she seemed to see it as another affirmation of her own innate rectitude. Thanks to various sponsors, she acquired use of a property in London for her growing group, 'The Society of the Inner Light', and took up part-time residence in the Glastonbury retreat, at the foot of the Tor. She had her staunch supporters, some of them, such as Charles Loveday, able to advance her cause financially too.

In Avalon her magicks took on a whole new lease of life. Here she garnered the inspiration for her classics of occult literature: the novels *The Sea-Priestess* and *Moon Magic,* and her prime text *The Mystical Qabalah,* amongst others. She was familiar with others involved in the spiritual quest in a number of new formats: from Spiritualism (with which she purportedly held little truck), to the resuscitation of mediaeval sorcery techniques thanks to translators such as MacGregor Mathers, through creative High Magick, to Mystical Christianity and tools for direct social change such as vegetarianism (she was vegetarian, at least in theory, though I can't help but note that her characters eat meat a-plenty); Feminism, the deconstruction of the class-system and concomitant loss of house servants in the UK, along with the emergence of a great deal of ground-breaking and inspiring literature. She was certainly aware of D.H. Lawrence and the controversy he inspired, for example, and her character 'Ursula Brangwyn' in *The Winged Bull* is named after his sexually liberated character in *Women in Love*. Lawrence, of course, was attempting to affect a sexual revolution, a freedom of expression not accepted in that era. It is quite obvious from today's liberal attitude to sex that these pioneers more than succeeded in their task.

In Dion Fortune's epoch, consciousness was newly expanding from the conformity of the Pisces Era to recombine Spirit with Ego, or even better, to dissolve Ego in Spirit without orthodox intercessors. There were many seeking an individual experience of Divinity, who were actively breaking the shackles of religion and spirituality as a patriarchal concern. The tides of the Goddess were on the rise all around her. In Glastonbury, Somerset, these energies are symbolised by the Chalice Well and the Red Spring that feeds it; by 1924 Dion was abiding much of the year at the literal Well-head of the Dark Feminine, latterly ascribed to the Sephirah Binah in Paul Weston's *Mysterium Artorius*, (within 'A Glastonbury Qabalah Pathworking'), and in my own *Magic of Qabalah*.

The World Wars affected Violet on numerous levels. During the First, she worked as a land girl, and one of the lesser known developments of her early agricultural training is her obscure book

The Soya Bean. Writing as V.M. Firth, she expounds the virtues of this humble legume as a source of protein, especially in times of dearth, easy and cheap to manufacture. Her ideas were taken up by others further down the line, and significantly embellished the wonderful range of affordable vegetarian foodstuffs available today.

During the Second World War, Dion and other esoterically-minded persons became aware that Hitler's Nazis were using national Aryan archetypes to induce a powerful, hypnotic response in the people of Germany. I currently live between Dion Fortune's old home in Glastonbury town, and her grave; it cannot be denied that she arrived in the latter earlier than was natural, possibly due to her relentless efforts in what is now termed 'The Magickal Battle of Britain'. She and other Golden Dawn members and magickally-minded citizens (her own activity by this time being primarily within the Society of the Inner Light), formulated visualisations set at the heart of Albion, or Avalon – specifically, inside Glastonbury Tor – designed to awaken the spirits of our land, such as Arthur and the Knights of the Round Table, to protect the UK from the pressing Aryan onslaught. It was obvious to those 'astrally awake' that Hitler, Himmler and fellow Nazis were invoking the spirits of their own mythos, and that in order to counter them on the all-important level of the Astral blueprint, doing the same here was necessary. Our real-life heroine put a great deal of effort into this project, and died following a very brief illness in January 1946, just after Anglo-American victory in the Second World War.

Dion Fortune remains a positive influence on many in the current era. Like Alice A. Bailey, she worked under a 'Hidden Master', her own being Melchizedek, but unlike Alice, she 'wrote' all of her books herself (apart from the final chapters of *Moon Magic*, which are said to have been scribed posthumously, via a cleaner temporarily overcome by Dion Fortune's spirit, and parts of *The Cosmic Doctrine,* allegedly dictated by Socrates).

Much may still be learned from Dion Fortune's quiet dignity and innate sense of Justice, and her novels and instruction manuals will withstand many a temporary Zeitgeist. We are bequeathed a sense of structure via fruitful toil and of the psychological and psychiatric value of the 'mystical' when wisely applied. Her words still stimulate the imagination and enrapture the soul. She is often 'seen' and spoken with in Glastonbury to this day: it is clear talking to other practitioners of the 'esoteric arts' that she continues to watch over her beloved Avalon of the Heart, and to abide by those who swim in her sacred waters.

For me personally she has been a most positive of evolutionary influences, and I thank her for it.

Recommended Reading

Benham, Patrick – *The Avalonians* (Gothic Image Publications, 1993)

Fielding, Charles and Collins, Carr – *The Story of Dion Fortune* (Samuel Weiser, 1985)

Fortune, Dion – (fiction) *The Secrets of Doctor Taverner, The Demon Lover, The Winged Bull, The Goat-Foot God, The Sea Priestess, Moon Magic*

Fortune, Dion – (non-fiction) *The Mystical Qabalah, Psychic Self-Defence, Avalon of the Heart, The Training and Work of the Initiate*

Richardson, Alan – *Priestess* (Thoth Publications, 2007)

Trobe, Kala – *Magic of Qabalah* (Llewellyn Publications, 2001), *The Witch's Guide to Life* (Llewellyn Publications, 2003), *The Magick Bookshop* (Llewelyn Publications, 2004)

Weston, Paul – *Mysterium Artorius* (Avalonian Aeon Publications 2007)

THE ALPHABET OF DESIRE: AUSTIN OSMAN SPARE (1886-1956)

By Steve Kenson

While the "fathers" of the modern Chaos Magick current(s) are still alive and kicking (as of this writing) the man who could be called its "grandfather" passed beyond the veil in 1956, nearly a generation before the magickal arts most strongly associated with him would be widely published or known.

Austin Osman (A.O.) Spare was born at the end of 1886 in Snow Hill in London. His friend Kenneth Grant later said Spare was "...not sure whether he was born on the last day of December ...or on New Year's Day..." likening his liminal birth to two-faced Janus, and calling his life "...a curious blend of past and future." His father, Philip Newton Spare, was a City of London policeman, and quite proud of his son's later artistic achievements. His mother, Eliza Osman, was the daughter of a Royal Marine. When A.O. Spare was seven, his family moved to Kennington, South London, where he attended St. Agnes School for the next six years.

Mrs. Patterson

It was during his time as a student at St. Agnes that Spare claimed to have met "Mrs. Patterson," an old fortune teller also known as "The Witch Patterson." According to Spare, Mrs. Patterson claimed (long before the popular television show *American Horror Story: Coven* or, well, television) to be a descendant of a line of witches from Salem, Massachusetts, not eliminated by Cotton Mather or the infamous witch trials. She told fortunes in her small parlor, accepting no payment save for the occasional symbolic coin, and displayed various occult powers, including divining the future, conjuring images, and the ability to change her appearance, going from wizened crone to beautiful siren.

Spare said Mrs. Patterson seduced him and initiated him into Witchcraft, and he referred to her as his "second mother." He later produced a number of portraits of her, both as old woman and young seductress, but these images are the only evidence we have of her existence. She is the classic "witch-mother" figure who initiates, but leaves little, if anything, by way of lineage for us to trace. Still, Spare clearly held an interest in Witchcraft and the occult from a young age, and apparently well before his confirmed contact with better known figures in those communities (like Kenneth Grant and Gerald Gardner, many years later).

Artwork

Also interested in art from a young age, Spare began taking lessons at the Lambeth School of Art at the age of 12. When he left St. Agnes School as a young teen, it was to work for nine months at a company that primarily designed posters, then as a designer at a glass-working business. Patrons of the glass-works Sir William Blake Richmond and F.H. Richmond, RBA, took note of Spare's work and recommended him for a scholarship to the Royal College of Art in South Kensington.

Spare was a fairly indolent art student, his own artistic style and interests clashing with the popular techniques of the time taught at the RCA. Still, his work was exhibited and he won a silver medal at the National Competition of Schools of Art in 1903 when he was sixteen. His first public exhibition was held in the foyer of the Newington Public Library in 1904, including works influenced by Theosophy and Spare's own occult ideas about what he called *Zos* and *Kia*.

The Zos-Kia Cultus

Spare's friend Kenneth Grant dubbed Spare's own magical and religious system the "Zos-Kia Cultus," after two of its primary concepts.

Zos, which Spare also used as a magickal name, is the self, the totality of body and mind. *Kia* is, in many ways, the opposite: universal mind, consciousness, or power, virtually unknowable in its totality, much like the concept of the Tao, and associated with the unconscious or atavistic parts of the mind.

The origins of both terms are open to debate, ranging from ancient Greek root words to influences from Eastern religion or Theosophy or word-games with Spare's own name ("Zos" being similar to "AOS," Spare's initials, replacing the "alpha" of the A with the "omega" of Z). Their pairing shows a focus on the relationship between the totality of the individual and the sheer vastness of the rest of creation, often represented by the repressed or primal impulses of the psyche. This is not unlike the ideas of Spare's contemporary, Howard Phillips (H.P.) Lovecraft, who once referred to the human place in the cosmos as, "We live on a placid island of ignorance in the midst of black seas of the infinity, and it was not meant that we should voyage far." (from his story "The Call of Cthulhu").

Zos & The Great Beast

A.O. Spare met Aleister Crowley, "The Great Beast" himself, after Crowley became an admirer and patron of his work. Crowley extended an invitation for Spare to become the seventh member of the newly founded *Argenteum Astrum,* but he never became a full member of the order. He claimed to dislike its strict hierarchy, and was quite critical of ceremonial magick (and magicians) in general. Crowley later claimed Spare was only interested in "black magic," which kept him from fully joining the order. Certainly, Spare's strongly ecstatic and inspirational tendencies in his magickal and artistic work clashed with the clear and methodical structures (and strictures) of ceremonialism.

Rumors also circulated that the split between Spare and Crowley was due in part to Crowley making sexual advances towards the younger Spare, although this was never proven. Indeed, Spare's sexuality was a matter of some uncertainty, as his work became popular amongst the gay *avant-garde* of London, some of whom became his patrons. The couple Marc-André Raffalovich and John Gray were two such, and Spare referred to Gray as "the most wonderful man I have ever met." Spare's friend Frank Brangwyn claimed the young artist was homosexual, but suppressed his desires. Spare himself, in spite of friendships with homosexuals like Raffalovich, Gray, and Irish novelist George Moore, proclaimed a varied and imaginative, but heterosexual, romantic life.

In 1911, Spare wooed and married Eily Gertrude Shaw, but their marriage was a strained and unhappy one. She was Spare's opposite in many ways, uninterested in philosophy or learning, and jealous of her husband's friends, particularly younger men. They eventually separated, although they never divorced, and Eily took up a relationship with another man.

The Book of Pleasure

Spare self-published *The Book of Pleasure,* his third, in 1913. It contained many of his ideas on the relationship between the conscious self and the unconscious, atavistic, mind as well as Spare's practices on the use of sigils in magick. It sold poorly, and Spare intended to produce a second, expanded, edition, which never came to pass. Much of the book's content went unnoticed by Spare's contemporaries, and reviews praised his artistic skills, while criticizing the book's occult imagery and ideas.

Spare served in the Royal Army Medical Corps during World War I, then was eventually assigned to working with other artists illustrating the conflict out of a studio at 76 Fulham Road. He was later strongly opposed to Nazism, proclaiming of Adolf Hitler, "If you are a superman, let me be forever animal." When the Second World War broke out, Spare attempted to re-enlist, but was rejected as being too old (he was 53 at the time). He lost his London flat—and all of the artwork in it—during the Blitz, leaving him homeless for a time.

Zos vel Thanatos

Austin Spare experienced a small resurgence of his career following WWII. In 1949, Steffi Grant introduced him to her husband, Kenneth Grant, and the two became friends. It was Grant who gave Spare the magickal name *Zos vel Thanatos* ("Zos or Death") and encouraged his writing and art in more occult directions once again.

Grant became the keeper of Spare's books, papers, and some of his art, and the primary preserver of his legacy, when Spare passed away in May of 1956 after arriving at a hospital with a burst appendix (and a variety of other complications from failing health).

Sigil Magick

Spare's single greatest contribution to modern magickal practice was his work with sigils, abstract symbols intended to embody or encapsulate desire and intention.

The essence of Spare's sigilization technique is to write out a particular intention, eliminating any repeating letters, and then combining the remaining ones into a single glyph or symbol. The sigil is then ritually empowered in order to fulfill the stated desire, which is still inherent in its structure, but in such a fashion that it interacts with the subconscious mind—which Spare believed to be the seat of inspiration and magickal power—rather than the conscious mind.

It's noteworthy that Spare's technique relies on nothing but the basic elements of written language, artistic inspiration, and altered or magickal states of consciousness: no "occult" or "secret" knowledge or magical lore is required; it is a pure magickal "technology". The gnosis to empower a sigil could come from as simple an act as self-induced orgasm. Spare suggested a magician could use his techniques to build up an extensive "vocabulary" of useful symbols or sigils, what he called "the Alphabet of Desire," essentially a do-it-yourself magickal system.

This home-brew approach appealed to the "punk" esthetic of the early chaos magicians. In his *Liber Null,* British magician Peter Carroll revisited Spare's concept of sigil magick and the creation of an "alphabet of desire," popularizing both concepts as part of the Chaos Magick current. Spare's essential technique remains a key tool in the Chaos Magick kit of paradigm-shifting technologies, and has found its way into other practitioners' "bags of tricks". Comic book writer Grant Morrison even included Spare's sigil magick in his pop conspiracy-culture opus *The Invisibles,* both integrated into the story, and asking his readers in an editorial to improve flagging sales on the book by empowering a sigil of his creation on a particular day and time by masturbating to it! Rather than being cancelled, the comic went on to be a success and Morrison was able to complete it as planned.

If A.O. Spare ever worked magick to ensure his techniques—and his work—were not forgotten, then we would have to call it a success, and one I am happy to be a part of.

Resources

Spare produced five books: *Earth Inferno* (1905), *A Book of Satyrs* (1907), *The Book of Pleasure* (1913), *The Focus of Life* (1921), and *The Anathema of Zos* (1927), many of which have been reprinted or republished in modern editions.

Ansell, Robert. *Borough Satyr: The Life and Art of Austin Osman Spare.* Holmes Publishing Group, 2005.

Baker, Phil. *Austim Osman Spare: The Life and Legend of London's Lost Artist.* London: Strange Attractor Press, 2011.

Yeats' Stolen Children: William Butler Yeats (1865-1939)

By Ruby Sara

WHERE dips the rocky highland
Of Sleuth Wood in the lake,
There lies a leafy island
Where flapping herons wake
The drowsy water rats;
There we've hid our faery vats,
Full of berrys
And of reddest stolen cherries.
Come away, O human child!
To the waters and the wild
With a faery, hand in hand,
For the world's more full of weeping than you can understand.

William Butler Yeats has been called one of the greatest poets of the Western world. His fascination with mysticism and the occult is well documented – he was a famous member of the Golden Dawn and the Theosophical Society, and his later works often reflected his thoughts on notions esoteric and the metaphysical structure of the world. In *The Triumph of the Moon*, Ronald Hutton describes Yeats as "possessed of a strong inclination to believe in the existence of a spirit world, and of deities, and to work with them" (p. 56). This enthusiasm for religion and the ineffable is evident in the body of his poetic work, but I believe that it is in his early writings, influenced by Irish folklore, that we see revealed the sorrowful, lilting romanticism – a longing to see and touch and experience the hidden worlds of Faery and the spiritual heart of Ireland – that seems to resonate so deeply with many in the contemporary pagan community, even today. Thus making Yeats not only a literal and literary ancestor, but a spiritual one as well – a man who wrote the pulse in the land he felt around him, who saw between the reeds and rushes to the parliaments of that secret country, and wrote songs for what he saw there.

Where the wave of moonlight glosses
The dim gray sands with light,
Far off by furthest Rosses
We foot it all the night,
Weaving olden dances
Mingling hands and mingling glances
Till the moon has taken flight;
To and fro we leap
And chase the frothy bubbles,
While the world is full of troubles
And anxious in its sleep.
Come away, O human child!
To the waters and the wild
With a faery, hand in hand,
For the world's more full of weeping than you can understand.

And how many of us can deny feeling that tug in the muscle of our chests at the mention of the hidden company Beyond the Fields We Know? When we wished as children, mightily and hungrily, for a glimpse into Faery. Dawn and dusk, we crept out to walk the dusty roads or pavement streets outside our homes, peering beneath bridges or under cold spring riverbanks. And don't we still? That golden hour, when the sun washes the grass in honey, and the trees become each a torch and a candle, every puddle and pond a mirror of glass, we make wishes. Every blue note of evening, when the mountains turn purple and the stars wink in the deepening hush, we lean in to catch the sound of silver trumpets in the far away. We remember, we dream, we summon. We leave biscuits and jam at the roots of blackberry bushes, and our hearts expand and contract in yearning and in joy. Hush, hush, it could be here, beneath this wet stone, by this rushing river. Or here, this hollow trunk, this patch of sacred earth. A secret door, a Faery store – "where dips the rocky highland," where we might find a clutch of "reddest stolen cherries." Yes, we would be Yeats' stolen children…for the world may indeed be "more full of weeping that you can understand."

Where the wandering water gushes
From the hills above Glen-Car,
In pools among the rushes
That scarce could bathe a star,
We seek for slumbering trout
And whispering in their ears
Give them unquiet dreams;
Leaning softly out
From ferns that drop their tears
Over the young streams.
Come away, O human child!
To the waters and the wild
With a faery, hand in hand,
For the world's more full of weeping than you can understand.

But we find, soon, that escape is no real option. And surely we would miss the mice and the lowing of the cows on the hillside. The realm of the People is, after all, as we are told in countless tales, the same as our own, just a step to the left or a chance wandering into Deeps, the following of marsh lights bobbing in the twilight – the worlds within worlds that get bigger the further in you travel. And to see the Hidden Country, witness to the marching of the Shining Host over and through the timeless hills? An anointing of the eyes or a holey stone perhaps. A difference of perspective – a difference of perception. So we rely on the fey words of those who See so that we might see also. We follow poets down muddy marshes and seek out storytellers in our midst. We ask not to be stolen, but to be returned. To the waters and the wild. And we understand that the world weeps only because it has forgotten how to see.

Away with us he's going,
The solemn-eyed:
He'll hear no more the lowing
Of the calves on the warm hillside
Or the kettle on the hob
Sing peace into his breast,
Or see the brown mice bob
Round and round the oatmeal chest.

For he comes, the human child,
To the waters and the wild
With a faery, hand in hand,
For the world's more full of weeping than he can understand.

— *The Stolen Child* by William Butler Yeats (1889)

Franz Bardon: 20th Century Magus (1909-1958)

By Rev. Bill Duvendack

When one looks at the bulk of the 20th century Western Esoteric Tradition, its depth, breadth, and mass are to be found firmly rooted in the Rosicrucian system that was improved upon and revamped by the Golden Dawn, in particular its founding members. This presents a very solid foundation to work from, as well as a particular focus. However, there are those in the 20th century that, while familiar with the Rosicrucian system, added their own tastes to the Western Esoteric Tradition in their own unique way. One of these individuals was a gentleman by the name of Franz Bardon. Another way to view this is that Franz was a Hermeticist first, and a Rosicrucian style magician second.

Franz Bardon was one of the greatest adepts of the 20th century in his own way, and what he gave to us is of the utmost value for the practical magick worker. He was born on December 1, 1909, in Czechoslovakia. Immediately one is drawn to the fact that most of the prominent adepts of the 20th century that are known about come from Western Europe and thus here is an individual that, culturally speaking, has a different background, which of course produces different results. It is also worth noting that he is a second generation Hermeticist, as his father also studied the Royal Art, which influenced Franz throughout his life. His life is a textbook example of someone that simply 'is' a magickal being, as it is profound in its symbolism. Besides being a second generation Hermeticist, his first job was at a company called Minerva! He grew to age during the tail end of World War I and into the postwar years. And to top it off, this was occurring in Eastern Europe. This should give sufficient insight into his character by itself. One of the things that this upbringing instilled in him was a sense of maturity which bled over into his magickal work, coloring his perspective in a positive way. He was the eldest of 12 and thus there were certain mindsets and behaviors that were present that reinforced this behavior.

After high school he became an apprentice at a sewing machine company called 'Minerva' as mentioned above. This is simply worth noting because Minerva is associated with weaving, and in some organizations, the idea and concepts that are associated with this goddess are used as beginning steps in religious development. While there, his father recognized Franz as his guru, and shortly thereafter the finer senses of Franz began to awaken. His magickal side began to spring to life. This included everything from clairvoyance to energetic healing work and healing work with various herbs and homeopathic remedies, and his reputation became quite profound in the 1920s and 1930s. Due to the degree of his sensory development his reputation began to spread out of his native Czechoslovakia, and he gained recognition or infamy, depending on whom you ask, in neighboring countries. When this occurred, one of the positions that he held was as a stage illusionist, and while touring through nations such as Austria and Germany he caught the eye of those that would have a direct and intense impact on his life, not only for the short term, but also for the long term. All of these experiences and more contributed to Frabato the Magician.

Frabato the Magician is a book that a student and close friend of his wrote that was delivered as fiction, but is commonly known to be biographical veiled behind a fictitious front. In that way it is similar to Gerald Gardner's novel *High Magic's Aid,* in that there is truth and teachings buried under the surface. Frabato covers the period in his life loosely beginning with his time in Minerva, but also covers his stage illusionist career during which he used the name Frabato, in Germany in the 1920s and early 1930s. Of course there is some embellishment that goes with it, but the overall themes of it are snapshots, so to speak, of his life. It is also worth mentioning here that events that occurred in his later life are also addressed in this novel, making it more of an overall tribute to his life rather than just focusing on one time period.

In magick, as most know, discipline and trust are two key ingredients not to be overlooked or taken lightly. I mention this here because it was a lack of both that led to one of the darker chapters in the life of Franz Bardon. While he was performing as a stage illusionist, traveling sage and mystic, he would arrange correspondences with select people that wanted magickal tutelage. One of the rules that he had was that the correspondences between himself and the student would be destroyed afterwards. A big reason for this was the rise of the Nazi party in Germany, and their oppression of anything that contradicted their ideology. A student of his broke this rule that he had and as a result, the Nazi party found out about Franz and his student, and both were arrested. This mistake made by the student ended up costing him his life, and brought hours of torture to both himself and Franz, as the Nazi party interrogated them. This correspondence caught the eye of Adolf Hitler, leader of the Nazi party, who wanted to know more about what they were doing sharing that information.

As the story goes, while the student was being tortured, he blurted out a qabalistic formula that paralyzed his attacker. When the paralysis wore off, the student was shot and killed out of revenge. Meanwhile, the Führer did his best to convince Franz to work with the Nazi party, particularly in the area of their occult work. He offered Franz high-ranking status in the Third Reich, and wanted to enlist Franz's aid following various global occult pursuits. Of course Franz said no, and that was the beginning of three and a half years of torture at the hands of the Nazis in a concentration camp. Eventually that resulted in a death sentence handed down by Hitler. But before the sentence could be carried out he was set free, and eventually made his way back to his hometown. Later on in life this time in the concentration camp would take a toll on his physical health, as he died at a relatively young age from various health ailments that compounded over time.

After the war, he resumed his travels across Europe, both from a stage illusionist perspective and as an energetic and herbal healer and teacher of Hermetic magick. However, one of the things he found was a much different Europe than the one that he was familiar with during the pre-war days. Once again, though, he found himself in legal hot water, as post-World War II Czechoslovakia was very closed to the idea of any sort of periphery work done in the fields that were Bardon's expertise, as much of the world was at this time, and because of this, he was arrested in 1958. It was during his imprisonment that he died at the age of 48. Even his death, though, is something of interest. The official reason for death that is listed is pancreatitis, and while that is one thing, it was the manner of his death that evokes a certain layer of mystery. While he was imprisoned he request that his wife bring him a piece of bacon, and it was shortly after ingesting this that he made his transition into spirit, which has led some to speculate that it was self-induced suicide, which is a strong possibility to those that are medically minded. Given his knowledge of the healing arts, it stands to reason that he knew that bacon would do this to him and thus is the reason that he requested it. His wife, son, and daughter all out lived him, and his son went on to become a major source of information about Franz in later years.

The Work of Franz Bardon

During his 48 years of life on this physical plane, Franz gave us some of the best work on Hermeticism from the 20th century. His strength lies in the fact that most of his material is based on practical occultism. While he does give a decent amount of space to theory, the bulk of his work is spent on practice. In only three short completed books, he lays down basic Hermetic practices that can be used by anyone. His inspiration for this is worth discussing briefly, too, as it was one of the first works to consider this idea.

His father was a Hermeticist, and because of that, the influence was always present in his life. An example of his dedication to the art can be found in the relationship he had with his wife. When they fell in love and got married, they discussed children. Franz didn't want any, but Marie did. So they made a deal. The deal was that they would have children, as long as she was the one that cared for them, because they way that Franz viewed it, caring for them and raising them would take away from his spiritual work. While to some this may seem like an extreme view, there was another magickal couple that approached their spiritual paths from a similar view and that was S.L. MacGregor Mathers and his wife Moina, who are believed to have never consummated their marriage. While rare, these types of ideas are not unheard of in the area of magick.

There are three complete published books that are considered the bulk of the work that Franz did during his lifetime regarding Hermetics. He titled the series the "Holy Mysteries Series", and each one correlates to one of the major tarot trumps, in sequential order, from the beginning of the major arcana. It is easy to deduce that perhaps he was considering writing a volume for each tarot card, and this pattern is not unheard of, as some years before, Aleister Crowley followed a same pattern when he wrote his volume *Magick in Theory & Practice*. Of course the main difference is that a chapter in Crowley's book was associated with a tarot card, while Bardon's work would be one book per tarot card. Franz made his transition into spirit before this could be completed, but the three books he left behind are an excellent testament to his work.

It is also worth mentioning that these books were published towards the end of his life, and thus the gift of his own hindsight came in very handy, as one could see that these volumes represent collected material from his decades of experience. He made his transition into spirit in 1958, and the first of these books were published in 1956. Thus, they also arrived on the occult scene during the 1950s, which I discussed in my essay on Kenneth Grant, to put things into context.

The first book in the series is simply entitled *Initiation into Hermetics*, and addresses exactly what the title claims. This book is an excellent primer regarding the Hermetic path, and lays down basic concepts to be aware of, as well as a clear and concise approach and revelation of the 5th element, which he calls "Akasha", which is another word that corresponds to spirit. This is an interesting tome because while he does address theory, the bulk of the book is focused around practice. One of the key points of this volume is that it lays down 10 basic practices and steps for personal and magickal development. By following these 10 steps, a practitioner puts himself or herself in a position to create their own magickal discipline without the necessity of a teacher. This is a key fact because that was one of the motivators for Franz, as other than what he absorbed from his father, he really didn't have a teacher of his own. The fact that these books are for the most part self-contained, also gives insight into his psyche, as it is evident that a spiritual goal of his was to help others help themselves, rather than putting others in a position to rely on others for spiritual advancement.

Initiation Into Hermetics brings through information that can also be adapted to any spiritual path, as it is so steeped in practice and specifically independent practice, that it can be modified as one's tastes may dictate. The 10 steps of development are there to assist one on their path, and while there may be some Hermetic dogma present, they address spiritual themes overall, rather than just what practices fit in that particular context. Franz was an individual that simply took what he had, improved upon it, and then disseminated it to the masses in order to be of service to the rest of the human race. His steps of development have been mirrored in many more recent works by various authors, ranging from Donald Tyson to Dolores Ashcroft-Nowicki, among others.

Also of note here is that he addresses elemental theory as well as the planes, and the different bodies that each person has. By addressing these topics, he not only gives the reader a firm grasp of practice in the development steps, but he also gives basic cosmological information that can be incorporated into individual practices, or can be used as stand alone material. Divinity, and interacting with divinity is also addressed here, and this is important to note because it fulfills the Hermetic axiom of "As above, so below." The subconscious mind is also addressed, and in a way that would've been revolutionary at the time of publication. Long story short, he examines the idea of autosuggestion, its potency, and how one can use the subconscious to create change in their environment.

At this point it is wise to enter into a tangent here into a brief discussion of fluid condensers. Franz Bardon did extensive work with fluid condensers through the course of his lifetime, and compiled a lot of material in this volume that addresses this. Wisely, he puts this information towards the latter part of his 10-step development process, and approaches things from an interesting and uncommon perspective, even to this day. His influences can also be seen here, as is evidenced by his language. He addresses a few magickal concepts that are not uniquely his, but rather are ideas that he learned that he could clarify in this volume. Let's look at them for a moment before continuing.

The first idea that he brings to the discussion is that of autosuggestion, and how it can be worked with. Keeping in mind that these books were released during the 1950s, let's approach this from a historical context. The idea of hypnosis that he brings to the surface to be addressed is one that was still, at that time, an idea that was not only circumspect, but also still in formation. Franz Mesmer originally advanced this idea approximately 100 years before Franz Bardon was born, and as he was learning Hermetics, Bardon was exposed to these teachings, and could apply the Hermetic theory to this scientific practice. There have been volumes written on this in hypnotherapy circles over the decades, but suffice to say here that Franz Bardon was one of the first modern magicians to address this directly, and to bring it into the light, so to speak, for others to use. Thus in some ways he was revolutionary at the time the books were published.

The second idea to address here is his work that covers fluid condensers and magickal mirrors. A lot of his work can be seen as based on the work of a 19th century occultist by the name of Paschal Beverly Randolph, who was a member of the group "The Hermetic Brotherhood of Luxor", a Rosicrucian, and a Spiritualist. He was also an influential factor regarding the use of magickal mirrors, and synthesization of Spiritualist and magickal ideas. Magickal mirrors are things that have been around for centuries, and have been used extensively in magickal ways. P.B. Randolph simply took this work and advanced it with his own spin. While Mr. Randolph was mostly known for sexual magick techniques, the ideas that are discussed here are ones that had a large impact on Franz Bardon, as well as a lot of the 20th century magickal scene. The basic theory behind the magickal mirror is that you use it as a tool to practice safe evocation. Another handy use of the magickal mirror is in the technique of scrying. Long story short, scrying is a technique that can be useful to look into other planes of existence, or even to other places of this third dimensional reality that we live in.

Fluid condensers, though, get a section all their own, as they are things that can be very potent. In essence, fluid condensers are tools that have been used for centuries in the secretive laboratories of alchemists, and because of this, there is a science in their creation. These are devices that are built, astrologically timed, alchemically matched, to store ingredients that can be used to facilitate particular results that can be of benefit to the magician. So, for example, depending on what one was working on manifesting they would look up the appropriate correspondences, alchemically, astrologically, and qabalistically, and not only create the condenser, but also the substance that would occupy it. It is worth revealing here that his work in this area is influenced by not only Randolph's work, but also Spiritualist teachings of the late 19th century as well. In short, Spiritualism teachings of that time talk of ectoplasm, and more physical manifestations of spirit energy, precipitating down to the physical plane via the astral plane. This is worth mentioning because while that idea was around before that time, Spiritualism took those ideas, writings, and principles, and codified them so that they could be used in a more common way, and so that they were available in a more accessible format. P.B. Randolph was well versed in Spiritualism as well as his magickal experience and because of this, he was in a position to bring the two teachings together. Franz Bardon took the work that Randolph had started, and took it to the next level by defining it more, and improving on Randolph's work.

Another interesting tangent that this discourse produces is the injection of Alex Sanders into the equation. Alex Sanders, the founder of his own tradition in the craft, and self-proclaimed King of the Witches, became familiar with the work of Franz Bardon in post-World War II Europe, when he was going through his own "Left Hand Path Phase" as well as expanding into ceremonial magick. Specifically, he worked heavily with fluid condensers as a conduit in conjunction with his mediumship skills that he had begun cultivating in his youth through various Spiritualist churches that he attended.

The second volume, *The Practice of Magical Evocation,* takes things up a notch and is more intense than the first volume. With this volume he takes things in a more proactive and creationist bent. In this volume he puts more emphasis on the magickal side of things. He covers tools, magick in general, and the evocation of spirits. The first section of the book delves heavily into the magick of what he has to teach. This is important to understand in context of his series, as one will observe that through the first two books he has taken the reader step by step through a personal empowerment process in a systematic way, and has done his best to not only be clear, but also analytical. For example, he does not begin his teachings by jumping straight into magick as other authors may do, but rather he walks the reader through the preparation that it takes to create the proper, healthy perspective that is wise to have when studying magick. Thus, tools are covered extensively, and while theory is still light in this book, it is present nonetheless, paving the way for a clear and concise practice.

Part of the value of this second tome is in the information that he provides regarding spirits of several different natures, and how, exactly, to work with them in a safe context. He approaches this subject in a very comprehensive and delineated fashion, and thus it is clear and concise to work with. Not only does he go into depth about the entities of the elemental kingdom, he also gives space to entities from other realms, specifically spirits of the planets, and spirits of the astrological signs. All of this information can be useful, and it is also nice to have all of this information in one book. During the 1950s this wasn't exactly common, and even to this day his organization can be an excellent reference for the practicing magician. Another pearl to come from this volume is that he also has sigils and seals for these entities as well in the third section of the book. Finally, in this volume, he also gives information on talismans, and how exactly one can work with them effectively. This volume is practically broken down into two parts as I mentioned above, but I'll address them here again from a different perspective. Basically, the first part is the tools of the art and the second section is dedicated to beings that exist that can be communicated with and worked with. I point this out because it is an excellent follow up to his first book, as it builds from within to without, as any practical set of working manuals would. Thus he is perpetuating the ancient axiom of "Know Thyself", codifying his emphasis on Hermetic teachings.

The third tome in his series becomes more specialized, but as is his true style, delivered in a practical and working manner. Entitled *Key to the True Kabbalah,* it is focused on just that, taking his writing style away from general Hermetics and focusing on just the Qabala aspect of it. The interesting fact to note about this book is that in some ways it is a return to his first book, and in other ways, it is the final statement to the legacy that he has left behind. It also validates his adeptship, and because of this it allows him and his work to stand on its own, rather than be seen as part of an incomplete project. It is a return to his previous style, as there is more of a delineated split between theory and practice. In essence it simply covers as many aspects of the Qabala as Franz knows of, and in its delivery, is revealed a profound magickal truth. The way that he approaches the Qabala is one of understanding it as a language of nature. In short, the main approach that he takes is that by understanding and working with the Qabala the adept can interact with the universe in a sovereign fashion. And in this fashion, his magickal legacy is sealed.

There is a part of the magickal tradition that simply states that a sign of a true adept is that the individual interprets every interaction with the universe as an interaction between the adept and divinity. So therefore, everything is simply messages to be interpreted so that a closer union can be achieved throughout life. This simple truth is a major basis for the teachings of this book, and because this is the stance that Bardon takes, it makes the Qabala a much more interesting subject. It moves the working with and familiarity into a dynamic force that can be potent in its simplicity.

He thoroughly explores different qabalistic formulae as well as addressing the power of the word, and of vibrations. This is an extension of some of the work that he discussed in the second book. In his second book he discusses magnetism as a powerful force, and in this book, he brings this to a new level as he discusses mantras and tantras from the Hindu tradition and the power of the voice. He also explores the esoteric meaning of numbers and letters, and thus takes a more intense turn into high magick ideas. By this point in the series it seems he feels confident that the reader is ready for these more advanced ideas, and because of this, he takes theory to a whole new level from that of the rest of his books. In his other two books he is light in theory, but in the third book, he adds in more theory, but with the express idea of giving this theory to the reader as yet another technique, and thus does not deviate from the exercises and techniques used up to this point.

There are fragments that exist of a fourth book in the series entitled *The Golden Book of Wisdom*, and it would thus correlate to the fourth tarot trump. The contents that survive of this book detail and clarify the Hermetic view of religion, mysticism, physiology, and universal laws, among other topics. While the book itself was never completed, there are sections of it that have and this is worth exploring should one choose to look at more of the meditative and religious aspects of Hermeticism.

While the volumes of material written by Franz Bardon may be only limited to three and a third books, he accomplishes something that was a shot in the arm to Hermeticism at the time, which carries through to this day. Through these books, Franz Bardon restores the "Royal" to "The Royal Art."

Kenneth Grant
(1924-2011)

By Rev. Bill Duvendack

Very few occultists of the 20th century evoke such a passionate reaction as Mr. Kenneth Grant. A powerful figure of the 20th century occult scene, Uncle Kenny, as some lovingly call him, gave us a whole new perspective on the subjects of the occult, tantra, and of course, magick. He brought to the collective consciousness of people everywhere a synthesis of eastern thought, the alchemical imagination, ancient Egyptian traditions, the expansion of consciousness, and an awareness of various occult figures that, until that time, were only known in small circles.

Kenneth Grant was born in 1924 to a mother whom he referred to as sainted, and for the first 20 years of his life lived as anyone else of that time would, but with two small exceptions: he fell in love with eastern thought and philosophy, deeply connecting with the consciousness expansion teachings of it. He also developed an interest in comparative and world religions. He became quite familiar with the writings of well-known authors of the time, including HP Blavatsky, John Woodruffe, and Sir E.A. Wallis Budge. Both of these interests would be more deeply developed during the coming decades, as more and more of his work would focus on both those subjects, with one other subject rounding out his spiritual toolbox: ceremonial magick. Part of his path was also receiving transmissions from beings beyond the physical, which he had already experienced by the time he went to work for Aleister Crowley.

In 1944, Kenneth Grant met Aleister Crowley, and they formed a working relationship in 1945. Their arrangement was Mr. Grant's services as secretary for Mr. Crowley in exchange for magical tutelage. Dr. Israel Regardie had also held the position of secretary to Mr. Crowley several decades in the past. However, this is where the parallels stop, as Mr. Grant and Mr. Crowley's relationship was of a much different nature. By the time he came to work for Mr. Crowley, Mr. Grant had already begun to absorb everything he could that Mr.

Crowley had written, and of course this increased during his tenure as secretary. Kenneth was initiated into the O.T.O. (Ordo Templi Orientis) in 1945, and then into the A.A. (Argentum Astrum) in 1946. Both of these groups are well known to be associated with Aleister Crowley, and at the time Mr. Grant was initiated into them, they were undergoing a transition period. Without going into too much technical detail here, the point to understand is that Kenneth was given a charter within that organization in 1951 to start a lodge, which he did. On an interesting side note, Gerald Gardner was given a similar charter, but chose not to act on it. Kenneth's lodge was called New Isis Lodge, and became active in 1955. As part of the group's manifesto, he declared the discovery of a current of 'set', which would be very defining not only for him, but also for posterity. This of course, was in sharp contrast to the current of Horus that the modern OTO is known as being aligned with. A current of energy is a style or a form of energy that can be tapped into. It is constantly moving and evolving in tune with those that work with it and Aleister Crowley delivered the news of this current of Horus in 1904 with the reception of *The Book of the Law*.

Prior to the establishment of the New Isis Lodge, Kenneth and his wife Steffi met and began working with the artist Austin Osman Spare to create the 'Zos Kia Cultus', which was another magickal group with a much different focus. The Grants and Mr. Spare formed a working relationship and friendship that was very successful, as is evidenced by the fact that this work was eventually chronicled in Kenneth's Typhonian Trilogies, which led to a resurgence of interest into the works of Mr. Spare. More on that though later. Suffice to say for now that in the early 1950s, in an era that saw Gerald Gardner publish his first non-fiction book on witchcraft in the form of *Witchcraft Today*, in 1954, and the repeal of the witchcraft laws in England in 1951, the Grants and Mr. Spare were tapping into the zeitgeist of the decade in their own unique way.

With the advent of the New Isis Lodge, which would later become known as the Nu-Isis Lodge, a new chapter was being written in his magical career, which would be fertile ground to draw from later in his writings. The New Isis Lodge would be active until 1962, at which point it was 'reabsorbed' into the OTO. Thus, the lodge lasted approximately 7 years. This is interesting because 7 is associated with a Saturnine cycle in astrology, and considering that the energy of Set is associated with Saturn, this is very profound, whether intentionally planned or not. Like humans, organizations have astrological charts associated with them, and thus, synchronicities like this can be pointed out and whenever possible, looked at for more insight into the energetics that are present in said organizations.

Once this magical work had been completed, it was only a matter of time before the tempo increased for Kenneth, as things were about to be turned up a notch in terms of intensity. In 1969, he, along with John Symonds, published *The Confessions of Aleister Crowley*, which had only previously been in serialized form. One of the things that made this a profound endeavor was that this time period, interestingly enough known as the 'Summer of Love', was the beginning of a revival of interest in all things magical and occult based, and thus Crowley's Law of Thelema was brought into the greater consciousness of the world. This opened the door for Kenneth to go full steam ahead in his unique direction. Shortly after this publishing endeavor, Kenneth wrote articles for the encyclopedic *Man, Myth, & Magic* series. One of the things that he did in conjunction with this is that he was able to secure a piece of Austin Osman Spare's artwork on the cover of one of the volumes.

In 1972, Kenneth published his first book, entitled *The Magical Revival*. In short, this was a book that was a catching up to speed, if you will, of the 20th century occult revival that had come about in full force in many areas. At that time, astrology, the occult, ritual magick, paganism, neo-paganism, and earth traditions had all been thrust back into the spotlight in the popular consciousness of people everywhere. Among the topics that were addressed there, one interesting topic stands out, as this is the first delivery of an idea that has led to many debates in occult circles worldwide since the publication of that book. This is the idea that the horror author H.P. Lovecraft received the Cthulhu mythos that he is known for via psychically transmitted means, and that the information contained therein is actually, among other things, ancient Sumerian and

Mesopotamian beliefs that are making their way back into the world now.

This book became the beginning of an epic 9-book saga that would span 30 years, and has become one of the most influential occult book series of the last few centuries. *The Magical Revival* is the first book in what is known as the "Typhonian Trilogy", which became the "Typhonian Trilogies" over time. In short, his Typhonian saga is a series of three trilogies, and while each trilogy has an overall theme to it, the bigger series of nine has common themes in it in general as well.

The first trilogy of books to be released was *The Magical Revival* (1972), *Aleister Crowley and the Hidden God* (1973), and *Cults of the Shadow* (1975). Following this was *Nightside of Eden* (1977), *Outside the Circles of Time* (1980), and *Hecate's Fountain* (1992). The final trilogy consisted of *Outer Gateways* (1995), *Beyond the Mauve Zone* (1996), and *The Ninth Arch* (2002). All nine of these books together constitute the bulk of Kenneth's work, but this list is by no means complete. Kenneth also wrote several other books, both based on the themes carried through in these books, and also having to do with the work of his close friend, the artist Austin Osman Spare. Without Kenneth's dedication to propagating the work of Mr. Spare, the 20th century might not have discovered the mad genius that was Austin Osman Spare. But that my friends, is a whole different essay in general. Not only did Kenneth share Spare's work with the world, he also shared information about Spare's personal and professional life, and went into the background of Spare's techniques.

The first trilogy in the series primarily dealt with matters of the 20th century, and thus was a contemporary view of the occult scene of approximately the last 70 years at the time of the writing. Most of the themes of the first trilogy are themes that contemporary occultists of that time could relate to, such as chapters on the newly budding Thelemic movement, as well as a variety of magical techniques not commonly discussed publicly until then. One of the more interesting techniques that he wrote about was the use of sexual magick. While most occultists were already at least passingly familiar with the techniques of sex magick at that time, they were not familiar with Mr. Grant's spin on it, which was the spin of the eastern philosophies that he was familiar with. Thus, he brought to occultists everywhere a synthesis of eastern and western sexual magick techniques. What made Kenneth's work stand out was the particular style of eastern philosophy that he was acquainted with, which was not the common eastern philosophy of the time. It is important to know here that most of the eastern philosophies that Mr. Grant was familiar with were those of the north east section of India, and most western traditions, even to this day, are centered in central and southern India. Because of this twist, Kenneth's writings were fresh and enticing.

Two other themes were birthed during this first trilogy, and those were the themes of the Left-Hand Path, and of the Typhonian tradition of ancient Egypt. In magick, the Left Hand Path gets a bad reputation. A lot of times it is seen as self-serving, or perhaps that of a more evil bent. In reality, its greatest strength is its greatest weakness, which is that it is 'self' focused, among other things. It focuses on taking care of the self. Of course one can see that this can be a scenario of 'too much of a good thing', and thus, with one wrong decision, one could easily turn selfish and lower negative ego in perspective and action. However, the Left Hand Path that Kenneth revealed was that of more of the hidden side of things. And in this way, he strongly connected with the lunar current that millions of people work with every day. The Typhonian tradition of ancient Egypt is another matter entirely. When it comes to this subject, it is of course prerequisite that one has knowledge of the entity known as Typhon. This equates with the Set tradition out of ancient Egypt. Thus, it is wise to be familiar with Set, which is the basis for the Christian devil, along with other influences such as Pan. Among other things, the Egyptian deity Set is associated with change, and more recently, tied into the Judeo-Christian personification of evil, and thus the devil. Set is the slayer of Osiris. Thus, he is the change element that is required for growth. In some ways, as Mr. Grant points out, he is the Great Initiator.

The second trilogy was more focused on the Left Hand Path, general magick techniques, the aeon of Ma'at, and the Cthulu mythos. With this trilogy, more emphasis is put on the idea of the alchemical imagination. By that I mean the fact that there is much debate as to the validity of working with the Cthulu mythos. Some say, ironically enough, that it is utter madness to consider the Cthulu mythos valid. Others work with it on a regular basis. Still others are skeptics, and consider the idea, but treat it as a sideline to other work. Whatever the facts may be, there is still the fact that Kenneth Grant brought it to the surface as an idea to be considered. So, let's consider it! To begin with, other than ancient writings that are sometimes obscure, most of the ideas associated with the Cthulu mythos date back to ancient Sumerian times. Various references can be found in the writings of H.P. Blavatsky. While this is true, this is also about the extent of the actual facts of the situation. On a more contemporary note, the horror writing of H.P. Lovecraft of the early 20th century fleshed out this ancient mythos. And it was enhanced by Kenneth Grant.

Without going into too much detail about it, there are several key elements that are to be considered in the context of the writings of Kenneth Grant.

The Cthulu mythos embodies that which is madness in all of its myriad forms. Another key note to know is that it is also associated with beings that come from beyond the stars, and now reside on earth. Of course one of their ultimate goals is the subjugation and even the eradication of the human race. Thus in some ways, the Cthulu mythos is the antithesis of everything.

The Maatian tangent is another matter entirely. This is based on the writings of Aleister Crowley, and thus requires a brief explanation to put it into context. One of the key notes of Aleister Crowley's writings was that of the aeon of Horus, the Egyptian warrior god, among other attributes. That is what we are entering now, in tandem with entering the astrological aeon of Aquarius. To Crowley, this is the aeon of Horus. However, the aeon to follow Horus is the aeon of Ma'at. Ma'at is the Egyptian goddess of justice, diplomacy, truth, harmony, and the idea of weighing things out. Considering the fact that each astrological aeon lasts approximately 2,500 years, on the surface, this seems like a far-fetched idea. But what Kenneth points out is something that was revolutionary at the time, and that is the idea of overlapping aeons. In other words, one of the main tenets of his teachings is that as the aeon of Horus is coming into being and forming, so, too, is the aeon of Ma'at overlapping the aeon of Horus. Now this idea was not completely his, as another student of Aleister Crowley's had come up with the idea before him. Rather Kenneth simply took the idea and expanded on it. Frater Achad, as he is known, made this correlation early in the 20th century, and Kenneth Grant simply moved the idea forward in a more cohesive and expanded way. Thus, when I say the focus is on Maatian ideas, this is to say that what Kenneth is revealing is that aeons overlap, and that one is forming and coming of age, so, too, is the next, successive one. Thus, by the end of the second trilogy of books, he has established not only a unique perspective on eastern thought, but he has also taken cutting edge ideas and brought them down to a more precipitated form.

Finally, in the third trilogy, Kenneth takes the reader in a very interesting direction, as he focuses in the direction of things that are from beyond. Thus, the easiest way to address this is through discussion of UFOs and beings from beyond. Did you notice how I didn't say 'aliens'? This is intentional, and is a key point of Kenneth's writings. By this point in the series, he is emphasizing communication with beings from beyond. And of course, to the average person, these are easiest understood as aliens. But, in accord with Kenneth's paradigm, these are simply beings that exist beyond our collectively understood paradigm and awareness. This is a result of his many years of consciousness expansion that he experienced, put into context of his spiritual toolbox. A large keystone of this is the fact that one of the things that Aleister Crowley emphasized in his writings was contact with beings of a preter-human intelligence. Kenneth took this idea and expanded on it to show his readers that there is truly no limit when it comes to trafficking with beings that are not physical. Also of a curious final note to his magnum opus is that the final book, *The Ninth Arch*, is based on a Masonic idea. During the third trilogy, there is also the very strong vibe of giving back to his readers, as he reveals experiences and transmissions that he had experienced over the years. These experiences, when looked at carefully, are experiences that can serve as insight and establish a certain intimacy with his readers.

While all of these are themes that can be looked at in a microcosmic way via each trilogy, there are also themes that run throughout the whole of the series. Some of these themes include the newly budding religion of Thelema, the work of Austin Osman Spare, the Maatian current, occult influences from the Middle East, the Left Hand Path, and eastern philosophy, especially sex magick. The interweaving of themes, both microcosmic and macrocosmic, is very interesting to consider. Like his idea of overlapping aeons, his themes overlap throughout the course of his books. Throughout the series, Kenneth paints a portrait of a very unique blend of ceremonial magick, eastern philosophy, sex magick, and ideas that are as cutting edge as you can get, and as controversial as you can get.

Controversy is something that has accompanied Kenneth Grant for most of his life. In an attempt to spare the reader too many technical details, I shall condense these events as best I can. After all, the facts are readily available to those that choose to pursue them in depth. The first controversy to surround his life came about from his association with Aleister Crowley. In 1945, Kenneth was initiated into the O.T.O., and in 1946, the A.A. After the death of Aleister Crowley in December 1947, there was much debate as to who he left the order to. There was a faction in California, and a faction in England, to put things simplistically. Kenneth was given a charter to start a 'camp' of the O.T.O. in England by a protege of Crowley's, and Crowley himself insinuated that he would like it if Kenneth was the head of the British O.T.O. Eventually, over decades, there were spread legal challenges and rights of succession that would make a sailor blush! Recently, after much legal maneuvering, things are finally settled, and, according to the law, things are clear cut and delineated. However, following in the footsteps of Crowley, controversy, publicity, and legalities were common and abound throughout the course of Kenneth's magical career. Originally, his organization was called the Typhonian O.T.O. Now, however, it is known as the Typhonian Order. But the central theme is the same, and that is the theme of self-initiation.

Another way that controversy has followed Kenneth is through another theme that runs through his magnum opus, and that is the idea of the 'Tunnels of Set'. To condense it down, this is a reference to the backside, or nightside, of the Qabalistic Tree of Life. So on the surface, this idea is related to the dark side, and another Qabalistic idea, which is the Qlippoth. All of this work is based on Aleister Crowley's *Liber 231*. Some parallels have even been drawn to this being the ceremonial magick equivalent of Satanism. The fact of the matter, though, is that this comes from some of Crowley's writings, and some of it comes from the scholarship of Kenneth Grant. With his background in comparative religions, Kenneth realized some things that are hidden for those that seek them, and took those and ran with them, exposing them to the masses for scrutiny. For example, he had a view of the Egyptian god Set as the grand initiator. To some Thelemites, therefore, Set is the one that brought forth the opportunity for *The Book of the Law* to be revealed to Aleister Crowley in Cairo in 1904. Grant took this idea and ran with it, pointing out that in the ancient Egyptian myths, Set went out in front of the midnight ark that RA travelled in, clearing the path for its traverses. Thus, Set cleared the way for the aeon of Horus to arrive and thrive. By taking this perspective, Kenneth revealed an alchemical principle, which is the idea of the 'sun behind the sun'. In other words, the idea behind the idea, and it is worth noting that to the average person this may seem forbidden or even *gasp* evil! Kenneth portrayed this by going into greater depth and detail about Atlantean spirituality, pushing the envelope even further to the conservative mind, and eventually discussing the realm of prater-human spirituality and sentience.

    Besides the Typhonian Trilogies, Kenneth also put out several works regarding Austin Osman Spare, as well as several fiction pieces. While the books on Austin Osman Spare are fairly straightforward, encompassing his relationship with Spare, and Spare's work, his fiction requires a second look. His books *Snakewand and the Darker Strain*, *The Other Child and Other Tales*, *Gamaliel Diary of a Vampire* and *Dance, Doll, Dance*, all espouse writings having to do with Left-Hand Path teachings, but in particular, concepts that are related to the Tunnels of Set. Thus, he called them *Nightside Narratives*.

    One particular book stands out among his fiction works, and that is one that fits the niche that he was discussing through his series. His fiction novel *Against the Light*, while fiction in theory, was actually more alchemical imaginative than fiction. In some ways, this particular volume stands alone, as there is a narrator that can be safely assumed to be a perspective of Kenneth by Kenneth. Thus, in some ways, it can be seen as autobiographical. A large portion of this text both ties into Kenneth's own personal mythology, and the connection between him and Austin Osman Spare. Worth mentioning here is that it also addresses witchcraft, and the influence of a particular wise woman of the woods. Its title alone reveals another secret to understanding Kenneth's writings, and that is the secret of the double entendres.

Double entendres are something that Aleister Crowley was well versed in, and Kenneth Grant saw this and ran with it, incorporating it into his cosmology and writing style, and used it selectively to guide the reader through key initiations that only they can deliver. This is most exemplified in his book *Against the Light*. On the surface, it appears to be something that is against the light, meaning anti-light, or alternatively, an adversary of light. However, the reader quickly learns that it is more akin to holding something against the light, as it were, to see its validity and authenticity. In other words, this means holding something up to the light for scrutiny.

Conceptually, Kenneth Grant said 'hey, we can take this farther, and there is no limit.' As was mentioned before, this was due to his eastern philosophical influence of consciousness expansion. Writings that he did in eastern journals throughout the years were collected in a book entitled *At the Feet of the Guru*. Through these writings, more of Kenneth's eastern philosophical views were revealed, giving the reader a more firm grasp on Kenneth's mindscape.

Kenneth also gave the world Starfire Publishing, which is 25 years young as of 2011. Starfire publishes not only the works of Kenneth, but also many other cutting edge magical publications. Starfire Journal is one of the most sought after journals that are out there today, and specializes in Thelemic topics, as well as high magick topics like sigil magick, working with the Qlippoth, and, to a certain extent, chaos magick.

It is also worth mentioning here that since 1946, he has been married to the artist Steffi Grant. She was the initiator in the friendship between them and Austin Osman Spare in 1948 that flourished for years, and has left a legacy in the occult community still present to this day. She has done many of the art pieces that run throughout the Typhonian trilogies, and has illustrated several of the other works that he has done, as well as many of the books that deal with Austin Osman Spare. She has a unique style that cannot really easily be compared to anyone in particular. Elements of different artists can be extracted from her style. In her artwork, one can see the post-impressionist influences of Van Gogh, as well as influences from her contemporaries, such as Salvador Dali, but it is safe to say that not one person or element in particular could be said to have an outstanding influence on her work. Her style could best be explained as abstract art, with a touch of painting basics, such as what was found in ancient artwork, predominantly cave drawings. While on the surface this may seem basic, on another level it is highly profound, as it shows not only the diversity of her style, but also the range. She could do artwork ranging from the abstract to the impressionistic to the highly linear, as is revealed by a lot of her drawings of the Qabalistic tree of life. In short, she can adjust her style and manifestation in tune with what the subject and/or focus is. Through her diversity, she can more accurately portray what that particular energy is via her art. Her style has influenced contemporary artists like Kala Trobe, among others. Steffi and Kenneth have had a magical relationship for over 65 years, and together they have left a legacy that is constantly pushing the envelope, even to this day. Steffi brought into the visual spectrum concepts that Kenneth wrote about in a very fluidly dynamic way. Her work is passionate, vibrant, and alive, to say the very least.

    Kenneth Grant made his transition into spirit on January 15, 2011. The public announcement did not occur until February 1, 2011. This is worth noting because even this plan was in line with Kenneth's spiritual practices, as two weeks is a sufficient amount of time for his soul to make its bardo journey, uninterrupted. The bardo journey is from eastern philosophies, and addresses the journey that the soul takes after the transition known as death. The metaphysics behind this journey are well documented throughout the publishing industry today in various forms and from various perspectives, and are readily available.

Of course this also illustrated how privately Kenneth lived his life, and the silence and mystique that surrounded his works. He was a devotee of keeping the private life private, and his public life public. Truly one of the greater adepts of the 20th century, Kenneth Grant gave us a legacy that will continue to influence those that seek it now and for many, many, years to come.

Special thanks go to Michael Staley, Nema, and Rich Brewer for their assistance.

Part Three: Crafters of the New Witch

Gerald Gardner
(1884-1964)

By Rich Wandel

"When you get to Castleton, go straight along Arbory Street until you see the old mill on the left; there is a large car park. In the ancient stone buildings you will find this unique Museum. Also a most beautiful old world restaurant, with its blackened beams hung with relics of the Past, and both it and the Museum are open 7 days in the week and you will receive a warm welcome in true Manx style.

Yours sincerely, G. B. Gardner."

The welcome would come from Gerald Brosseau Gardner, Director of the Museum of Witchcraft, a thin man with a shock of white hair behind his high forehead and an equally white mustache and triangular beard tapering to a rounded point at the end. Blue-eyed and angular he was custodian of a lifetime's work of collecting, reflection and practice of what he considered a surviving strain of Britain's ancient Witch cult.

Opening the museum at the age of 67 he had been born of a well to do merchant family in Blundellsands, a suburb of Liverpool, England, on Friday the 13th 1884. His father William was a timber merchant, his mother, Louise Burguelew, an American, but more important perhaps than either was his nursemaid Georgiana Harriet Wakefield McCombie better known as "Com." By the age of four, school age, Gerald was frail and asthmatic. On the advice of Com his parents decided that it would be better if their son spent his winters in a drier, warmer climate. He went with Com first to Nice and then the Canary Islands. With no formal schooling, and little from Com who showed more interest in partying and men than in the four year old, he taught himself to read and continued throughout his life to be inquisitive and self-taught. From his first days in the Canaries, the young boy noticed and was intrigued by the common site of men carrying weapons – knives and swords. He obtained his first pocket knife, but quickly lost it to Com's disapproval. The fascination would continue and later become Gerald's first entry into the world of archeology and folklore. It wasn't long before the two travelers moved on, first to the Gold Coast of Africa and then to the Portuguese colony of Madeira. Here they would return each winter for the next nine years, Com to enjoy her parties and young Gerald, left pretty much on his own, to investigate this part of the world and to read the books left behind by European visitors at their hotel. Among these were the works of Florence Marryat. In 1891 she published *There is No Death*, Gerald's first introduction to the ideas of Spiritualism.

During summers back in England, Gerald remembered how he was entertained with family tales of his grandfather who had married a Witch, a second wife known for her occult interests, especially her healing powers (which he later recounted for J. L. Braceline's *Gerald*

Gardner: Witch). There was also a family pamphlet claiming as ancestors a number of Gardners, including Grizell Gairdener who had been burnt as a witch in the 1600s, and a few other less than reputable naval men, a possible bigamist, and several smugglers. According to Philip Heselton, in his biography of Gardner, the grandfather was more likely his grandfather's nephew and while it is unlikely that the others were all actual blood ancestors, the family viewed them as such and counted them as part of the family lore and history. Then there were the Sergeneson cousins, Christian churchgoers and believers in the occult.

In 1901 Com decided to marry David Elkington. She had met him in Madeira during one of their winter excursions, and after a back and forth romance decided to go with him to his new tea plantation in Ceylon (now Sri Lanka). Gerald was old enough to learn a trade so it was decided that he would accompany them as a sort of apprentice to David. Gerald's father continued to pay for his son's upkeep in an annual stipend to Elkington. The teenage Gardner was well on the road to manhood and was soon immersed in the monotonous life of a tea plantation in the British colonies. For most colonialists contact with the local people was minimal, only enough to take care of the business at hand. Gardner did mix with his British compatriots, going to parties although he himself did not drink, joining the Freemasons in 1910 and at one point becoming a member of the Ceylon Volunteers, a colonial army group formed to guard against invasion and if needed to assist in the Boer Wars of South Africa. He also began to study the local cultures, interacting with the Buddhist population and learning something of their strong belief in reincarnation and their certainty of the presence of many spirits both good and evil.

Within a few years Gardner was no longer satisfied with being an apprentice and still dependent on his father, it was also time to separate from Com who was more of a parent than his mother and father were. In 1908 he left Ceylon and went to Borneo by way of Singapore. This time he was paid for his work. Here he met yet another culture, the Dyaks. As usual he engaged the local culture and belief system, including their custom of a specialized shaman or pawang communing with the dead in order to affect healings or to gain needed information. By 1911 he was again ready to move on, this time to Malaya at the age of 26. Here he worked with a long time British planter who had become a Muslim and married several local women. Islam was the dominant religion of Malaya and to know and be trusted more readily by the Malays Gardner swore the Islamic oath: "There is no God but Allah, and Mohamed is his prophet." As a member of the Islamic community Gardner was introduced not only to the overarching Muslim beliefs but also to the more local cultural beliefs, lore and magick. Included were tales of the Malay knife or kris, especially the majapahit kris, a magical knife which could both protect the holder as well as slay an enemy simply by pointing the blade at him. Gardner had begun to study the subject that would get him known among anthropologists and archeologists. By 1923 he left plantation life in favor of government employment as a plantation inspector and later as a customs official. This increased his ability to travel around Malaya, continuing to collect knives and information. He made contact with the indigenous population, the Senoi, called by the Malays "Saki." They lived deep in the jungle and had their own traditions of magick which they regarded as simply part of what is, something effective, and so they used it. According to Heselton, three of Gardner's later associates maintained that his financial security came in part from his time as an inspector of opium sales when he took bribes to allow the dealers to produce more than the law allowed. Gardner believed opium to be not only benign but actually helpful and therefore had no qualms in looking the other way for a price. In all Gardner would spend 20 years in Malaya, collecting, learning, and ultimately publishing his findings.

In speaking with the Malays Gardner heard tales of a lost fortress and of ancient gold coinage. The British thought these only tales, in their mind the Malays were simply liars. Gardner wasn't so sure. In traveling along the Johore River he thought he saw evidence of an old man-made embankment. Further investigation and some digging found an old fort and in time he discovered the gold coins the Malays spoke about. At first British officials and archeologists simply refused to believe him, or even to go to Johore to see for themselves. Later they were forced to accept his findings. In the early 1930s Gardner presented his findings in several specialized journals and attended conferences in Britain and the Philippines. In 1936 his *Kris and Other Malay Weapons* was published in Britain. His discoveries, along with his work on the Malay kris gained Gardner a measure of recognition among scholars and archeologists of the Far East. In 1936 he was elected a Fellow of the Royal Anthropological Institute.

During his time in the Far East Gardner would return to visit his native England every few years. He returned in 1905 and again in 1916 during the First World War when, too frail to fight, he worked in a hospital. Perhaps his most significant return "home" was in 1927 when he married Donna Rosedale whom he met through his brother-in-law. While in England he carefully investigated the truth of Spiritualism. At first he looked to a local group but being unimpressed he traveled to London to investigate and there happened upon the London Spiritualist Alliance. Although a believer in life after death, Gardner took a scientific approach to examining the claims of this group of mediums. He told no one of his trip to London, not even Donna who he was fast courting. He borrowed some letters from a friend which he placed conspicuously sticking out of his pocket. If a fake medium were to examine his pockets he/she would come to some false conclusions. Arriving at their headquarters he demanded to see a medium immediately and two more shortly after. He was discouraged from seeing so many without any intervening time to regain strength after the experience, but Gardner insisted and finally saw two mediums that day and one the following. All three had messages from the same three "relatives", an Uncle John and cousin Anne. He had heard of neither of these people. The third was his mother. They also predicted that he would remain in England several months longer than his government leave would allow. In the next few days he found out from living members of his family that those indeed were the actual, though rarely used names of an uncle and a cousin. He also proposed to Donna Rosedale and quickly arranged a wedding which by government regulations automatically entitled him to extended leave time thus fulfilling the final prediction. Gardner return to the Far East convinced of the truth of Spiritualism but cautious of any particular medium who might still be a fraud.

In 1936, as a retired civil servant with pension, Gardner left the Far East for good. The 56 year old had spent 36 years in the Far East.

He first went to Palestine to work with archeologist Sir Flinders Petrie at Tell el-Duweir. He had met Petrie on a trip to Gaza in 1932. Here he saw ancient temples that contained two altars, one to Yahweh and a second to the goddess Astaroth. This may or may not have been Gardner's first encounter with the divine female but it made a strong impression on him. By now Donna wanted to return permanently to England, and so they did. As usual Gardner got his return-to-England illness. England's cold and damp were always a trial for him. His doctor recommended the naturist cure of sun and air and Gardner spent some time at a nudist club, becoming convinced of the health benefits of naturism. In the meantime Gardner had begun to have recurring dreams of an ancient landscape and in a 1938 trip to Cyprus he discovered what looked very much like that dreamscape. The result was his novel *A Goddess Arrives* published in 1939. He and Donna were living in London across from Victoria Station. As the Nazi threat increased, Gardner realized that living in London, across from a prime target was a threat to his by now very large collection of artifacts, so he and Donna moved away from London, settling in Highcliffe in Britain's New Forest region. Here he advocated for the establishment of what would become England's Home Guard, became a Civil Defense Warden and when denied entry into the Home Guard because of his status as a warden, used his weapons expertise to become the local Guard's armorer. Officially armed he was ready to defend the home front in case of the expected Nazi invasion. While cycling one day he noticed a building, which according to the words cut into its stone façade was "The First Rosicrucian Theatre in England." Curious, Gardner joined the group. Its leader was a man who claimed to be immortal and the current persona of a long line of famous magicians and seers, including Cornelius Agrippa. At Christmas time in 1939 Gardner showed him an ancient bracelet which he had among his collections. The bracelet had some strange magical writing. The Rosicrucian leader looked at the bracelet carefully and using all his wisdom gained through so many lifetimes announced to the group that the bracelet was ancient indeed and that he could tell from the mysterious writing that it was Celtic in origin and very magical. At his point Gardner revealed that actually he had made the bracelet in the past few weeks and that the writing was in Theban, an alphabet often used by Cornelius Agrippa.

Gardner, of course, left the theater, but he had become friendly with a smaller group within the theater who seemed to be genuinely knowledgeable and interested in the occult. He asked them why they remained and they told him that it was a way for them to stay together and share their interests. Shortly afterwards they brought Gerald to a home owned by Dorothy Clutterbuck; an older woman and according to Heselton "probably strongly bi-sexual." In short order he was stripped naked and initiated into what they called the Craft. Gerald Gardner was now in contact with a surviving remnant of Britain's old Witch cult. Gardner continued meeting with the New Forest group. He also continued collecting artifacts relating to magick and to Witchcraft, publishing in a 1939 issue of Folk-Lore a description of his Witchfinder General Matthew Hopkins relics. Gardner's time in the New Forest area was also a time of war and fear of imminent invasion.

According to Gardner, Dorothy Clutterbuck called together a network of witches, who, meeting in the New Forest on four separate occasions, worked magick to keep Hitler from invading. In a 1952 interview quoted by Heselton, Gardner says that seventeen witches came together in a clearing in the New Forest. They met four times, and using a form of dance as well as other means they raised a cone of power to keep Hitler out of Britain. The energy raised for this was exceptionally great and exhausting for the participants. Four of them would die in the next few weeks as a result of the depletion of their energies.

The close of the war in 1945 saw Gardner joining the Ancient Druid Order. For the most part this merely meant an annual ritual at Stonehenge. He also moved to a new home, The Witch's Cottage, which Gardner bought from a folk lore park and had dismantled and then reassembled in Bricket Wood. Here he joined others in the establishment of a nudist club and by 1951 the Bricket Wood Coven was also meeting here, joined in 1952 by Doreen Valiente one of the most important of the various High Priestesses who would work with Gerald. Also in the 1940s Gardner continued his investigations, meeting Aleister Crowley in 1947, a few months before Crowley's death in December of that year. Crowley, perhaps concerned with the survival of his Ordo Templi Orientis, presented Gardner with an OTO charter which Gardner never activated, although he did use the charter as a means to collect OTO rituals from other members. He visited America, including New Orleans in 1947/48 and published a second novel *High Magick's Aid* in 1949. At about the same time he began to look for a permanent place for his large collections, eventually cooperating with Cecil Williamson in opening a witchcraft and magick museum in Castleton, Isle of Man. The museum opened in 1951, the same year that Britain's anti-witchcraft law was repealed. As the Museum's "resident witch" Gerald became a leading voice on the subject, speaking of its true nature and long history. Three years later he gained sole ownership of the museum and became its director. His 1954 book *Witchcraft Today* joined with the 1950s witch craze in the British sensationalist press to make Gerald B. Gardner the man to see on the subject. He spoke to press and seeker alike, maintaining the Craft's ancient origins and separating it from any idea of devil worship. More often than not, reporters who promised to tell an accurate and sympathetic story would do the opposite, or their editors would turn a sympathetic story into a lurid exposé. Regardless of the accuracy and whether or not the reports were accusatory or laudatory, they attracted new members to the two covens that Gerald was familiar with. Characteristically, seekers would write to Gardner in care of the Museum or his publisher. He would respond and in a number of cases invite the seeker to visit him in Casteleton or in London where he maintained an apartment. Sometimes he would invite men or women to meet with the Coven in Bricket Wood, on other occasions he simply initiated them and took them into the Coven without letting the other members know ahead of time.

Some of his fellow witches, upset by the often negative press, objected to his notoriety, preferring the old way of hidden meetings and quiet magick. They also objected to his initiating newcomers without referring them first to the rest of the Coven. Led by Valiente they drew up a set of coven laws requiring consultation before admitting new members and calling for an end to the publicity. Gardner countered with his own set of newly discovered "ancient" laws mandating among other things that older high priestesses step aside for younger women to take over. In 1957 Doreen led her group away from Gardner and they established their own Coven. Despite the "bad" press, or perhaps in part because of it, Witchcraft spread not only in Britain but also to Europe and ultimately the Americas. In later years Doreen Valiente, who was one who objected to the publicity encouraged by Gerald, came to believe that perhaps it was best after all in that it spread the worship of the old gods far and wide.

Throughout the 1950s witchcraft was very much in the British press, usually portrayed in a negative light, and often as a threat to the British way of life. Gerald stayed in the limelight, often referred to by the press as the leader of the witches although he always disclaimed any such title. He continued working at the Museum, leading covens with a succession of High Priestesses at his side. The last of these was Monique Wilson who in a sort of correspondence course trained Raymond Buckland, a British expatriate living on Long Island. Buckland then traveled to Scotland and, with Gerald in attendance, Wilson continued the training in an intensive few weeks followed by an initiation. Buckland became the means for Gardner's Witchcraft being spread to the United States. Gardner would never accept any money for teaching the Craft or for initiating seekers into its mysteries.

He also continued his frequent trips to warmer climates in the wintertime, sometimes giving lectures and always increasing his knowledge of local people and customs. On a 1953 trip to the Gold Coast (now Ghana) he gave a sold out lecture using the local YMCA as a venue. Later in visiting the local market he was mobbed by some of the local women with shouts of "Master, you give me baby!" Gardner simply replied "I'm too old." His last trip was to Lebanon in 1964. Returning to Britain aboard the SS Scottish Prince he took ill and died while the ship was in port at Tunis on February 12, 1964 at the age of 79. He was buried in North Africa, and later when that cemetery was closed his body was moved to another plot in Tunis. His grave remained unmarked until 2007 when Patricia Crowther and the American Larry Jones located the grave and erected a tombstone.

The grave is in the Christian Cemetery on Keiredine Pacha Street in Tunis, Section F. Carre 4, Plot 246.

Who then was Gerald Gardner? He was anthropologist, archeologist, nudist, priest and curator, a man at least comfortable with ideas of free-love and possibly quite capable of straying from his marriage bed with the knowledge and apparent agreement of his wife. Self-taught, he never stopped seeking more knowledge. He combined a firm belief with an always present skepticism. He was strong and determined, but insecure enough to acquire a doctorate from an American mail-order diploma mill. Determined to bring about a true image and continuance of the Witch cult he saw as going back to the stone-age and not above using storytelling and occasionally outright deception to bring that about. He was a man of contradictions, but after all maybe no more so than most of us. He kick-started the neo-pagan revival not only in Britain but also in Europe and the Americas. To believers such as me, a strange man whose life produced just what was needed to bring back the old gods, an apt illustration of the truth that the Gods always choose the person with the right faults to get the job done.

DOREEN VALIENTE: MOTHER OF MODERN WICCA (1922-1999)

By Matthew Sawicki

Now I don't know about you, but when I first became interested in the Craft of the Wise at the impressionable young age of 13, I soon found that I couldn't read enough about my new fascination that would then become my life's spiritual path. Like all seekers of wisdom, an insatiable thirst for knowledge is part and parcel of the true path of the Witch. In the early 1990s, when I started my quest, I remember slyly wandering off from my parents in the mall to venture into the bookstore where the "New-Age" section then consisted of one bookcase, unlike today, where it has its own aisle! Of the books then available, most were personal astrology guides and self-help books or something safe like Gustav Davidson's *Dictionary of Angels*. Very few on Wicca or Witchcraft but at least I was able to find some classic authors like Scott Cunningham and Raymond Buckland. I guess I was lucky back then in small town Northeastern Pennsylvania.

It wasn't until a few years later, while working in an actual occult shop in Manhattan, that I was afforded a selection which was far greater and also much more refined as to what was worth reading and what was not. It was here that I came across my first Doreen Valiente title, *The Rebirth of Witchcraft*. By this time in my craft training I was working towards my first degree in the New York Wicca Tradition – a Gardnerian offshoot from the late Edmund Buczynski. While learning about Wicca, the history of its elders was just as exciting as the work itself and so *The Rebirth of Witchcraft*, a sort of autobiography of Doreen's life in the occult, proved to be a fascinating title to start with. I soon realized that not only was I reading a good book by a good author but a book by *the* High Priestess responsible for most of what I was learning! But the unique thing with this particular book was that the writing style was different from what I had experienced with other authors of the occult genre. Most were either dry and academic or simplistic and instructional. Doreen seemed to want nothing more than to tell you a story and hope that she could present it well enough that you'd learn something along the way. She reminded me very much of my own great grandmother and the conversational style of stories my grandparents would tell. It was comforting and yet informative and I absorbed it a lot more quickly than a "how-to" book. Her writing style made me want to experience the things she was describing and not just read about them. I came to love this style and found myself seeking out whatever books I could find by her. Little did I know how much I would stop to reflect on her, on my path in years to come, even well beyond my Gardnerian training period.

I was thrilled with the opportunity to write this little chapter on Doreen as a way to thank her and honor her for the influence she had in my life and on my spiritual journey. Doreen seemed to always be a bit of a rebel and did what was necessary to achieve the life she wanted. The tell-tale signs of a true witch from the beginning!

At the risk of reading like an obituary, Doreen Edith Dominy was born in Mitcham, South London on the 4th of January in 1922 to her parents Harry and Edith. She was raised in the west of England in a town called Horley in Surrey. Little is known about her childhood other than that her parents were Christians and very religious. It was there, in the West Country, surrounded with the old folk customs and close ties with the land that young Doreen grew up.[1] Folk dances and honoring sacred sites are still common practices in the West Country to this day, especially in Cornwall. A lot of traditional and hereditary crafters reference the West Country in their work.

Doreen started having psychic experiences as early as age seven where she would gaze at the moon and start to be able to sense the Otherworld was closer than just in the fairy tales. At age thirteen she performed her first spell to protect her mother from a bullying woman at work. Though the spell worked, her parents were far from thankful, sending Doreen off to convent school for fear she would want to continue dabbling in the craft. But, like a true witch who reshapes her fate, Doreen walked out of the convent school at age fifteen never to set foot in it again.[2]

As she became more aware of her psychic abilities and became more proficient with them, she began her quest to learn more and so started to find books at her library by all of the classic occult authors available at the time. She began with works by Charles Godfrey Leland, Margaret Murray, and even Aleister Crowley.[3]

At age nineteen, she was working as a secretary in an office in South Wales and it was there that she met and married her first husband, Joanis Vlachopoulos, who was in the merchant navy. Only six months after their marriage he was reported as missing at sea and presumed dead. Doreen moved on and continued working as a secretary until she later moved to London.[4]

---

[1] "Childhood Years" – *www.doreenvaliente.com*

[2] Doreen Valiente by George Knowles – *www.controverscial.com/Doreen%20Valiente.htm*

[3] Doreen Valiente by George Knowles – *www.controverscial.com/Doreen%20Valiente.htm*

[4] Doreen Valiente by George Knowles – *www.controverscial.com/Doreen%20Valiente.htm*

In the spring of 1944, at age twenty two, Doreen met and married the man with the name we'd come to know her by, Casimiro Valiente, a refugee from the Spanish Civil War who was wounded while fighting with the French forces during WWII. He was sent back to England to recover and while there, met Doreen. With their marriage, Doreen was now a Spanish national and she remained with him until he died in the spring of 1972.[5]

After the war had ended, Doreen and Casimiro moved out of the bombed out remains of London and went down to Bournemouth, just outside of the New Forest. This part of the south of England is also a place steeped in legend and folklore and it is here that Doreen's interests for the old ways were renewed. While living there, she had read an article by a Mr. Cecil Williamson, who was advertising the opening of his "Museum of Witchcraft and Magic" on the Isle of Man. The article mentioned a coven that was still operating out of the New Forest area, of which Mr. Williamson was in contact. Intrigued by this discovery, as this was practically in Doreen's backyard, she wrote to Mr. Williamson to inquire and Williamson forwarded her letter on to a man named Gerald Gardner, who was looking for new potential students for his coven[6]. The meeting that followed was the beginning of what was to become the movement of Wicca as it was passed down to all of us today.

After some correspondence, Doreen met Gardner at the home of Dorothy Clutterbuck who was known simply by the pseudonym "Dafo". At this meeting, she was given a copy of his book *High Magick's Aid*. This was Gerald's way of screening the candidates and he would ask them what they would think of the story and the rituals played out within the book. As the "year-and-a-day" tradition would have it, Doreen was initiated a year later at Midsummer of 1953 by Gardner at Old Dorothy's house and given the new name of "Ameth", by which she would be known in the circle from then on. She became

---

5 Doreen Valiente by George Knowles – *www.controverscial.com/Doreen %20Valiente.htm*

6 Wicca: Gardner and Initiation, 1952-1953 – *http://en.wikipedia.org/wiki/Doreen_Valiente*

part of Gerald's first coven – the Brickett Wood Coven in the New Forest – in which she quickly rose up to become High Priestess.[7]

During Doreen's work with Gardner, she began to recognize things in his ritual grimoire, or "Book of Shadows" as he referred to it, that she had previously learned from the various sources she had studied years ago while reading Leland and Crowley. One particular passage she recognized was taken directly from Crowley's Gnostic Mass. Confused and a bit concerned, she asked Gerald about his sources and when confronted, admitted to having to supplement the broken pieces of lore passed to him from the New Forest coven with things he had considered suitable from different sources. Doreen didn't care much for Crowley as his reputation always preceded him and she wanted to avoid such influence in the craft. Gardner asked Doreen, "Can you do any better?" [8] The rest of this story is well known in that many of us have experienced the beauty of Doreen's prose that became the Gardnerian Book of Shadows passed on from her forward. Whether your craft training is of Gardnerian background or not, Doreen's "Charge of the Goddess" is probably the most well-known and beloved of all modern craft liturgy and is a beautifully concise way to sum up the spirituality of the Wicca. It was through Doreen's work and the influence that writers like Margaret Murray and Charles Leland had on her that she was able to shape Wicca into the Goddess orientated religion that it has become today. Several of her other poems have become well known and also incorporated into the work of covens far removed from the Gardnerian tradition. Her "Witches Rune" poem is often times used by many groups for raising power and working magic. Doreen continued to work with Gardner as his High Priestess for several years. Though Gerald initiated several people, Doreen is only known to have initiated one man, Jack Bracelin, into the Brickett Wood Coven.

Eventually Doreen's relationship with Gardner deteriorated as Gerald continuously sought out publicity and press and Doreen

---

7 Brickett Wood Coven, 1953-1957 – *http://en.wikipedia.org/wiki/Doreen_Valiente*

8 Brickett Wood Coven, 1953-1957 – *http://en.wikipedia.org/wiki/Doreen_Valiente*

preferred to remain in the shadows. "As the coven's High Priestess, I felt that by speaking to the press, Gardner was compromising the security of the group and the sincerity of his teaching." [9]

She eventually parted ways with him in 1957 and took several of the original group with her to form her own coven. She continued to practice the craft as she came to it by Gardner, leading her own group for many years.[10] Over the years, she mended her friendship with Gardner and was known to have said that even though they did not work together again, things were never quite the same.

In 1964, with the death of Gerald and also her mother, Edith, Doreen was re-evaluating her own life. She decided to move on from the Gardnerian craft that she herself helped to create and began working with a man she had met that year at a summer solstice gathering at Glastonbury Tor named Robert Cochrane. Cochrane ran a coven called the "Clan of Tubal Cain" and claimed it to be a hereditary tradition from his own family dating back to the seventeenth century. Shortly after their meeting, Doreen was initiated into the Clan. With Cochrane, Doreen was known to have experienced some of the most raw and powerfully profound rituals she had known, up to that point.[11] Having been self-taught by her own research and then with her experience of Gerald and his hodgepodge early Book of Shadows, Cochrane's approach was refreshing to Doreen, if a bit troubling. Though the workings were powerful and undeniably effective, Doreen was uneasy with Cochrane for making much of it up as he went along and not using any sort of written materials or keeping any specific book. They worked mostly out of doors and she enjoyed the closeness to nature that it inspired. Overall, this experiential, shamanic style intrigued Doreen and she loved the atmosphere it would conjure in their working space, out in the woods. She had fond memories of many rituals she attended while working with the Clan of Tubal Cain.

---

9 *The Rebirth of Witchcraft,* Doreen Valiente

10 Brickett Wood Coven, 1953-1957 – *http://en.wikipedia.org/wiki/Doreen_Valiente*

11 "Robert Cochrane, Magister" – *The Rebirth of Witchcraft,* Doreen Valiente

Doreen practiced with the Clan for almost two years when she had become disillusioned with Robert Cochrane as well. Unfortunately, though Cochrane was wise and seemed to bring through a style of Craft Doreen had never seen up to that point, he was also a human being. He strongly opposed the work of Gerald Gardner and called him an outright fraud, and stated that several other traditional groups were not happy with what he was labeling as "witchcraft." He would get so enraged about Gerald's ongoing press and sensational nonsense in the newspapers that it was actually Cochrane that coined the term "Gardnerian" in an anonymous letter he had written which was published in *Psychic News,* a popular occult magazine of the times [12]. It was obviously not meant as a complimentary term, yet it stuck. One particular night, while having a jab at Gardner, he made mention of wanting a "night of the long knives with the Gardnerians". With this final nasty comment, Doreen had had enough and "rose up and challenged him in the presence of the rest of the coven. I told him that I was fed up with listening to all this senseless malice, and that, if a 'Night of the Long Knives' was what his sick little soul craved, he could get on with it, but he could get on with it alone, because I had better things to do" [13]. This was the end of their relationship and unfortunately, Doreen had little contact with him after this point. Cochrane had a penchant for dabbling with herbal blends that included poisonous herbs like Deadly Nightshade, a curiosity Doreen did not much like. He took his own life (though some say it was an accident) at Midsummer of that year from an overdose of Belladonna. He wrote a final letter to Doreen telling her that he planned to do this and unfortunately, due to a stay in hospital, she didn't receive the letter until much later than intended. When she had written him back, pleading with him not to do it, the letter was too late.

Doreen continued practicing on her own and also began writing. Her first book was published in 1967 entitled *Where Witchcraft Lives.* She wrote it as an outsider being granted special access to the work of

---

12 "Robert Cochrane, Magister" – *The Rebirth of Witchcraft,* Doreen Valiente

13 *The Rebirth of Witchcraft,* Doreen Valiente

the witches. She does thorough research into the craft and presents it in a clear and straightforward light. Now, looking back, we can see the influence of Wicca in her writings as she related everything back to it. To any outsider I'm certain it was informative, yet to an insider, we read between the lines to see that this was no ordinary researcher. This book is one of her best and was recently republished in a limited edition. Ronald Hutton, an academic and historian known for his book *The Triumph of the Moon* reveals that it was "one of the first three books to be published on the subject" of Wicca, and that the "remarkable feature of the book is that it remains, until this date [2010], the only one produced by a prominent modern witch that embodies actual original research into the records of the trials of people accused of the crime of witchcraft during the early modern period." [14] It makes me happy knowing that there are now more copies floating around out there for people on the path to access. She continued writing over the next thirty years, including four more books and many more poems, chants and invocations. A collection of these poems was published in a small book to fulfill one of her last wishes. It is through her books and teachings that many of us are here today including you, reading my story. Her books have become the backbone of Wiccan training and the younger generations really should seek her out when they are studying their craft. There are so many books available now on the mass market as compared to twenty years ago, yet Doreen's are classics that all Wiccans need to be aware of.

I'm not trying to re-tell Doreen's life story here, as it is documented in several places, both in her own book and in various others that use her as a reference. Her name has since generated several web pages including even *doreenvaliente.com*, which was set up as a memorial after her death. It's a great place for information on her life, as well as some photos of her large collection of occult paraphernalia. Her legacy of books, tools and magical knick-knacks were all passed on to become a large part of the Museum of Witchcraft and the Centre for Pagan Studies in the UK. At least we

---

14 Writing, 1967- , *http://en.wikipedia.org/wiki/Doreen_Valiente*

can still go visit Doreen and see the beauty of the traditions she left behind through her collection.

My own experiences of Doreen were usually during some of the most profound moments on my path of Wicca and Witchcraft. My story as I began it above, marked a definite turning point and the true start of my journey. Doreen was, of course, prominent in the beginning of my path as she is in most new students to Wicca, who are reading her books as part of their training, or I would at least hope that they are. As I discovered more of her books, my life was on a very interesting express route through Wicca and the training of a witch. Being able to work in an occult shop was a very rare and unique experience that I remember fondly and I continue doing apothecary work to this day. The requirements of working there were that everyone who worked in the shop also belonged to the shop coven. So, if I wanted to work, I had to train with them as well. This of course was a no-brainer for me because, how does a kid from rural Pennsylvania find his way to an occult shop in Manhattan? This chance was once in a lifetime for me, and so I began at Enchantments, Inc. in the East Village of New York City. What an amazing place it was, back in its prime. Here my journey into the Gardnerian Craft began and also my literary meeting with Doreen.

As I grew older and continued to learn both at college and out of the back Apothecary section of Enchantments, I devoured any books by Doreen that I could find, which weren't too many. At that point, many of her books were from British publishers and once the initial run of American copies was gone, it was out of print for quite some time.

For my Junior year of College, I went to London on a study abroad program with my school and while there, I made the most of the occult scene, which was thriving at the time, as opposed to New York where it seemed to suffer from disorganization and apathy. London was a breath of fresh, sooty air. Everything about it was old, but at the same time filled with wisdom and mystery. The very buildings had eyes that watched you walk down the street in return for your wonderment. It is a magical place for me. I got involved with the open groups run by the Pagan Federation and also met some wonderful people that I was able to attend private workings with.

Many of the American students were scared to be so far away from home and so they stayed together and went to pubs with other American students. I, on the other hand, and on the other side of town, was always off on my own, meeting people and taking in the ancient beauty of this place. I finally made my way to the Atlantis Book Shop, where so many famous occultists of our past have met and mingled. While looking through titles of occult lore and magic I had never seen nor heard of, I also came across some new Doreen titles as well. It was there that I bought copies of her *Natural Magic* and *Witchcraft for Tomorrow*. It was also where, on this fateful day, I saw the first advertisement for a lecture coming up later that year. The keynote speaker of the Pagan Federation's Annual convention that fall would be Doreen Valiente, in person, to give a talk on her life in the craft. This was SO meant to be!

The Pagan Federation is the UK's largest organization that supports paganism of all varieties. In addition, they work to see that pagans are afforded the same benefits of followers of other religions. The Pagan Federation has chapters across the UK and Ireland with groups and covens connected to each chapter. They sponsor events of all sizes, usually for the seasonal festivals. Their annual conference, a big affair with workshops and speakers and vending, is usually held in London. To be the keynote speaker of such an event was impressive enough, though this time around it would be legendary. And I would be there, in the third row.

I cannot describe exactly how excited I was that this was all happening while I was living there. I COULD NOT WAIT until this particular Sunday in November of 1997. I took the bus down to Croydon, which is a part of South London. The bus ride was over an hour and I remember being nervous and anxious and extremely excited. I entered the building that the conference was being held at and walked into the large room of vendors and readers and was overwhelmed by how much cool stuff was there. I was in Witchcraft heaven! I'd never been to a large pagan event and to have my very first one be THIS one, in London, with Doreen Valiente to boot was simply surreal. I looked around but knew I had to go get a seat for Doreen's talk coming up in only an hour. Being new to London's transport system and how to gauge the distance between places, I was, needless to say, a little late getting there. I was not late, however, for Doreen's talk. I entered the large auditorium as people were all bidding for spaces for themselves and their friends. Luckily, being by myself, I could slip into any number of singular empty seats. I managed to get a spot right in front in about the third row. Perfect! I settled in and waited for the lights to dim.

After an excessive announcement from the PF President, Doreen was introduced to a thunderous applause. She entered the stage and sat in a chair in the center. Doreen gave a talk that is still remembered to this day. This is due in part, not only to it being one of her last public appearances before her death, but also because she covered many topics and several of them were quite controversial to the crowd. Doreen is regarded in the greater Wiccan community as a sort of saint – the "Mother of Modern Wicca". The audience hung on every word. It was like seeing the pope give Mass. I was not above it either – listening with bated breath to see what she'd talk about next, and what juicy tidbits she'd reveal. She began by talking about Gerald Gardner, whom she worked with and who is basically responsible for the Wicca movement as a whole. She praised Gerald for his knowledge and wisdom but also was very frank about the reasons she decided to move on from him. She disagreed with the act of swearing to secrecy of the work, while Gerald constantly sought out publicity. She continued on about also not agreeing with Gerald's rules of Wicca and how she was certain he made them up. The next thing that happened was quite unexpected for everyone. It was 1997 and the issue she was about to address was not new, but it was still an issue. The next thing Doreen mentioned got both roaring applause and straight up boos and cat calls.

"At first I did not question anything Gerald told me about what he said were the traditional teachings of the Old Religion. Eventually, however, I did begin to question, and to ask how much was really traditional and how much was part of Gerald's prejudices. For instance, he was very much against people of the same sex working together, especially if they were gay. In fact, he went so far as to describe gay people as being 'cursed by the Goddess.' Well, I see no good reason to believe this. In every period of history, in every country in the world, there have been gay people, both men and women. So why shouldn't Mother

Nature have known what she was doing, when she made people this way? I don't agree with this prejudice against gay people, either inside the Craft of the Wise or outside of it." [15]

As she finished this sentence, half the crowd, myself included, stood up and screamed with our applause. To have an elder (THE elder) of the Gardnerian tradition sit up there in front of a room of hundreds of her followers (more or less) and say this, was history in the making. I, as a young gay man, never questioned two things in my life—that I am a witch and that I am also gay. When training for my Gardnerian degrees, I had struggled with the heterosexual emphasis in the tradition at that time also. I was training with a group in New York City that labeled themselves as "Neo-Gardnerian". This was the term we preferred to use, for though we practiced Gardnerian Wicca, by the book, we were a huge group of homos, there with our lovers and partners by our side. This was how I thought it was everywhere, especially in this day and age, but soon learned that outside our free-loving city, the other Gardnerians still were not in agreement.

Though many might say they had no problems with gay practitioners, the actual amount that would work with us was very slim. And yes, even though we were over 25 years into the Gay Rights movement, we weren't quite as accepted as we are today. We still had another year until the fun loving gay guy was a household name with *Will & Grace* premiering on TV. This anti-gay prejudice was still a part of the craft in pockets here and there, and supported mostly by Gardnerians of the "old guard."

With one fell swoop, Doreen not only stood up against it, as she herself had developed several gay and lesbian friends over the course of her life, she knocked such archaic beliefs off the table. She did live, after all, in Brighton in the south of England. Known for its antique shops, and those who frequent them, the seaside town of Brighton is still the Fire Island of the UK. Doreen lived just off the High Street, and only a few blocks from the beach. I'm sure she was no stranger to the "happier" crowd. It was amazing as I sat there continuing to

---

[15] From transcript of Doreen PF Talk, 1997 as printed in "Wiccan Wisdomkeepers" by Sally Griffin.

applaud through the other occasional boos. As they continued, we continued, and the applause was in stark contrast to the awkwardness of the rest of the room. I had to turn around finally and look up the lengths of auditorium seats to see just whom the cat calls were coming from. I was amazed to see who was slinging what words at whom. This all lasted for only a minute, but it was a noteworthy moment in craft history. It was mostly the older crowd who had the disgusted looks on their faces and the younger set, with me screaming along with my peers, in favour of Doreen's denouncement.

As if this weren't enough, always being a touch rebellious, Doreen went on to then very publicly challenge the well-known "Rule of Three". The Wiccan "Rule of Three" is taught to be the basic guiding point for all Wiccans, which is the belief that what one puts out, one attracts back to themselves three times over. This was later revealed to be installed by Gerald Gardner as a security system to reinsure that no one would accuse him of practicing black magic. If anyone questioned a witch's practices, they need only remind their accuser of the "Rule of Three" and explain, "Why would I curse you, if I'm only then cursing myself in return?" This sounded perfectly fine, and of course, did exactly what it was intended to by calming people's fears. This rule was one of several that Gerald had incorporated into the Book of Shadows without any point of reference but a loose play on the eastern concept of Karma and his own personal morals. However, we have come to understand, that in more traditional, pre-wiccan Witchcraft, the law was truly: Do what is necessary and be prepared to pay the price. And I will back this up by the old maxim: A Witch who can't Curse, can't Cure.

Doreen continued:

"Another teaching of Gerald's which I have come to question is the belief known popularly as the "Law of Three". This tells us that whatever you send out in Witchcraft, you get back to you threefold, good or ill. Well, I don't believe it! Why on earth would we assume that there is a special law of Karma, which only applies to Witches? For the Goddess' sake, do we really kid ourselves that we are that important? Yet, so I am told, many people, especially in the United States, take this as an article of faith. I have never seen it in any of the old books of magic, and I think Gerald made it up."

This was another comment met either with a mixed round of applause or otherwise looks of confusion and even disbelief. So many people having simply gotten used to this as an easy cushion from assault, and yet again, here sat our Matron, debunking it! This was an interesting moment as well, and one that had the wheels in everyone's head turning.

And though I'm not one for flinging curses, the idea of the rule of three always did seem foreign to me as a practicing witch, and this only confirmed my gut feeling which was more of "an eye for an eye" approach when it came to the old craft. I sat back and smiled as I applauded her.

Doreen went on to talk about her relationship With Robert Cochrane, the traditional Witch she worked with after leaving Gerald Gardner and how potent his rites were. She discussed the concepts of the mysteries of Wicca being far deeper than simply fertility and death and that to truly be a witch you must understand the layers of these things to the deepest level. Overall, she concluded with the message that it is our differences that should unite us instead of divide us under the banner of witches and pagans.

After the talk and the applause, Doreen was escorted to a small side room behind the stage where she would sign a few autographs. I had one of my books with me for exactly this moment and I somehow managed to race to the door and be the second person in line. I didn't want to get her when she was tired, after all. I didn't know what I was going to say or ask but I knew it would be right at the time. She was also overwhelmed with camera flashes and pictures. I decided that I would not ask for a picture out of respect. I will of course refrain from telling you all how regretful I am even to this day. I'm sure her eyes could have endured one more flash.

Finally it was my turn. I was escorted into the room and she was seated in a folding chair at a table and was receiving people for about five minutes at a time. As I walked into the room, my head started to spin. It wasn't because I was about to sit in front of Doreen Valiente, if maybe only part of the reason. It was more so because I was having one of the strongest olfactory memories that I'd ever had. The power of scent and it being able to recall memories is something we've all experienced at some point or another. As I walked through the small room to the vacant seat, my nose was overwhelmed by the very familiar scent of what turned out to be Doreen's perfume. A deep and heady fragrance, Estee Lauder's "Youth Dew" was introduced by the American company in 1953 and is what put the company of Estee Lauder on the map. The perfume was first sold as bath oil with a fragrance so strong that it could last up to 24 hours! It was absolutely unmistakable. Deep rose and patchouli with sandalwood and musk. Haunting and beautiful, it's the classic "old lady" perfume!

Now you will remember that when I first read Doreen's books, I was reminded of my great grandmother, who was known to enter the room by her perfume first. And it was of course, Estee Lauder's Youth Dew. As I sat down in front of Doreen, there was so much going on in my head, I completely lost track of everything. Why I was there, what I was going to say, or anything I had wanted to ask. As I sat in front of her and she greeted me hello, I opened my mouth but no words would come out. She then asked me "are you alright, dear?" I luckily pulled myself together and remembered to talk. She then complimented me on the Green Man t-shirt I was wearing and him being one of her favourite aspects of the old God. I then realized that I had just heard her say some pretty major things and so I thanked her for her outright support of the gay pagan community. I mentioned the way the Neo-Gardnerians worked in New York and she was very excited to hear that such a group existed. I also mentioned the existence of groups like the Minoan Traditions, which were developed for the gay witch community by advanced thinking people like her, which also seemed to intrigue her. I was clearly a young sprite filled with enthusiasm and she was glad to have the excitement and entertainment, if also a bit overwhelmed. She signed my copy of *Natural Magic* and shook my hand to bid me goodbye. As her older hand grasped my younger hand, I honestly saw flashes of so many of her working partners past and realized just how many legends of the occult world had also grasped that same hand. Gerald Gardner, Robert Cochrane, Cecil Williamson, Evan John Jones, and countless others! I did not ask for a picture as I said I would respect her space. Oh well...

In the autumn of 1999, I was now living in New York City full time having graduated from college that spring. On a rainy afternoon in late September, I walked into Enchantments to see my friends, eat my lunch, and check the schedule. I immediately noticed a newspaper clipping posted on the bulletin board behind the front door that was new since the last time I had been in. When I glanced at it, I noticed a picture of Doreen as printed in one of her books. I looked more closely and then read the headline of the article: "Doreen Valiente, 77, Dies; Advocated Positive Witchcraft" from Sunday October 3, 1999 in The New York Times. As my eyes took in exactly what I was reading, my heart sank a little, yet I knew she wouldn't be around forever and I remembered my time with her and the rare moment I had while in London. I was saddened yet also at peace because though she touched many on their paths, I had the rare chance to actually meet her and express my gratitude. I left the article up for about a week then I photocopied it and took the original for my own safekeeping. I still have it today.

Even though she was gone, Doreen still was a strong influence in my life and I like to think that now having crossed over, I could chat with her more easily by calling out to her in the spirit world. Over the years to come, I had several visitations with Doreen. Sometimes I would arrive home and upon entering my living room, suddenly smell the overwhelming headiness of her perfume and feel her around. I would say hello and have little chats with her. Though I sometimes felt as if I were slightly crazy, I did hear answers that lead me in the right direction.

In 2003 it was announced to me by my teaching High Priestess that I was ready to receive my Third Degree elevation. This was welcome news after almost three years as a Second Degree, a time considered by Gardnerians to be the equivalent of the Underworld journey. Let's just say, I was more than ready to greet the light once again. My High Priestess was a wonderful friend and instructor, both in the Craft and in her career as an elementary school teacher. She was tough and required a great deal from her students. As members of her coven, we had to know our rituals by heart and no book was used in circle except for the occasional reference at a sabbat. She felt that doing things by heart was the purest way to pull the energy through. She had a degree in theatre along with her teaching credentials and had a flare for the dramatic, to say the least. Her parents had a wonderful piece of land in the mountains of Pennsylvania not far from where I was brought up. We would do rituals there all year round, whenever we could get out of the city. Working outside was a favorite of ours, as it was with Doreen and she was often in my thoughts whenever a particularly charged night was awaiting us. We used to line the paths of the woods with Jack-O-Lanterns for Samhain and hang chandeliers with lit candles in the trees for Midsummer. We loved to create magick!

It was determined that since our good friend had recently relocated from New York City to Ireland that we would visit her. And since we would be together with her, another 3rd degree, we would do my elevation at her family's castle in the Irish Midlands. This was a lifelong dream come true for me. And only after the fact did I realize the symbolism of making it to the castle for the ritual of my rebirth. Something I would later learn to be very significant in the Clan of Tubal Cain's mysteries. We flew to Ireland in February of that year and I was elevated to the Third Degree on the night of the full moon. It was truly magickal and a night I won't forget. The trip didn't bode well for my High Priestess however, who kept having very disturbing dreams of not being able to get her breath and a woman on a white horse that was coming to collect her. We were all a bit worried but were mostly chalking it up to possibly something she ate that didn't agree with her. The woman on the white horse is any number of representations of the Goddess but we immediately recognized her as Rhiannon, who comes to collect her own when it is time. Unfortunately, her omens and dreams were accurate and three months later, just after the full moon in May, she was killed on her way to work, her motorcycle having been hit by a tractor-trailer truck whose driver didn't see her and ignored the red light. She died instantly, her very breath being taken from her lungs.

Needless to say, I was devastated. I had never felt the grip of death's grief like this before. I had lost several older family members but never someone that I knew so well, lived with for a time, and considered as much a sister as a teacher. But she was gone, and it seemed, at least for me, that she took all the magick of our work with her. I couldn't perform the rites without her, it was just too painful, as I was the High Priest and my working partner in circle was gone. I lost all interest in my crafting, and didn't know what to do. The Gardnerian work was unsavory to me without someone of a like mind to work with. I was no longer at Enchantments and our coven more or less fell apart. Yet, here I was, over 10 years into the Craft, with so much time and devotion behind me, yet I was ready to walk away from it all. Yet, knowing that this was my life's journey, I knew I couldn't abandon it. After a few months and some time to hurt and heal, it was another full moon and I wanted to do some craft work. I knew it had to be simple and from the heart. I decided to put the tools of my Gardnerian craft aside and start from scratch. I needed to start from a place that made me feel the sparkle of magick in my heart that I remembered as a kid.

I created a simple altar on a shelf in my bedroom and lit a single candle and asked for help. Shortly after that night, I came across a book I had bought that Doreen had helped to write with her friend from the Clan of Tubal Cain, Evan John Jones. It was called *Witchcraft: A Tradition Renewed* and contained a loose explanation of the rites of the Clan of Tubal Cain. When I had originally picked it up almost 10 years previous at a used bookshop while attending college, I tried to get through it yet it was beyond me at the time. So, I shelved it, of course, and knew I'd get to it when the time was right. Upon seeing the title again, I realized that Doreen started working with the Clan of Tubal Cain after Gerald Gardner had died while finding herself at a similar point in her life. I decided to pick up the book again and read it. It suddenly clicked, as the main point of the rites of the Clan of Tubal Cain are about working intuitively and from the heart, using The Sight to guide your way. They followed the seasonal cycles and observed them in a much more shamanic sort of way. I remembered Doreen's experiences of the profound rituals with very little written down – all spontaneous and divinely inspired. The book resounded with me very clearly and I felt as if Doreen had inspired me to find my way yet again when I needed her. I continued to study this particular style and figured that if it were meant to be, I'd see some signs.

As life went on, and I continued forging my new path, I came to regard Doreen as a sort of spirit guide. I would light a candle in front of her picture and ask her questions and for her help. I always got answers. I had eventually met some interesting fellow witches who practiced a form of traditional craft similar to the Clan of Tubal Cain. They had experienced a ritual of mine that I had offered at a public gathering and after getting to know me a bit better, encouraged me to pursue the path of the Clan, saying that though it wasn't their path, they could very much see my work already bringing it through. I eventually moved my life from New York to Los Angeles to start fresh and also because I understood that a branch of the Clan of Tubal Cain existed in southern California. I came to contact this group, which was not actually Clan but styled after it, and through it, met some like-minded people who wanted to work the Clan materials with me. Together, we were able to contact the current Maid of the Clan of Tubal Cain, Shani Oates, in England and started a working correspondence with her. She would give us suggestions for our work and we would do it, completely feeling it out as we went. We would receive amazing insight and inspiration into our experiences and became acquainted with what we came to learn was called the "ancestral stream". This stream of consciousness that had to be tapped into was the direct connection to the Clan members who had passed on. I feel Doreen was what helped me to be drawn into this stream and it is with the Clan that I still work to this day. I truly feel that I've come full circle in my journey.

This year marks 20 years for me in my involvement with the craft and only a few less before I discovered Doreen in the mid 90s. Doreen has been with me for quite some time over the years and I am thankful for her influence to know just when to turn my head and see something or to engage my Sight to the awareness of things outside of the mundane. I am thankful to Doreen for helping to guide me to this place as only she could. I realize I am the ultimate guide of my spirit on this journey, but I need to give thanks to the spirit of Doreen who was there in a way that was very unique to me.

I encourage those who have yet to discover Doreen Valiente on their path of the Old Religion to seek her out and to also get to know her. She can both enlighten and amuse and I hope she guides you on your journey as she has done for me on mine.

And as we witches say: Merry Meet, Merry Part, and Merry Meet Again!

References

"Childhood Years" – *www.doreenvaliente.com*

Doreen Valiente, by George Knowles – *www.controverscial.com/Doreen%20Valiente.htm*

Wicca: Gardner and Initiation, 1952-1953 – *http://en.wikipedia.org/wiki/Doreen_Valiente*

Brickett Wood Coven, 1953-1957 – *http://en.wikipedia.org/wiki/Doreen_Valiente*

Brickett Wood Coven, 1953-1957 – *http://en.wikipedia.org/wiki/Doreen_Valiente*

The Rebirth of Witchcraft, Doreen Valiente

Brickett Wood Coven, 1953-1957 – *http://en.wikipedia.org/wiki/Doreen_Valiente*

"Robert Cochrane, Magister" – *The Rebirth of Witchcraft*, Doreen Valiente

Writing, 1967-, *http://en.wikipedia.org/wiki/Doreen_Valiente*

Transcript of Doreen Valiente Pagan Federation Talk, 1997 as printed in "Wiccan Wisdomkeepers" by Sally Griffin.

ALEX SANDERS
(1926-1988)

By Jimahl di Fiosa

Alex Sanders, "King of the Witches," was born in Liverpool, England on June 6, 1926. He was the eldest child of Harold Carter and Hannah Bibby. Harold was married at the time and was unable to pass his proper surname to his new son. Consequently, he and Hannah picked the name "Sanders" from a phone book and went about creating a large family together. Little is known of Alex's early years. It would seem by later accounts that Alex was somewhat of the "black sheep" of the family.

The principal influence in Alex's young life was his maternal grandmother, known in popular media as Mary Bibby. She lived in North Wales and Alex went to stay with her for a period of time when he was a child. Mrs. Bibby apparently had hereditary ties to

Welsh Witchcraft and was known to many as the village "wise woman."

Alex insisted that she was a witch and would later tell the story of how he went round to her house for tea in his seventh year and found her standing naked in the middle of a magic circle. According to Alex, the result of this impertinent discovery was that she initiated him into Witchcraft on the spot and proceeded over several years to teach him the ways of Welsh magic. While many have been inclined to dispute the "grandmother story," this writer considers such debates to be purely academic. Additionally, some recent scholarly evidence has surfaced which lends credence to the connection between Alex's grandmother and hereditary Welsh magic, taking some wind out of the sails of the detractors who for whatever reason have been heretofore determined to punch holes in Alex's firsthand account of his early introduction to the Arts Magical.

The lessons received from his grandmother were well learned and Alex devoted his life to building upon the magical foundation laid early in life by the elderly Mrs. Bibby. In the 1950s, Alex was well known throughout the Manchester England area as a healer, psychic, and trance medium.

In the early 1960s, Alex was initiated into Gardnerian Witchcraft, a contemporary form of Witchcraft made popular through the work of British witch, Gerald Gardner. Differences in opinion between Alex and other prominent Gardnerians of the time created a schism and Alex branched off to form what would later become known as the "Alexandrian tradition" of Witchcraft. The Alexandrian tradition, standing shoulder to shoulder with the Gardnerian tradition, is one of the major branches of Wicca today. Although it is generally thought that the name of the tradition is derived from "Alex", it is believed that it was named instead after Alexandria, the ancient city of learning.

Alex Sanders met Maxine Morris in the mid-1960s and it was a match well made. As High Priest and High Priestess, the couple went on to initiate and train hundreds of witches throughout the British Isles and around the world. In the late 1960s Alex and Maxine moved to London where they would later marry and celebrate the births of their two children, Maya and Victor.

The 1960s were a decade of social change and revolution on many levels. Witchcraft provided an alternative to established religious practices and interested people of all ages and backgrounds found their way to the London Coven seeking counsel, teaching, and initiation. The media loved Alex and Maxine and once the publicity machine roared into gear, the couple found it impossible to escape attention wherever they went. Several high profile publicity opportunities presented themselves to the couple in a short period of time which further catapulted them into a worldwide spotlight. The first was a very early biography of Alex entitled *King of the Witches* by June Johns (1969 Pan Books), followed closely by a documentary film, *Legend of the Witches* (1969), a vinyl recording of actual witchcraft ceremonies on the A&M record label called *A Witch is Born* (1970), and a non-fiction account of the work of the London coven entitled *What Witches Do, a Modern Coven Revealed* by a well- known journalist named Stewart Farrar (Phoenix Publishing 1971.)

The basic tenets of Alexandrian Witchcraft are very similar to other branches of modern Wicca. However, the emphasis in the Alexandrian tradition has always been on the quality of training. Alexandrian covens are considered to be autonomous and each is encouraged to contribute to the basic body of lore passed down from Alex. While core principles and beliefs are shared by Alexandrian covens, specific rituals and training techniques may vary from coven to coven. For example one coven may exhibit a proclivity toward ceremonial magic while another might have expertise in the working of spells. The basic core practices of the Alexandrian tradition include, but are not limited to, the worship of both the God and Goddess, the use of a "Book of Shadows" which is passed by hand of write from initiator to initiate, a sincere and unapologetic belief in magic of all types, the awareness of the unseen spirit world, a working relationship with the elemental forces of nature, the effectiveness of spells, the transformative power of ritual, and perhaps most importantly, the acceptance of personal responsibility for all actions taken within the Art Magical. The rituals of the Alexandrian tradition are enacted within a consecrated magic circle. These Rites are usually officiated by a High Priest or High Priestess or both. Alexandrian covens may consist of an unlimited number of witches. They may have as few as three (two coven leaders and one other member) or as many members as the group feels is appropriate. A full coven is generally believed to contain between seven and thirteen witches.

Although Alex and Maxine separated in 1974, both individuals remained active as Elders of the Craft. Maxine remained in London, while Alex found a new home in Sussex where he lived until his death on May Eve 1988.

Alex Sanders was both charismatic and controversial. He lived his life without compromise and cared little for public opinion. He was simultaneously an extraordinarily public and yet very private person. He inspired a wide range of emotions in everyone he met. Those who knew him well either loved him or hated him. Some consider him to be the ultimate showman, always ready for front page news. Others know him as a quiet introvert, painfully shy, an individual who despite the fact that he was one of the most photographed men in all of England hated to have his snapshot taken.

The inherent danger in writing a biographical piece, however small or large, about a historic figure is twofold – despite the most valiant efforts of the writer, the man himself can become lost in the seemingly endless list of facts and statistics that despite our best efforts inevitably become the sum of our lives. And secondly, the person becomes a "thing" who is loved, hated or objectified in some way for the sake of history itself, rather than remain what he obviously was and always will be – a human being like all the rest of us.

The irony is that Alex never set out to be a historical figure. He did not create the Alexandrian tradition. He never set out to be a leader. The title "King of the Witches" was not one he took upon himself but was an honorary title given to him out of respect by hundreds of his witches. While the many newspaper photographs and journalistic references over the years may paint a portrait of a flamboyant showman, there is a frailty to Alex Sanders that undermines the flash and glamour. He, like the rest of us, was decidedly human.

Two years before his death, Alex wrote in his personal journal "I had to do something because I couldn't refuse. I couldn't refuse because no one else in the world could do what I had to do and a job had to be done." He lived his life by example, demonstrating the importance of following one's personal vision and staying true to one's highest ideal, despite sometimes insurmountable odds. Alex's tireless love for the Goddess and his dedication to the Craft would influence thousands of seekers who would come after and inspire a new generation toward the Inner Mysteries.

Alex had a vast knowledge of the occult. Yet he shared this wisdom with others in the most practical ways. He once said to a student "If you learn nothing else from me, learn this," as he stamped his foot three times on the earth, "This is where all witches stand."

Perhaps then the true measure of Alex Sanders can be summed up best by looking at his human legacy. Twenty two years after his death, the Alexandrian movement is still going strong with witches around the world continuing the work that Alex inspired.

The magic of today is just as vibrant as it was in the 60s, although it is understandably very different. The sense of energy within those who are touched by the power raised within the Circle of the witch will always be available to those who have the magic within themselves. Part of today's magical work is enabling those who have the potential to teach the Art Magical which is made possible only through the awareness of the sacredness of the work of the Priesthood.

Recognizing the magic within a potential student of Witchcraft was one of Alex Sander's many talents. Helping others develop magical ability, finding ways to draw it out from the subconscious to conscious manifestation was perhaps his greatest gift.

Alex always said that 1 in 1,000 may have the magic within. But 999 have the potential for it to be awakened.

Charles Godfrey Leland
(1824-1903)

by Raven Grimassi

When people think about the origins of modern Wicca and Witchcraft, they often focus on a man named Gerald Gardner. Gardner wrote several books in the early to mid 1990s on such topics. Many people refer to him as the "Father" of today's practices, beliefs, and concepts. However, decades prior to Gardner, an author named Charles Godfrey Leland was the first to introduce the public to the idea of contemporary practitioners of Witchcraft.

Leland was a scholar, folklorist and author who wrote several classic texts on English Gypsies and Italian Witches. He was born in Philadelphia on August 15, 1824 and died in Florence, Italy, on March 20, 1903. Leland was fascinated by folk lore and folk magic even as a child, and went on to author such important works as *Etruscan Roman Remains, Legends of Florence, The Gypsies, Gypsy Sorcery,* and *Aradia: Gospel of the Witches.*

In 1888 Leland landed in Florence, Italy, where he lived out the remainder of his life. It was here that he met a woman whom he always referred to as Maddalena, although some people believe that her real name was Margherita. She made a meager living as a "card reader" telling fortunes in the back streets of Florence. Leland soon discovered that Maddalena was a Witch, and employed her to help gather material for his research on Italian Witchcraft. In Leland's biography, his niece Elizabeth Pennell mentions running across his manuscript notes in which he writes of Maddalena:

"...a young woman who would have been taken for a Gypsy in England, but in whose face, in Italy, I soon learned to know the antique Etruscan, with its strange mysteries, to which was added the indefinable glance of the Witch. She was from the Romagna Toscana, born in the heart of its unsurpassingly wild and romantic scenery, amid cliffs, headlong torrents, forests, and old legendary castles. I did not gather all the facts for a long time, but gradually found that she was of a Witch family, or one whose members had, from time to immemorial, told fortunes, repeated ancient legends, gathered incantations, and learned how to intone them, prepared enchanted medicines, philtres, or spells. As a girl, her Witch grandmother, aunt, and especially her stepmother brought her up to believe in her destiny as a sorceress, and taught her in the forests, afar from human ear, to chant in strange prescribed tones, incantations or evocations to the ancient gods of Italy, under names but little changed, who are now known as folletti, spiriti, fate, or lari the Lares or household goblins of the ancient Etruscans."

Maddalena was very poor, and Leland describes her in his letters as living in stark poverty. Leland hired her to collect Witch lore from practitioners in and around Florence, paying her 5 francs for delivering material to him. Some commentators feel that paying Maddalena for material brings into question the validity of what she supplied to Leland. This suggests that being paid for services renders the service questionable, in which case anyone working for a living should be suspect by their employers.

Over the years Maddalena gave Leland the material that formed his books *Etruscan Roman Remains,* two volumes of *The Legends of Florence, Legends of Virgil,* and *Aradia: Gospel of the Witches.* The last title is the strangest of all his books related to Italian Witchcraft. It was also his last. In its appendix, he writes:

> "*So long ago as the year 1886 I learned that there was in existence a manuscript setting forth the doctrines of Italian Witchcraft, and I was promised that, if possible, it should be obtained for me. In this I was for a time disappointed. But having urged it on Maddalena, my collector of folk lore, while she was leading a wandering life in Tuscany, to make an effort to obtain or recover something of the kind. I at last received from her, on January 1, 1897, entitled* Aradia, or the Gospel of the Witches".

It took about ten years for Leland to receive the material that ended up becoming his Gospel of Aradia. The material is unlike anything Maddalena had previously given to Leland, and its depiction of the Witch is in sharp contrast to this figure in his earlier books on Italian Witchcraft. This strongly suggests that Maddalena had not been familiar with it beforehand. Instead, she was previously presenting Leland with her own understanding of Witchcraft being the society of "The beautiful Witches of Benevento" (as Leland once put it).

There is some evidence to suggest that Leland may have been initiated into Italian Witchcraft at some point. One example appears in his book *Etruscan Roman Remains*, in which he writes: "True, there are witches good and bad, but all whom I ever met belonged entirely to the buone. It was their rivals and enemies who were maledette streghe, et cetera, but the latter I never met. We were all good." His use of the term "we" indicates something noteworthy.

In a letter to his niece, Elizabeth Pennell (written on April 6th, 1895) Leland states:

> "*There is a difference between collecting folklore as a curiosity and living it in truth. I do not believe that in all the folk lore societies there is one person*

who lives it in reality as I do. I cannot describe it – what it once was is lost to the world – you can not understand it at second hand."

It appears he is saying that his involvement is not that of an investigator or observer.

Leland and his niece were very close throughout his life. She gives us some insight as to the nature of her uncle in this passage from his biography, which she wrote after his death:

"...and he was so serious in his superstition that I used to think he prized it as a symbol of the strange, the spiritual things always lurking somewhere in his thoughts and his conversation, the things he cared for most. He was never happier, nor his talk more eloquent, than when he was lost in speculation where I could but dimly follow. I doubt if such a true mystic had walked and talked in the streets of Philadelphia since Penn, and Pastorius, and the early seekers after the Inner Light. It often struck me that, could they have come back, they would have understood him, as I am afraid his contemporaries did not".

Leland was often burdened with being misunderstood. There is an old saying that the price of genius is to be misunderstood; this seems to have been Leland's lot in life. He was often plaqued by the dismissive attention of his work by the scholars of his period. Their academic blinders and sense of personal correctness prevented them from seeing the truth of what Leland brought to public attention.

Despite the challenges undertaken by Leland, he remained steadfast in his beliefs to the every end of his life. His 19th century writings remain in print and continue to be studied and debated to this very day. Perhaps there is no stronger vindication of the man than the endurance of such a legacy.

A Pellar's Fate: Robert Cochrane (1931-1966)

by Shani Oates

*I know that I hung on a windy tree
nine long nights,
wounded with a spear, dedicated to Odin,
myself to myself,
on that tree of which no man knows
from where its roots run.*

Found comatose, wrapped within a sleeping bag upon the sofa in his council house on the Britwell Estate in Slough on Midsummer's Eve 1966, Roy Leonard Bowers, died nine days later in hospital without regaining consciousness. An inquiry into the actual cause of his death confirmed it as an overdose of librium, belladonna and hellebore – a lethal cocktail ingested to invoke the 'faerie rade,' and seek a trial in which he might resolve his fate.

His controversial suicide over forty years ago has raised many theories regarding the life and death of one of the Craft's most gifted exponents. But even the facts cannot reveal the torment of frustrated genius and anarchy within the mind of this most tragic of poets, who'd dared to eat from the table of the gods. Inspired through joyous intoxication of Odin's honeyed mead received as manna to his ravenous soul, he was also soured by bitter strife from the herbs of Eris that peppered his dish a little too frequently and liberally for his irate sense of justice. But importantly, precious moments of grace revealed to him the philosopher's stone or kernel, whose secret heart within wisdom's fruit when pressed, produces the Hermetic Elixir of Immortality. For indeed there is no doubt he has received immortality through his work and the stream that flows steadily from it and serves it.

Why Roy Bowers chose to sever his connections in this life to those he knew and loved was very much determined by his choices in life. He would have said that such things are fated. Yet he would have also added that it is within our grasp to overcome even the worst of fates to achieve and fulfill a destiny beyond its dictates. There has been some ill-considered theories presented that suggest it was yet another carefully orchestrated hoax, a prank that escalated beyond its designer's purpose. A note, handwritten by Roy was found close to the body which clarified his intent without reserve:

"This is a carefully prepared suicide. This has been a mixture of Belladonna, Hellebore – terrible tasting stuff –and a dose of sleeping pills to counteract the movements, jerks, actions and all the rest, of my muscles caused by the high quantity of atropine in the Belladonna...This is to indicate, though that must be your opinion, that I took my own life while of sound mind."

Perhaps if we explore some of the ideas and ideals Roy was working on, we might better see the man through that work. During the phenomenon of the early part of the 1960s, a huge groundswell of philosophy, spiritualism, astro-sciences and political anarchy prevailed, the context in which Roy Bowers was honed into the free-thinking, anarchic seeker of answers he believed were within grasp, if one could only reach out far enough. Possessed of an intense charismatic and seductive charm, he exuded an unmistakable 'alpha male' stream of pheromones such that both men and women alike were drawn to him. When Doreen Valiente eventually met Roy Bowers in 1964, she could not help but describe him as 'strikingly handsome.'

He was undeniably arrogant and opinionated, but it is clear that while ever this served the best intentions of those around him, it was tolerated – barely. This became increasingly harder as all bounds of tolerance disintegrated into the mire of ego, delusion and absolute absorption of self-serving provocations that escalated his eventual alienation.

In spite of this, he was without question a unique figure, possessing a keen sense and presence of the 'other' within, without and around himself; he was a magnet that drew others to gravitate in his orbit. Some people are followers, but Roy Bowers was a natural leader, a trendsetter, a 'mover and shaker,' whose innovations still resound within the occult world to this day. One of his distinguishing ideas, unprecedented in the 1960s, was of belonging to a stream of traditions very different from the contemporary ideologies of Wicca as presented by Gerald B. Gardner. So here are a few more words by Roy used to describe himself, with particular regard to his shunning of 'labels' and priorities of focus:

"I describe myself as a Pellar. The People are formed in clans or families and they describe themselves by the local name of the Deity. I am a member of the People of Goda – of the Clan of Tubal Cain. We were known locally as 'witches', the 'Good People'. 'Green Gowns' (females only). 'Horsemen', and finally as 'Wizards'."

It is apparent that one title he did not use by choice, infers here that "witch" is not a title proclaimed of oneself:

"What do witches call themselves? They call themselves by the name of their Gods. I am Od's man, since the spirit of Od lives in me."

And, even more explicit, he expands upon that by saying:

"Now, what do I call myself? I don't. Witch is as good as any; failing that 'Fool' might be a better word. I am a child of Tubal Cain, the Hairy One."

To quantify those remarks, Roy then feels it necessary to expound "wisdom" as the lure:

"...since talking about the People (we describe ourselves as such) ...The religion is even more mystical than most – so words are very poor approximations of what we actually discover or feel about our beliefs...so we come to the heart of the People, a belief that is based upon eternity, and not social needs or pressures — the 'witch' belief then is concerned with wisdom, our true name then is the People and wisdom is our aim."

In his pursuit of this elusive wisdom, Roy Bowers has been consistently described by even his close friends and associates as egotistical, prone to violence and melancholia, yet also distracted and vengeful, whose earnest approach to everything within his life was far from superficial. In fact as a 'serious occultist' he chose to focus on a 'Higher Truth' accessed through a spiritual path within the Mysteries. His expression of 'Truth' has become subject to much debate over this past decade in particular, and his detractors have claimed his system of belief to be disruptive and contentious to anyone following a path already. As heir to his work, I would refute that unmitigated, and as a serious student of the mysteries, I would then second it. However reception of his praxis may add some degree of chaos, dependent upon prior belief, but not one that cannot be easily resolved.

Because he was primarily a serious occultist, we focus on the 'Work' as journeymen within a 'gnostic' legacy that seeks the evolution of spirit, in preference to the regression of it through mundane distractions. The 'craftsmanship' of Roy's system is indeed an 'Arte.' And yes it is agreed that both Gerald B. Gardner and Roy Bowers ardently promoted their occult philosophies as bound within 'religion' and yet, much to the chagrin of both founders, this fundamental tenet of their belief has been rejected by many of their practitioners. Overall the 'Craft' remains, forty years later, as divisive as ever. Yes the Arte is 'Truth' just as Roy declared, all else is illusion – deny this he believed, and all is lost; here it is where the path becomes perceived as 'crooked.' Conversely, Truth however, is as straight as an arrow. He asserted that the Ancient Mysteries, whilst not being secret, hold the means by which man may come to know himself and God, which is again the Highest Truth.

As for Witchcraft, it has always been a system hidden within others, including somewhat ironically, paganism and is practised widely throughout, including Wicca. But lest it be misunderstand, I myself, like Roy and John before me, remain fully aware that the roots of Wicca and Traditional Craft are different, but we must not miss the point of the Mysteries within them and which Roy affirmed beyond all else. No-one may own the Higher Truth, only their own and perhaps the ways and means of its discovery. So we certainly need to promote the depth of the Craft in order to admonish the popular image of it, and as a serious occultist working Roy's legacy, it has become one of my main objectives to succeed in that particular mission, close to his own. But I have to state the caveat, that unlike Roy, I do not believe that the Craft should be termed a 'religion' for many reasons. Not least of these is the restrictive and proscriptive dogma overarching the extreme spectrum of practice to which it would apply. My own path is deeply spiritual, but I would never say it was religious, whereas this term was used indiscriminately by Roy, I think perhaps to inject some deeper elements into the Craft he believed was too concerned with spell-work and little else of any worth or value.

Each journeyman, in accord with the gnostic principles set in motion by Roy, must decide for themselves what measure or ratio of theurgy and thaumaturgy they factor into their praxes. Each person works alone on this path, even within the Clan. As for gnosis in preference to logos, again there is here another case where semantics obfuscate purpose. For myself, there is little practical distinction, as logos can be understood as the mind or wisdom made manifest – which is after all what gnosis is. Nevertheless, it was the primary concern of Evan John Jones, Roy's right hand man, that everyone down the line avoids 'misappropriation by misadventure.' By this I understood it to mean that Roy's own failings should not be taken up and perpetuated within any campaign, especially where his insights could conversely shed light for at least some able to reflect it. Of course many things require breaking down to evolve, expand or mature. We are indeed all very different and must remain so; it is not my intention here to suggest that Roy believed that we blend or merge, diluting the potency of all involved within that evolutionary process. No-one's integrity should ever be compromised.

But we do need to also be mindful that we are correct in how we choose to present those differences, which I do not deny exist; for example, witchcraft as a practice within almost all cultures and religions stands as one that is not independent and cannot therefore be presented in any perceived 'pure' form. Yes we all need to confirm and maintain our individual boundaries, which we may attempt without derision. This prejudice ate into the very soul of Roy Bowers, poisoning his rationale until he saw 'witch-hunters' behind every active political campaign or policy. But is not Ma'at also Cosmic Truth, higher than our mortal perceptions, and does not Her wisdom enflame us all to higher principles? Each of us must take up the tools of the smith and forge our own destiny, preserve our own honour and destroy and release that which does not serve our evolution in Truth, Love and Beauty.

Yes, new letters, previously unknown, may occasionally turn up over the next few years to reveal a unique individual, whose expression of the Craft he devoted his life to, and to his newly discovered and fast evolving identity especially prior to his later mystical shift. Certainly the two most recent letters discovered in a cache to Robert Graves reveal a political, vulnerable and somewhat cynical man, cleverly 'fishing' a known authority on mythology, testing the waters. They enquire, yet cajole Graves. Most of all, they offer us a chance to know the man before the myth developed the ego which created the catalyst for his mystical epiphany and despair.

Throughout his letters, many of which are published, Roy shrouds his early life in mystery, alluding occasionally to his own desolation in his enforced denial of what he called the teachings of the blood, until his late teens. Then picking up the colourful threads of his life, he weaves a tale of experience gained in the occult field through his work in a foundry and on the canals, both close knit repositories of folklore and alternative beliefs.

Later still, duty and responsibility called him to the more settled employment of 'artist' a designer of printing fonts and typefaces, which sorely tested his free spirit. His many claims regarding his 'Craft' heritage included a lineage reaching back five generations into the 18th century, where he boldly asserts his great-grandfather as being the once 'Grand Master of the Staffordshire Witches,' that his father was a Horse Whisperer and his mother the Maid and scryer for an old local coven in Windsor during the reign of Queen Victoria, that two unnamed ancestors had been hung for witchcraft, and finally, that he'd had childhood experiences of the Goddess, who had called him to Her.

Further incidents somewhat later, complimented a no less profound experience of the Horned God, a brooding, dark and vetivert scented form who had seemed to Roy to be as old as time which left a lasting impression upon him. As to the fact of these matters, it is an issue of faith, for to paraphrase Professor Ronald Hutton of Bristol University who stated: 'he was either genuine or a genius.' His 'genius' was fundamental to the current and wave of influence absorbed by all those touched by its flow. His light was the sharpness, the clarity of vision that invigorated and illuminated all the disparate shards and fragments of lore he hungrily consumed along the trail of his own tragic argosy.

Around November 1963 he began writing a spate of articles for occult magazines, first for *Psychic News*, with 'genuine witchcraft is defended,' then later in 1964 after the death of Gerald B. Gardner, four more pieces were penned for *The Pentagram*. Here he became involved in some very unsavoury polemics along with his associate 'Taliesin' against Arnold Crowther, a well-known witch of the Sheffield coven and husband to Patricia Crowther, the group's High Priestess, both of whom had known Gardner very well. Somewhat harshly, he promoted the concept of what he termed 'grey magic' which allowed him to expertly weave yarns into circumstance, leaving the recipient bewildered and uncertain about where the boundaries of fact and fiction began and ended. In fact he was not beyond pulling off a major 'hoax', a regrettable scenario the author Enid Corral [A.K.A. Justine Glass] was subject to with regard to an incident involving a Copper plate that he allegedly attempted to pass off as a family heirloom; in another discussion he gave her his interpretation of symbols carved upon a French Menhir. Both subjects were later featured within her book.

Nonetheless, he was a flawed anti-hero, untypical and revolutionary. Being a thoroughbred non-conformist was never going to win him the approval of the middle-class establishment he despised and held in contempt. These 'good' folk of the fashionable set, who take tea, have sherry and cake, who seek only the flaccid rudiments of his passion were to him, less than approachable, less than tolerable, and yet, he did, in spite of himself garner their good graces. With gritted teeth he attended cocktail parties, book launches, gallery viewings all with an eye to being perceived well for his innovative views or be scorned for their lack of vision.

His scathing candour and propensity to mock those he considered beyond approach is well attested. And yet he attracted a number of known and respected occultists to work with him. Clearly he radiated a profound sense of the other detectable and tangible to all who met him; in fact without exception, they all record this most remarkable vibrancy and luminosity about him.

Having an empathic awareness of this, he utilised it to great effect, manipulating those around him towards his vision. Working outside, in what would now be deemed as shamanically, he kept the ritual form close to his chest. In effect, he became the 'supreme Master of Ceremonies,' orchestrating each musician to their finest tune. To date, none of those who worked with Roy Bowers, or who had been present at one of his rituals has since found its measure. Leading his Clan, he declared himself its trickster and master – the 'devil' explaining that the occult truth mirrored the outer plane where the Creatrix reigns supreme upon the inner plane. Choosing dramatic locations, high on hill tops, open to the winds, his many haunts and working sites included:

"Burnham Beeches in Berkshire, Witney Clumps in Oxfordshire, the Sussex Downs, Cheddar Gorge in Somerset and the Brecon Beacons in South Wales. Black and hooded robes were worn and power was raised by pacing or dancing in a circle around a central fire. The ritual tools used included a knife, a cord, a stone, a cauldron, a human skull, a cup or drinking horn and a forked staff called a Stang."

Many sources fed into and advanced the development of the Clan of Tubal Cain, particularly the wide ranging experiences and knowledge of Evan John Jones who brought the threads of 'The Rose Beyond the Grave,' among other curious lore, and George 'Winter' who brought threads of the 'Cave and the Cauldron Rite' through whom the final stages of its creation were formulated. Certain rites and methods of working along with codes and law were constructed in adherence to old formulae known to the proponents of that lore, bound together under the guiding light of Roy Bowers. They marked their working area with ash and soot, but not as a boundary, rather it delineated the main area to be used for ease, to keep all participants together. Sabbat fayre was also traditional, consisting of easily transportable foods such as bread, meat, cheese, butter, apples and wine.

On the surface, to outsiders, it appeared that their focus was upon the 'Horned God,' when in fact it was ultimately the Creatrix behind him who received their adoration. The Horned One was to them the presence in the Stang, the guardian of the 'dancing floor,' the bridge and link from one realm to another – the 'Lord of the Dance' himself! Their calendar was one that reflected the Christianised Folklore round of celebrations and observances called 'knots' by the Clan. Specifically, he was most insistent to assert how genuine witchcraft is not paganism, despite an overlap in the path towards the Mysteries. He used terms such as 'telling the maze' 'the skull and mound' 'crossing the Lethe,' all adding to his glamour and beguilement of those seeking a key to that pathway in him.

Quite often, more than one working area would be set up, and with more than one fire. Always outside, open to the wind and all elements. The Clan's Tutelary deity, a god of civilising arts of music, poetry and agriculture was shadowed by his twin, the psychopompic god of death, often given as the divine smith, Tubal Cain. Pale Leucothea, the cold, ambivalent and ruthless godhead was perceived as the femme fatale, the fates, sirens, harpies, but also as the graces, and ultimately as 'Truth.' This 'Wyrd' triplicity presented Her in accessible form. Her hidden aspect is Nox, the dark goddess Night, from whom is drawn the 'child of compassion,' the lamp of wisdom and guide to mankind. Placing Her Compass point in Magnetic North, he adhered to the Anglo-Saxon tradition where the souls of the dead become taken up by the wild geese upon the bitter winds in her train. Another tenet of this Traditional Craft, was concerned with the 'Luciferian' or Promethean aspect of Tubal Cain, who in choosing to advance mankind, became subject to punishment by the other gods, who alone wished to retain this knowledge. These comprehensions were to Bowers, profound truths upon which his die was cast.

Another, now common belief Bowers expounded was of the union in the annals of time, of the gods of the stars with the creatures of earth. Many myths, legends and lore throughout numerous cultures subscribe to this ideology to explain the subsequent drive for our return through acquired gnosis and of course mankind's curiosity towards the magical arts. The unusual form his unrehearsed rites took may be found exampled in the works of those authors present for them. They presented an alien world, of shadows and fleeting song, of silence and visionary prophesy, of horn and hoof; effectually a spell-binding combination hitherto unknown. His own injection of gnosis elevated the purpose and intent of these seeming primitivisms, a heady trance-inducing mix that he insisted distinguished his work from that of: "pagans, being naught but 'dancing peasants'." Inspired gnostic elements, aspects of eschatology and a cosmological mythos became collectively modeled upon philosophical and heavy theological truisms, gleaned experientially from the rich well-spring of company, and the revelatory works they achieved.

But Roy was to die alone, perplexed, bereft of his grand title, a recluse at odds with himself and the world; falling foul of his ego-driven dictatorial manner, his friends and family abandoned him, one by one. Feeling without hope of achieving his destiny in this life, he made his gambit, exploiting his belief in reincarnation, wherein the Pale –Faced Goddess would return him once again to his fold to complete the work he'd failed to fulfill in that incarnated form. In one of his many letters to me, John, writing in August 2000, cautioned us regarding commitment to a magical path:

"Once you embrace a dedicated magical path, you must live within its bounds and mythos; to forget that mundane and profane are one, to step out from its boundaries, is to invite chaos."

I am pain, grief, sorrow and tears,
The rack, noose and stake.
The flayer and the flayed,
The hunted and the hunter.
The Head without a body,
Thrust upon a stake.
The body without a head,
Hung upon a tree/
Yea! All this, but still am whole.

References

Books written about Roy Bowers/Robert Cochrane and his Clan of Tubal Cain:

The Roebuck in the Thicket: An Anthology of the Robert Cochrane Witchcraft Tradition, Evan John Jones and Robert Cochrane. Edited by Michael Howard (Capall Bann 2001).

The Robert Cochrane Letters: An Insight into Modern Traditional Witchcraft, Robert Cochrane with Evan John Jones. Edited and introduced by Michael Howard (Capall Bann 2002).

The Old Sod: The Odd Life and Inner Work of William G. Gray, Alan Richardson and Marcus Claridge (ignotus press 2003).

Witchcraft: A Tradition Renewed, Evan John Jones with Doreen Valiente (Robert Hale 1990).

Sacred Mask, Sacred Dance, Evan John Jones with Chas S. Clifton (Llewellyn USA 1997).

"A Hereditary Witch's Revelations" by Robert Cochrane in *Witchcraft, the Sixth Sense – and Us*, Justine Glass (Neville Spearman 1965).

"Robert Cochrane, Magister" in *Rebirth of Witchcraft,* Doreen Valiente (Robert Hale 1989).

"The Man in Black" in *The Triumph of the Moon: A History of Modern Pagan Witchcraft,* Ronald Hutton (Oxford University Press 1999).

Sybil Leek
(1917-1982)

By Adam Sartwell

When I was in college I loved to search the stacks of the college library for anything about Witchcraft, astrology, or anything that had a whiff of magick about it. It was rare to find one but still I would look. Most libraries will keep their books about the occult behind the desk because they are usually stolen or never returned. I have a clear memory of searching the stacks and a bright orange book caught my attention. *The Diary of a Witch* by Sybil Leek. This was my introduction to Sybil. I found every book that she wrote in the library that day and signed them all out. They only had three and I can't remember the other two, but I know they were on astrology and reincarnation, two topics she wrote a great deal about. Reading her journalistic style to her writing was enjoyable and informative. I later found out how prolific her writing was: she had written more than sixty books.

Sybil claimed lineage to a line of hereditary Witches on her mother's side that could trace its roots back to 1134 in Ireland. On her father's side she was related to the occultists that were close to the Russian royalty. She was said to be related to Molly Leigh, the Witch of Burslem, reported to live from 1685-1746, though some sources say different dates. Molly had a familiar of a black bird that lived with her. She didn't get along with the minister of the town and he accused her of cursing the beer in the local pub to go bad and many other ailments of the townsfolk. The more shocking manifestation of her power was after she died. After her burial the minister and the town folk went to her cottage to find her apparition with her pet, a black bird sitting waiting for them. The minister exhumed her up put a stake in her corpse through her still living blackbird in the coffin with her and reburied her going north to south in the grave yard to keep her down. It became a local legend to be told to children. Children are still daring each other to bring back her ghost by chanting "Molly Leigh, Molly Leigh, chase me round the apple tree" and circling her grave three times. Supposedly Molly had an apple tree in the garden of her cottage. Sybil visited that town taking pleasure in walking around it with her jackdaw, Mr. Hotfoot Jackson, on her shoulder as her reported relative would have.

Her family had many famous friends. She met Aleister Crowley who was a frequent visitor to her house when she was nine. She gave a report of their encounters in a Diary of a Witch. He supposedly told her that she would do great things. She also got to meet H.G. Wells who took her to her first eclipse.

She grew up in the New Forest area near Hampshire. She claimed that the area was home to four covens that had survived the burning times. Gerald Gardner also claimed an ancient lineage from a group in that area. She also spent time living with the gypsies in her area learning about herbal potions and gypsy lore.

She ran an antiques store in the Burley area until after the Witchcraft law was repealed and she came out as a Witch. She found that she was quickly hounded by the media and tourists and her landlord didn't want to renew her lease. By then she had written a book and was going to America to tour. She found that she loved America and moved there. She was author, astrologer and made many media appearances promoting Witchcraft. By the time she died in Melbourne Florida, she was a millionaire.

Her age was confusing because she said she was born in 1922 on February 22nd. In her funeral handouts it said 1917 to 1982.

As this article is going into a book about the ancestors of the Craft who may have become Mighty Dead to support the teachings of the Craft to this day, I have to share an experience that I had with a spirit who presented herself a Sybil Leek while on spiritual retreat to England. The group was meditating in the Chalice Well Gardens and trying to connect with the spirits of the Mighty Dead. The Mighty Dead are people who have reached an amount of what I can only term as enlightenment and are able to guide traditions of people on this side like saints, ascended masters or the Great White Brotherhood of the Theosophists. In my meditation Sybil came forth and in a jolly way she told me that she was glad that we were "following in her footsteps" meaning she had been to all the sacred sites we were going too. She then told me she had to go visit the other one. When I came out of meditation and we shared our experiences I found that another person in the group had had Sybil show up to speak with them.

This introduction meditation was followed by a teaching when we went to do ritual at Stonehenge. There she came to share with me a reaction she had to the way that we go about things in the Temple of Witchcraft: "In my day our magick was all about our will. Rarely did we see the fact that will must be tempered by love and guided by the wisdom of the spirit and past ages" giving me a message about how the magic of our age should be a tapestry of will, love, and wisdom.

DAUGHTER OF THE NIGHT: ROSALEEN (ROIE) NORTON (1917-1979)

By *Gede Parma*

Rosaleen Norton, infamously and fondly remembered in Australia as "the Witch of King's Cross"[1], is perhaps one of the most underrated and misunderstood public Witches of the recent centuries. She was an artist with a penchant for vivid and visceral detail, an occult genius with a deeply intuitive insight into the Otherworld/s and perhaps most importantly to Roie herself, a devotee of Pan and a Witch.

On the 2nd of October in 1917, Rosaleen Norton was born during a 'violent storm' in Dunedin, New Zealand. It has been noted that the circumstance of her birth was characteristic of Roie's tendency toward the dramatic. She was the youngest of three girls and the daughter of a seafaring father and a housewife mother. Religiously,

---

[1] The King's Cross (the Cross) area of Sydney (Australia) was once notoriously Bohemian; a refuge and play-ground for the 'outcasts' of society. Today the Cross is simply a dilapidated night-club district with only a vague resonance of its former 'glory days'.

while the family was not overtly indoctrinated, they still maintained an orthodox Protestant family (Church of England). It was in 1923 that the Nortons migrated to Sydney's affluent North Shore suburbs. There Rosaleen shared in a happy and comfortable childhood. It was also in the North Shore that she had her first totemic encounters.

For three years Roie slept outside of the house in a small tent that became her private sanctuary. She enjoyed her solitude from an early age and though the tent became tattered by the culmination of those three years of hermitage, Roie took the greatest pleasure in it. She was protected by an orb-weaving spider who she named Horatius. This spider had taken it upon herself (Roie believed the spider to be female) to weave a web across the tent's entrance. When Roie had to leave the tent she would of course have to destroy the web, however Horatius would diligently reweave the web. Safely contained within the inner sanctum of her tent, her family would never bother her within for fear of the giant spider. Roie and Horatius were connected by web and by wyrd, it seemed.

If communion with Nature came easily to Roie, then her art came unbidden from a hidden realm within. From the age of three onwards Roie was giving flesh and form to otherworldly creatures on page. She knew these presences as palpable and named them 'Nothing Beasts' and 'Flippers'.

> *"The latter looked rather like the conventional sheeted ghosts, and were hostile to me; but they were kept at bay by my friends and protectors the 'Nothing Beasts', who had animal heads surmounting a mass of octopoid tentacles, with which they seemed to swim through the ether." (Norton's own words)*[2]

It can be seen that Roie's artistic skill and her magickal knowledge seemed to be interdependent; one comes to the question whether she would have been quite so talented without one or the other.

---

2 Nevill Drury, *The Witch of King's Cross* (Australia: Kingsclear Books, 2002), 7.

Nevill Drury[3] is of the opinion that Roie's self-identification as a Witch grew after the media began to refer to her in such a way, however it can be seen that Norton's embracing of the mythos and prototype of the Witch is decidedly and deeply personal. Roie often cited her witch marks as proof of her destiny to Witchcraft. At the age of 7 two blue spots appeared on her left knee. She also possessed elfish ears – tapering points that are characteristic of 'darwin's peak'. Another physical 'abnormality' was the 'long strand of flesh which hung from underneath her armpit to her waist'.[4] It is rare these days for Witches to claim 'witch marks', however the belief in them or their providence is not necessarily restricted to the 'inquisitorial' fantasies of the witch-hunters during the Persecutions. Witch-marks or identifiers of magickal skill are present within the stories of the Italian Benandanti ('good walkers') who are born with cauls. Interestingly, Australia's other well-known and public/media Witch (Fiona Horne[5]) attests to having a third nipple, which began to become more formed as her prowess in the Craft grew.

At 14 years of age Rosaleen was expelled from the Church of England Girl's School for, what was termed, socially-disruptive behaviour and continuous 'grotesque' drawings. Roie did indeed admit that she was excessively disruptive, but maintained that she always claimed responsibility for her waylaying. After her expulsion from the Girl's School, Roie attended East Sydney Technical College. It was here that she gained the confidence to become Australia's first woman pavement artist. It was during this time, though she was still living at home with her family, that Roie began to indulge in private rituals which she had intuitively pieced together. Drury comments that Roie used joss sticks, robes and wine. Doreen Valiente expands on this by repeating the story of Rosaleen's private ritual of allegiance to Pan (the Greek God who Roie described as 'Pan the Elemental'

---

[3] To this date her only official biographer. Drury is an acclaimed academic of the occult and the magickal and has published more than twenty books on related subject matter.

[4] *The Witch of King's Cross* (2002), iv.

[5] Fiona Horne now makes her home in Los Angeles, California.

and as the God of 'Infinite Being'). Valiente cites Roie's usage of wine, green leaves, incense and 'a little of her own blood' in a ceremony performed when she was thirteen years old. Valiente comments that this could indicate a previous incarnation as a Witch; I would also dare to suggest genetic or archetypal memory (both are equally valid, in my mind).

The Persecutions

It was to be Rosaleen's relationship with the precocious poet Gavin Greenlees, with whom she shared a romantic and sexual relationship that would truly transform Roie's personage in the public eye. Originally her art had been praised by various publications, and the following quote from a journalist reviewing one of her early Sydney exhibitions illustrates this:

"...[Rosaleen Norton] had developed a most exceptional ability to actually enter the psychic sphere, to transport her personality to other planes than the physical one, and to sensually perceive that which, to most of us, remains forever hidden."[6]

I believe that the phrase 'sensually perceive' is truly indicative of Roie's approach to Life in general.

Unfortunately in 1949, an exhibition of Norton's art held at the University of Melbourne in Victoria, proved disastrous. Several police officers arrived on the third day of the exhibition which intended to run for several weeks and charged Norton with decadence, obscenity and arousal of 'unhealthy sexual appetites' through the medium of her art. When they questioned her concerning the meaning behind the artwork originally entitled *Witches' Sabbath* (later *Black Magic*) Roie replied that the female figure represented the Witch, the panther with whom she was seemingly dancing embodied the powers of darkness and their embrace was initiation into what she termed the 'infernal mysteries'. Nowadays, this explanation would invite curiosity more so than revulsion and yet the police rejected any notion of merit to the art and a court case ensued. Fortunately, Rosaleen and Gavin Greenlees won and were awarded costs.

---

6 *Pertinent* June (1943), 33.

In 1952 the book *The Art of Rosaleen Norton* was published. Originally 500 copies were published; they were leather-bound by a professional and included Roie's artwork with poetry by Gavin Greenlees. Some of the pieces in the book were Lilith, Fohat, Eloi, Rites of Baron Samedi and Black Magic. Again, it is clearly indicated by the titles of these works that Roie had a broader knowledge of the world of magic and the occult than is generally assumed. However, and again, the Australian government prosecuted the publisher of the book (Wally Glover) for producing an obscenity. In defense of the publication in court, Roie invoked the providence of Jung and Freud in establishing a precedent for the exploration of such themes as delved into through her work. In conclusion two of the artworks were ordered to be blacked out from future copies of the book (The Adversary and Fohat; both images contained overt phallic imagery). On the other side of the world, US customs decided to burn all incoming copies of the book and Australia prohibited the importation of the book; if someone in Australia already possessed a copy and left the country with it on hand, it would not be allowed to return. Roie, however, was not to be turned away by such limitation. She sent out copies of the book to those individuals she greatly admired including T. S. Elliot, Dr. Carl Jung, Professor Albert Einstein and C. S. Lewis.[7]

In 1955, yet again, police charged the owner of a Sydney café in Potts Point (near to modern-day King's Cross) with obscenity for displaying 29 Norton works. Roie and Gavin were again called into court and convicted and fined, more so for photographs which had come to police attention earlier in that year. The photographs depicted Roie and Gavin before the altar of Pan performing an 'unnatural sex act' (photos from one of Roie's recent birthday parties, taken as a joke, and presumably by their friend and fellow magical practitioner, Sir Eugene Goossens).

Sir Eugene Goossens, an Englishman who arrived in Australia in 1947 with his American-born wife, was an internationally-renowned

---

[7] To whom she wrote an involved letter conveying her belief that the cosmogony/cosmology as described in Lewis's works was parallel to that which Roie had encountered in her own trance experiences. She also challenged him to qualify how he reconciled his mystical insights with orthodox Christian doctrine.

conductor and was instated as a permanent conductor of the Sydney Symphony Orchestra. He was credited with the original idea for the Sydney Opera House and was a knight and quite well-to-do (he and his wife lived in the North Shore Sydney suburbs). Goossens was also heavily fascinated by Paganism and Magic from being introduced to it by earlier colleagues. In the early 1950s he came to know Roie through discovering the book *The Art of Rosaleen Norton* (1952) and after meeting her in person quickly became a working and dedicated member of the coven which honoured Pan and performed unique Pagan rituals (which Roie, according to Drury, defined as 'the heathen worship of ancient Greek Gods').

In March 1956, Goossens was stopped by police waiting for him at Sydney airport as he returned from London. In his bag they found over 800 erotic pictures (which were considered pornographic), a further film spool, and several ceremonial masks which were later confirmed by Gavin Greenlees as having been used in the magical rites of their group. Sir Eugene Goossens was charged under a Customs act which prohibited 'blasphemous, indecent or obscene works or articles'. Rosaleen Norton was seemingly caught in a perpetual whirlwind of accusations, which would, in this day and age, have never been leveled at her in the first place. Australia in the 1950s was obviously a very concerned and conventional country.

The Goat Fold – Rosaleen Norton's Tradition/s of Witchcraft

"...this held the essence of all that called to my inmost being: Night and wild things and mystery; storms; being by myself, free of other people. The sense of some deep hidden knowledge stirring at the back of consciousness, and all about me the feeling of secret sentient life, that was in alliance with me, but that others were unaware, or afraid of, because it was inhuman."[8]

Nevill Drury's comments that Roie's Witch identity was a reaction to the media's representation of her, I feel, are largely untrue. As early as 1955 we find that Norton is self-identifying as a Witch and apparently as one of the earlier (October, 1955) news

---

8 Rosaleen Norton, *Witches Want No Recruits* Australian Post (10 January, 1957), 35.

articles on her states (Australasian Post) Norton had written a letter to the editor in response to a series of articles speaking on the 'evils of devil-worship'. Norton goes on to say, in this same article, which came out only a year after the British publication of *Witchcraft Today* (Gerald Gardner) that she is a Witch and an active member of a King's Cross coven. In this article three witches/warlocks are interviewed (Rosaleen herself and two men, presumably her initiates). Each wears a ceremonial mask (Roie dons a cat mask, the men, a toad and a rat) – they declare that the wearing of these masks heightens the 'psychic atmosphere'. When asked whether their coven (comprising of seven members at the time) was the only one in Sydney, the answer was that it was one of half a dozen. When asked about 'certain cruelties' performed in the honour of deities, the Witches reply that no human or animal is ever harmed as part of their ceremonies. In fact, Rosaleen was staunchly against the idea of animal sacrifice, as she considered herself more kin to the animal world than the human.

According to Roie, and considering the first Gardnerian initiate did not arrive in Australia until 1959[9], she discovered contacts in the occult world (including other covens) from age 21 onwards (the late 1930s and early 1940s). When Roie spoke on discovering covens or

---

9 Both Doreen Valiente and Nevill Drury comment that there had been some (but necessarily limited, considering the circumstance and geography) correspondence between Norton and Gardner, in the early 1950s and that Norton had sent him a copy of *The Art of Rosaleen Norton*. Gardner is also quoted as suggesting that Norton had implored him to magickally aid her so that she would be acquitted of charges against her – Gardner claims many Witches across England prayed and worked magick for her nightly to aid in the effort which was apparently successful. However, in considering all of the evidence thus far, it can be clearly seen that Roie's form of Witchcraft in Australia actually predates the publication of *Witchcraft Today* (1954) and in studying the elements inherent in her Craft as discussed above we discover that Rosaleen's Witchcraft differs from the Gardnerian in many significant ways – including the emphasis on ceremonial masks, Welsh titles such as 'consurier' and Welsh initiatory oaths, a secret handshake known only to initiates, and a kind of apron which covers only the front and back of the person from the waist-down. One of the similarities was that Roie referred to it as the 'Witch Cult', though Drury comments that one of the only two books explicitly concerning Witchcraft in the bibliography of *The Art of Rosaleen Norton* was Margaret A. Murray's *The Witch Cult in Western Europe*, and this may have influenced Roie, considering the usage of that very term liberally throughout Murray's book.

groups for oneself she repeats the generic occult attitude that when a student is ready the teacher will come. She also speaks on the fact that a Witchcraft adept has the sense to know when another is also a Witch and also when another is a potential initiate. Also, that often the wandering spirits of Witches will discover each other on the 'inner planes of Being' and then go on to meet in the flesh (Victor and Cora Anderson of the Feri Tradition would agree with this completely; they met and made love on the astral years before they met in the flesh). Roie's story of her discovering that she was a Witch at age 13 never changed and she never embellished this with any lie of initiation by a family member or any Craft initiate[10]; in fact, Roie maintained that if you are a naturally-born Witch no one has to teach you anything, you simply know! I certainly understand what she is speaking of here, but would also suggest that training aids us only insofar as it offers forms, techniques, concepts and philosophies with which we may deepen and strengthen our personal spirituality, as well as offering the springboard of objectivity in that other humans are available to provide reference points, context or criticism (as well, of course, as support and advice on many levels).

Drury incorrectly asserts that the first Australasian Post article on Rosaleen was published in 1956. In actual fact, that article was the third, the first being a 1952 article written by a sympathetic friend and journalist entitled *'Rosaleen says she could be a Witch'* which also coincided with the release of *The Art of Rosaleen Norton*. The 1955 article is far more telling of Roie's Witchcraft style or tradition (as seen above). Drury also asserts, based on the apparent 'first' article that Rosaleen believed in all religions, however that is not what she is suggesting at all. Roie responds to the question, "Do you believe in God?" by declaring that in 'Infinity', a concept of which she perpetually propounded, there is room for all deities, including the Christian God. The reporters then asked Roie if she would ever be a Christian, and she replies, "Well, hardly, would I?" This is a very typical Witch answer to such questions – that we believe in the

---

10 In a 1957 *Australasian Post* article Roie repeats the story of her 'confirmation' as a Witch sealed by her ceremonial allegiance to Pan which has been mentioned above

providence or existence of all possible deities, but that in saying that, we would not necessarily abide by any or all religious dogmas.

Another interesting distinction made by Roie is that while the term 'Witch' is appropriate for both sexes (as well as sorcerer), Roie notes that generally a male witch is called a warlock, and for those warlocks who are adepts – wizards. This is in stark contrast to the Witchcraft of Gardner which never uses (or used) the terms warlock or wizard for male initiates (Magus however was/is used for a third degree male in some lines of Wicca).

Roie describes initiation rituals as having different forms from group to group, but that there are similarities in that after a period of time/probation the 'neophyte' is asked several questions and then kneels and places one hand on the crown of their head and the other under the sole of one foot to vow all between to the Gods (in this case Pan and Hecate)[11]. She also mentions that a ceremony to the four Elements is also performed either during or after (somewhat akin to the Gardnerian initiation). A new name is given, as well as a charged talisman and a ceremonial cord which Roie calls the Witches' Garter.

Doreen Valiente, in her book, *The Rebirth of Witchcraft* (Phoenix, 1989), refers to Rosaleen Norton and her tradition known as the 'Goat Fold' in her chapter on Leslie Roberts, the occult 'investigator'. It was in 1959, when working as a waiter on a cruise-ship that Leslie docked at Sydney. He hastily sought Roie out because Doreen had previously spoken to Leslie about her. Doreen mentions that Roie had contacted Gerald Gardner and that she had sent him a copy of *The Art of Rosaleen Norton*. Therefore the communication must have occurred after or during the latter half of 1952, after the publication of the book. In the communications Roie spoke of working with her coven in Sydney. This shows that she knew of and was celebrating Witchcraft rites in a group presumably before knowing of Gardner and certainly before writing to him. It can also be ascertained that Gardner would not have sent any oath bound material of his tradition to her, and in fact this is made more plausible by the fact that the

---

11 This appears time and again in most forms of traditional Witchcraft and is in fact enshrined in the second degree Gardnerian initiation, however the High Priest/ess is the one to place his/her hands over the head and under the knees (not the feet) of the initiate.

terminology and the majority of the techniques and themes relating to the 'Goat Fold' were not Gardnerian in the least. To further consolidate the case of Rosaleen's tradition existing in Australia prior to the arrival of Gardner I have gathered evidence from newspaper articles relating to a man named Anton Miles, who in 1959 (four years after the media began to publish articles about Roie's form of Witchcraft) was initiated as a Gardnerian Witch in the Bricket Wood Coven in North London. He then moved to Sydney, Australia and soon founded a Gardnerian group there. According to one article in People (February 15th 1961) Anton Miles states that the Witch Cult in Australia dates from August 1959 onwards (his arrival in Sydney). It is quite obvious then that he either had no idea that Rosaleen Norton existed (which is hugely unlikely) or that he did not consider her coven to be authentic Witchcraft (or it simply slipped his mind). Undoubtedly, as I have hopefully demonstrated, it certainly was authentic and just as valid.

Valiente sheds more light on the Goat Fold when she mentions that Roie told Leslie that the Goat Fold came to Australia with the early convicts. Whether there is any authenticity to this claim cannot be vouched for; however it is quite possible Roie simply assumed this because she did not know from when or where the tradition derived. The name however is very in line with traditional Western European Witchcraft which often embodies the Witch God as a Goat (Pan is also considered to be half goat). Valiente notes a Welsh influence in the 'first degree' title ('consurier'); she asserts that its meaning is akin to 'wise woman' or 'cunning man'. The ritual contains the following phrase which is also reproduced (with Rosaleen's permission) in Valiente's book:

> *"Walking on the heath, I met some friends. I have been in the cauldron and out again. They told me I am one of the green shoots of Pryderie."*

I personally feel a much older resonance with this ritual phrase than most of those I have read in Gardnerian rituals (though they are as equally poetic). It embodies the death and rebirth journey of all true initiatory experiences (in and out of the cauldron) and further affirms this by referring to the 'green shoots of Pryderie' – the underworld contains within itself all powers of fertility and regeneration and Pryderi has underworld associations as his father is Pwyll Pen Annwfn, meaning Pwyll, King of the Underworld.

By this time Roie's coven was celebrating the four Greater Sabbats derived originally from the Celtic fire festivals of Samhain, Imbolc, Beltaine and Lughnasadh (and though it was not mentioned by Roie in the media until 1969, the coven may have been celebrating these festival prior to Leslie's initiation in 1959, indeed it would be assumed that the group had been doing so for several years if they thought it important enough to pass on to Leslie). Like the Gardnerians, 'working tools' were used, but only five – the athame, the chalice, the censer, the pentacle and cord (each representing one of the Five Elements including Spirit). They too partook in a sacred meal of wine and cakes; the wine was drunk from a horn passed around the Circle. Also included in this chapter of *The Rebirth of Witchcraft* is a piece called 'The First Knowledge' given in the initiation ritual of Roie's coven. It reads as both practical and deeply evocative simultaneously, and I urge all to read this section of Valiente's book to enjoy the words. Valiente passed on the First Knowledge to a British Gardnerian High Priestess, and at the time of the writing of the book it was apparently being used in rituals in the UK (from Roie to Leslie to Doreen to the unnamed Gardnerian High Priestess).

Decline and Death

Throughout the 1960s Roie began to amass a small clientele to whom she sold charms and hexes for a charge (the role of the cunning woman/wise witch). She also began to paint occult paintings (either completely new subject matter or repeats of Pan and Lucifer symbology) for between five to one hundred pounds. In 1964 she and Gavin (who was on temporary release from hospital – for schizophrenia) were again charged with vagrancy and though Roie was acquitted of that charge, she was fined two pounds for 'indecent language'. Gavin Greenlees was convicted and sentenced to one month of jail for the crime of carrying a knife with the intent to harm (Nevill Drury comments that this sentence is ludicrous considering Gavin's mental state).

In 1974 the Anglican Archbishop of Sydney proclaimed a Commission of Inquiry into the Occult. As Drury writes, "It was only the second such enquiry in a Protestant country since the Middle Ages."[12] This was the same year that the film *The Exorcist* was released in Australia. This movie had a terrifying impact on the subconscious of the culture at large. In response to the media and society furor and comments that the occult was a dangerous pursuit, Rosaleen came out to make her own comments:

> *"Magic can send you round the bend. It is as dangerous as drugs...They can release various entities that they don't know anything about, and such people have no idea how to handle these entities..."*[13]

Towards the end of 1978 Roie fell very ill and it was discovered that she had colon cancer. An operation was conducted, however it was not successful, and Roie was taken in November 1979 to the place in which she would die – the Roman Catholic Sacred Heart Hospice for the Dying. To her friend Victor Wain, shortly before she died, she uttered these words, firm and resounding, "I came into this world bravely; I'll go out bravely." Roie was a proud Pagan to the end and though she was surrounded by Catholic iconography, dying in a bed surrounded by crucifixes, she was devoted to her mighty Pan for what would seem eternity. Rosaleen Norton died on the 5th of December, 1979. Exactly four years later on the 5th of December, 1983, Gavin Greenlees, beloved of Roie, was found dead in his home.

Rosaleen Norton was infamous, fascinating, dark, sardonic, devoted, intelligent and hugely in touch with the Unseen. She was undoubtedly a Witch. She has inspired fictional books, several biographies, documentaries, stage-plays, art and the experimental film-maker Kenneth Anger even announced in 1993 that he wished to make a feature film about Roie's life because it contained all the 'ingredients' of a good film. And yet, for me, the most beautiful and, I believe, resonant story relating to Roie is that she once slipped into a pond and emerged holding a little turtle in her hands. She sincerely

---

[12] *The Witch of King's Cross* (2002), 86.

[13] Gus de Brito, "A Witch's Warning" *Sunday Mirror* (Sydney, 17 August 1975).

believed that this turtle was a gift of Pan and I wholeheartedly agree. Christopher asked me to write on Rosaleen Norton because I have lived in Australia for the majority of my life and would therefore have a better feel for her. I had known of her, of course, for many years prior to writing this entry on her, but researching and writing this piece has provided me a deeper insight and a greater fondness for Roie. To close, and in honour of Roie, now one of the Mighty Dead, I have written and offered this poem:

O Rosaleen

Your eyes stare into mine and a stirring unfolds,
You tell me it is Infinity and that I am One with It.
You take my hands and smile; your face broadens,
And for a moment you become a cat.

As we leave our 'mortal coils' behind,
We rise upon the Inner Planes of Ether;
I laugh because I would never use those words,
You laugh because you would not either.

You sing to me that beyond all else is Pan,
And I whisper back that Pan is but one God of Many.
Your eyes glow with a knowing eclipsing the moon's wisdom,
And you sing an invocation to the Mighty Horned Man.

As we come to the peak of a palace of stars,
As the spirits we are climax, crescendo,
We behold the vision of the Lord of Infinity,
And though we wish to kneel, it is he who bows.

Pan! IO IO IO! PAN!
Your wild shriek into the night coalesces,
And forms an altar upon which we place,
Our memories, our stories and our secrets.

The Horned One grins widely and I tremor,
You hold my hand and tell me all is well;

And I perceive the horns upon him,
And like an aura the goat-like smell.

The Horned God begins to laugh and swell,
And as he does so, so do we.
A terrifying clamour of music,
Illumines the heavens with majesty.

He speaks to us of his holy name,
That Pan means All and All is All,
That one God he may be until,
We come to know I AM the ALL!

A name, a power, a deity,
Has shared with us his secret rites,
And so we take our secrets back,
Into the soul's resplendent night.

She turns to me in the Singing Chasm,
And as silver stars spin all around,
She thanks me for the sacred time
I have given her upon the ground.

I tell her I will light a candle,
For her spirit at Samhain,
That she will know I do remember,
The blessed Witch – O Rosaleen.

Felicity Bumgardner

By Christopher Penczak

Felicity is the seemingly mythic ancestor to the Cabot Tradition of Witchcraft, holding a special place in our hearts not unlike the figures of "Old" Dorothy Clutterbuck and "Old Daffo" (Edith Woodford-Grimes) unproven until fairly recently, for the Gardnerian Branch of British Traditional Wicca. Felicity Bumgardner is the teacher and initiator of Laurie Cabot, the founder of the Cabot-Kent Hermetic Temple, the founder of the Cabot Tradition of Witchcraft and the "official Witch" of Salem, Massachusetts. She has been active publicly as a Witch, operating various Witchcraft shops to provide outreach and magickal tools to Witches and non-Witches, educating the public through interviews and appearances, performing activism work, counseling others as a minister and educating Witches and those seeking to be Witches in the art, science and religion of Witchcraft.

As a child, Laurie experienced some profound psychic events, and they didn't stop when she and her mother moved from California to Boston. Her mother was desperate to understand and control Laurie's abilities, and their search started at the Boston Public Library. They began hunting down any books on psychic experiences and the paranormal. They delved into precognition, fortune telling and ghosts. Her mother struck up a conversation after several visits with one of the librarians. She was gray haired and short, and though a very comely woman, her age was difficult to determine as she seemed quite vital. Laurie says, "At first the librarian was very standoffish. I remember that clearly. She seemed a bit shocked and didn't want to talk. She sat behind a big desk, and finally she led my mother to what would amount to the 'occult section.' " [1]

After several more visits, Felicity began to open up to the mother and daughter. She said, "I think I can help you." The librarian gave them a copy of Sir James George Frazer's *The Golden Bough* and took the mother aside and whispered that she was a Witch. Laurie's

---

[1] Private Interview with Laurie Cabot. Salem, Massachusetts, April 16, 2009.

mother was stunned, but since they had already talked quite a bit at this point and had determined that Felicity was a kind and helpful woman, they accepted she was a Witch. She then said she felt she could help Laurie because she believed Laurie was a Witch too. She offered to train her as a Witch, and her training could help control her ever growing psychic abilities. Surprisingly her mother agreed and they both began attending classes at Felicity's home in a brownstone on Commonwealth Avenue in Boston, not far from the Public Library. She began her training at age thirteen.

Felicity was obviously from England, still having a bit of an accent, but had married an American of the last name Bumgardner. As far as they knew, she had been living in Boston for quite a while. Their home was quite lavish and beautifully decorated. The home had oriental carpets and expensive wall hangings. Her husband had a wood paneled study with a full library, where he would read and smoke his pipe while his wife practiced Witchcraft. In retrospect, she couldn't have lived there on a librarians salary, so Laurie and her mother assumed that the husband must make quite a good living or come from a well-to-do family.

Felicity would lead them upstairs where she taught Laurie and two other American women, Felicity's coven. While they were more experienced than Laurie, they were still students. She didn't know if they were Witches previous to meeting Felicity, and had just found someone like minded, or if she was the source of their Witchcraft training. Laurie isn't certain of their names anymore, though when telling the story to students, she often called one of them Betty, though she is not sure if her name was really Betty. The memories of childhood can often be vague. One was a musician and the other was a college professor locally. Laurie's mother observed and learned the theory, but did not take part in the rituals.

The Teachings

Felicity taught Laurie the magick of the Witches of Kent. She was the first to tell Laurie that coven is a group of Witches, numbering three to thirteen. Their little coven was three ladies and a little girl. This teaching was echoed in the trials of Isobel Gowdie, where the first concept of the coven in this format appeared in Witchcraft literature.

The Lord and Lady were the God and Goddess of Witches, described as primal, not personal, forces. The Witch God is the Lord of the Woods. The Witch Goddess "has three sides" [2] but was not specifically maiden, mother, and crone. The Goddess manifested in flowers, which is where she could be best "seen" though she didn't talk about Bloudewedd specifically. Laurie later read the myth of Bloudewedd and made that potential connection. Magick and psychic ability were more of the focus of the Witch, rather than the worship of gods.

The Fey are a race of people, and the Witches and the Fey are one. Felicity taught us that if you were Celtic at all, then the Fey is in your blood, your lineage. She would say that being a Witch is in your blood. (Laurie also believes that as the races mingled, we all have the blood and can call upon it.) There were no special rituals of communion for the Fey. You simply had to be aware of your connection to them.

King Arthur, Merlin and Morgana Le Fey were important to the traditions Felicity taught. She believed that her tradition was pre-Christian, and remained so despite the coming of Christianity. She was spiritually descended from that time and place. The Witches of Kent are the keepers of the light of Excalibur. Initiates would have some sword-like tool, such as a knife or letter opener, to receive the light of Excalibur. Felicity did have a sword but the other members of the coven did not. Felicity also used a double edged knife with a bone handle.

Witches do their magick in the magick circle. She taught four ways of casting a circle. It did not include calling the quarters or elements formally. All the forces of nature were automatically present in the circle. You can cast a circle by laying your knife outward, pointing outward and stepping three feet in to make a circle. There would be one blade for every Witch in the circle. You can cast a circle through a circle of salt on the floor, like a magician, but instead of chalk, you use salt. Felicity used ordinary table salt. You can point

---

[2] Private Interview with Laurie Cabot. Salem, Massachusetts, April 16, 2009.

your knife to the center of the circle and then slowly bring the blade upward and outwards, all the way to the edge of the circle, the rim where we envisioned the boundary. This method worked best with a group of witches, three or four. You can cast with a wand, a simple blessed stick, three times clockwise. Everyone in the circle adds to the power of the circle, even if it's not their specific intention being cast in a spell.

While the classical elements were not important, she taught about the power of nature as manifest through water, wind and fire. Animals can act as guardians. They do not necessarily come when called, but come when they are needed. She taught about the crow, owl, bear and badger.

The waters of the chalice could be blessed and stirred with your finger or your knife. You first poured out a libation to the gods, either outdoors upon the ground, or in a little bowl of dirt if indoors, before you drink. The chalice blessing was not the Great Rite or Cakes and Ale of Wicca. It had no overt sexual connotation. It was a simple sacramental act to unite you with the gods.

The Magick

Words such as intuition, intention and energy were not used. Felicity simply called those things your "magic" or your "power." You used what you had around you, and your magick would make the herb or stone do whatever it needed to do. She did not teach about exotic herbs or medicinal properties for the most part.

The Moon was an important factor in magick. The waxing moon was used to gain things, bring blessing and make things happen. The waning Moon was used to get rid of things, like getting rid of enemies, illness or anything unwanted. Petition spells written out on paper in accord with the Moon phase would be burned in a pot or cauldron. You should envision the spell when reading and burning it to make it clear in your mind so your magick will give you exactly what you want. The burning releases the spell to the ethers. You can carry some of the ash in a pocket or bag until it manifests.

The waning moon can be used to erase the past, to erase bad things from your past. While in circle, name what happened in your past and say, "This happened in the past, but it shall not be drawn forward into the future." Knowledge of Sun signs was also important to Felicity. She taught a Sun sign astrology and encouraged her students to know the foundations of astronomy, but it was not required.

Felicity didn't teach anything about color in magick. Candles were white. You could put herbs or symbols beneath them, but she did not dress them with oil. Crystals were not available, but rocks from the river or beach could used to hold your magickal wish. Felicity used a cord, but never taught them why she wore it or how to use it. She did some knot magick with simple string, but nothing with her more formal cord. The rest of the coven never made cords or wore them in ritual. Felicity never used an image of a pentacle. She made charms of very simple symbols, such as the moon, a cat or an equal arm cross. Other tools included a broom to sweep the ritual area before circle or to protect a threshold and seldom used cauldron.

Felicity taught spells, including a simple love potion of basil leaf and vanilla bean in almond oil to be worn like a perfume. She taught the common folk wisdom of an iron horseshoe over the door for protection. Iron shavings can be mixed with water, along with Frankincense and Myrrh, for a protection potion. They were available at the Catholic Supply shop. Felicity used a small amount of dragon's blood resin, obtained from violin makers. She used it sparingly but it added power to any working. Animal fur can be used in potions and spells as well.

Tea was infused with magick for healing. You'd sip the tea, think about who you wanted to heal, and send that healing with your thoughts. Spells can be infused in water, tea or wine, ingested and sent forth. Food magick can be infused in the same way, particularly earthy thing such as vegetables and potatoes. Potatoes could be used for anything. Lemons were to cleanse and banish. Meat was not used.

Felicity could summon the winds, and used feathers to demonstrate their strength. Feathers could be omens. A gray or white feather meant good news coming if you saw it on the ground in front of you. Good news was coming your way. Black feather, like crow feathers, were for protection or warning. Blue feathers, of course, were happiness if you ever found one. Cardinal feathers were good luck.

She trained her students in using their "mind's eye" to see things first internally before doing your magick. She did use the term "third eye" at times, but never referenced the chakras. Through the casting of stones, scrying in ink and water, tea leaf reading, she taught the arts of divination. She never used cards or other symbols. She could seemingly see colors in the aura.

This little coven celebrated the seasons, but not the full eight neopagan holidays. They learned about Halloween, and mentioned Samhain, but more often referred to it as Halloween. There was May Day and the harvest. Very simple observances occurred in Felicity's brownstone. She encouraged her coven to reflect upon where they were, where they are going and the changes in nature. The changes in nature reflected the changes within you.

The Tradition

Laurie never received a book with this material. The lessons plan was not formal and clear with a neat progression. It was organic. New things were taught when they came up. Felicity claimed connection and lineage to people she referred to as the Witches of Kent. They were the source of her own education and training, though obviously she was well read and very familiar with available occult and mythological literature of her time, being a librarian. She lived in Kent, a county in southeast England, prior to coming to America.

Kent includes Canterbury and Dover, as well as the famous White Cliffs of Dover. Populated since Paleolithic times, it has a large number of standing stones. Legend says that the megalithic tomb Kit's Cooty was created by Witches. Witchcraft trials abounded in Kent as well as other parts of England. Felicity spoke of the elders in Kent, seemingly very different from the current public group of Wiccans and modern eclectic witches in Kent today. She emphasized this linage, their connection to Excalibur, the faeries and their Celtic ways.

There was no Wiccan Rede in the Kent Tradition. Some spontaneous poetry and rhymes were used in ritual, but nothing like the Charge of the Goddess. There were no degrees, titles or papers. While the tradition was respectful, it was much less formal than other traditions. Felicity never worked skyclad. Being naked for ritual would have been scandalous for Felicity. They did wear black at times, but it was not required. Divination was stressed by her teachers, and in turn emphasized by her as a means to control and refine psychic ability.

Initiation was a rite of passage for a Witch. Laurie received initiation at about age sixteen, and soon after her training stopped. Today Laurie initiates her own students much like she was initiated. It was at her initiation that Felicity spoke more deeply about the Witches of Kent as the keepers of the light of Excalibur. They have kept it burning for centuries, passing the light, and she continued their tradition here in America. Initiation consisted of the magick circle and an evocation of the Lady and Lord. She blessed the chalice and poured a libation. Felicity initiated Laurie with sacred oil and had her kneel. She then "dubbed" Laurie with the sword upon the shoulders, as they do in a knighting ceremony and proclaimed her a Witch. She then struck Laurie's letter opener sword with her own larger sword, to transfer the light of Excalibur to it, and with a small pot of Earth, she struck the earth with her own blade, saying, "I return my wisdom to the earth," representing the cycle of exchange between the Witch and the land, the reciprocity. The earth, the land was very important in what Felicity taught. The Lady could be seen everywhere. The ceremony was soon over. Though being a Witch would guide Laurie for the rest of her life, she was a sixteen year old girl, now with greater control over her psychic ability and went out to live her life. She soon became a dancer, got married and had two children. It was not until the dissolution of her marriage that she truly reclaimed her identity and mission as a Witch.

The Search

Felicity disappeared into the mist of obscurity, not really coming to light until Laurie's more public career as a Witch in Salem, Massachusetts and her own writing career. Some initiates of the Cabot Tradition claim psychic contact with Felicity at times, or simply feeling a presence they recognize as hers. In my own work communing with the Witches of Kent in spirit, I commune with an entity known as Margaret, who claims to predate Felicity in the chain of initiation. I have not been able to tune into Felicity specifically myself, in any way that can be corroborated or aid in my quest to document her existence.

Research to verify her existence has been difficult to obtain. If she taught other Witches in the Boston area, predating the modern Wicca movement, none of them or their own students have made any public connections to modern Pagans besides Laurie Cabot. If any of the elders in the Kent Tradition back in England survive, they have been very quiet. Modern researches on the Craft in England have not turned up any corroborating evidence despite a flurry of other traditions claiming non-Wiccan origin.

Out of all the Witches Laurie Cabot later encountered in her career, only the late author Stewart Farrar said he had heard anything about the Witches of Kent. Sadly no further information was forthcoming and he makes no mention of them in his public or private correspondence or papers. [3]

Her immigration to the United States, and her marriage to an American makes original records hard to obtain without knowing her maiden name or hometown. Kent is a wide territory and it is assumed that Bumgardner is her husband's last name. It is uncertain if they married in the U.S. or in the United Kingdom. Even the spelling, with variations of Bumgarner, Baumgarner, Baumgardner, Bumgartner and Baumgartner have been suggested with no avail. Some aiding my own research have suggested that at the time Felicity was rarely a first name, but a possible nick name for another "F" name, or a middle name.

Although she met Laurie and her mother while working at the Boston Public Library in the 1940s, the library has no record of anyone with any similar name, first or last, in that time frame on the payroll or annual reports for the 1930s-1950s. [4] Local census and city reports do not list any variation of Bumgardner on Commonwealth Ave. or nearby in Boston. Her name does not show up on any electronic registered grave finder websites as of yet.

---

[3] Farrar, Janet. Personal Electronic Correspondence, 2009.

[4] Private email correspondence with Gail Fithian, Curator of Social Sciences Boston Public Library, dated October 26, 2011.

A possible connection is a Mrs. E. F. Baumgartner on a boat passage manifest from England to America, stopping in both Boston and New York. She is listed on the boat Scythia, arriving Feb 18th, 1933 from Liverpool to Boston. A John Bumgardner is listed in the Boston Directory in 1936 on Queensberry, possibly as a chauffeur. [5] Could this be her husband? He seems to be conspicuously missing from later directories.

While it is assumed that Bumgardner is Felicity's married name, it comes from an ancient aristocratic family from East Prussia with associations to the Teutonic Knights. The family name means orchard or worker in an orchard and their coat of arms consists of three feathers of the Prince of Wales and a tree surrounded by a circular fence. They arrived as a family to the United States in Pennsylvania in 1732. I wonder if the orchard association plays any part to the emphasis on Avalon, or the land of Apples, in the Arthurian lore of these Witches. [6]

Though I initially wondered about the origin of the Arthurian material in Felicity's teaching, remarking some similarity with Dion Fortune's work on the holy grail, as Laurie's learning focused upon the sword of Excalibur, and Fortune's "first degree" work in the grail mysteries were focused upon the sword, Witchcraft expert and author Michael Howard commented, "I don't find it strange that there might be Arthurian material in relation to the Kentish witches as that is something I've come across. Sometimes it is a safe and acceptable 'mask' for Luciferian beliefs." [7]

While Kent is not connected to the New Forest of Gerald Gardner, Gardner tended to favor the sword as a tool along with the athame. In his *Ye Bok of ye Arte Magical* the magus uses the sword to cast the circle. Doreen Valiente mentions the New Forest sword that was used to initiate her. While it is in the style of *The Key of Solomon*,

---

[5] Boston City Directory, 1936, p. 774.

[6] http://www.houseofnames.com/bumgardner-family-crest: April 22, 2012.

[7] Howard, Michael. Personal Electronic Correspondence. 2012. Used with Permission.

it might also point to a connection in folk belief and traditional Witchcraft customs.

The only written material specifically focused upon the Witches of Kent that is not based upon more recently Neo-pagan traditions is the booklet *The Witches of Kent* by Kelvin I. Jones, first published in 1991, detailing the transcripts of the Witchcraft trials in 17th Century Kent. While it does point to the possibility of traditional Craft groups in the area surviving if Witchcraft was so prevalent in the area, it can also point to if any of these groups are still surviving, they would still be underground and have no contact with the modern neopagan moment. [8]

One can also wonder what resources Felicity had in working her own magick and mythos if it was completely unconnected to the Wicca revival of Gerald Gardner. If teaching Laurie Cabot in the 1940s, and a librarian, she most likely had access to the standard classics of the time. Laurie said that Felicity gave her and her mother a copy of *The Golden Bough* from the library, by James George Frazer. It influenced the modern Pagan revival, right along with *The White Goddess* by Robert Graves, though that was not published until 1948. Margaret Murray's *Witch Cult of Western Europe* was published in 1921 and *The God of the Witches* in 1933, though the later did not see an American edition until 1952, as her books reached popularity as best sellers in the 1950s and 1960s. Of course, depending upon the date of her emigration and contacts back in the UK, she could have had easy access to Murray's work. While the Theosophical classic *Isis Unveiled* had been available since 1877, there doesn't seem to be any influence of that more eastern esoteric work on Felicity's craft.

In the Boston area metaphysical scene for the first half of the twentieth century, there were a number of resources for Felicity, if she explored them. Her secrecy with Laurie and her mother suggests that she was most likely very private about her own Craft, but in the area were active groups of Spiritualism, Rosicrucianism, Theosophy and New Thought.

Spiritualism was split into several factions, with some more "magical" than others, and two of the best known advocates were

---

8 Jones, Kelvin I. *The Witches of Kent*. Oakmagic Publications. Penzance, 2001.

Paschal Beverly Randolph and Emma Britten. Randolph was a spiritualist, as well as a magician and Rosicrucian, and his writings influenced much of the ceremonial magick movement. He had students and advocates in Boston as his Rosicrucian Society in America was formed in Boston, and had links with the Anglia group, giving it a connection to the same occult circles as the Hermetic Order of the Golden Dawn.

Art Magic: or, Mundane, Sub-Mundane and Super-Mundane Spiritism: A Treatise...Descriptive of Art Magic, Spiritism, The Different Orders of Spirits in the Universe Know to Be Related to, or in Communion with Man, by Emma Hardinge Britten (1823-1899), a British Spiritualist living in Boston and New York, synthesized Spiritualism and Mesmerism with Ceremonial Magic and Witchcraft. Emma once referred to herself as a Witch and wrote and worked in Boston.

New Thought Movement, known in the late 1800s as the Mental Science or New Metaphysical Movement was active in Boston. Mary Baker Eddy, part of the movement, published her book *Science and Health* in 1875 in Boston. She taught the basic principles of "mind over matter," particularly for healing. Her own movement eventually became known as The First Church of Christ, Scientist, believing that Jesus taught these same mind over matter principles.

Likewise, the controversial figure of Adriana Porter, grandmother of Lady Gwen Thompson, and Gwen Thompson herself were both in the Boston area when Felicity was actively teaching. Thompson claimed her grandmother passed her an ancestral tradition of Witchcraft and is best known for claiming a version of the Wiccan Rede from this tradition, supposedly unrelated to the version from Garnderian Wicca. If this family tradition had any connection to Felicity, there is no surviving evidence of it, but it is an interesting coincidence. [9]

Similar concerns of verification were leveled at the Gardnerians, and while there is still great debate on the origin of Gardnerian Wicca, Doreen Valiente proved the existence of Old Dorothy and later biographers and historians verified Old Daffo, though what

---

[9] Matheisen, Robert and Theitic. *The Rede of the Wiccae*. Olympian Press, Providence, RI: 2005.

happened behind closed doors in terms of initiation is still kept sub-rosa. Anyone who wasn't there in the room won't really know what, if anything, happened, much like the initiation of Laurie Cabot. Will Felicity's existence bear out historical authenticity as the potential initiators of Gardner's eventually did? Perhaps. I'd like to think so. Was there something more mysterious and magickal being set in motion there, making the myth more important than the verification? I'd also agree with that, for it is the magick that has come from the Kent heritage of Felicity Bumgardner, the mythic history, that is far more important than the names, dates and records.

Biblical traditions certainly emphasize what can charitably be called mythic history, so much so that they have convinced much of the Western world to look at it as factual history with little physical evidence. When looked at with a critical eye, the First Temple of Jerusalem, King Solomon, the Egyptian enslavement of the Jews and even the existence of, let alone the resurrection of, Jesus of Nazareth must be looked at as speculative myth.

The Eastern traditions often take for granted their mythic history with much less literal tension, where Bodhisattva shows up, materializing and changing the course of history. While we can historically trace the origin of Buddhism in Tibet, the Tibetan religious history has it retroactively a part of their ancient history.

Our precise scientific guides to history, culture and anthropology were not present in such ancient cultures, so we can only look at them retroactively, while today, the resurgence of modern Pagan traditions are under a finer microscope much earlier on, giving us a different set of challenge in the information age. Perhaps this is one of many seeds of mythic wisdom and history setting the stage for modern Witches. We must actively hold the paradox of our mythic history and verifiable history. Together, the doors of enchantment swing open and we can be better magical people in a modern world.

Special thanks to Laurie Cabot for sharing this treasured material about her teacher, to Paul Cummins for his excellent genealogical research help and to Michael Howard for generously sharing his insight in surviving Traditional Witchcraft groups in the United Kingdom.

Searching for Pearls: Dorothy Clutterbuck (1880-1951)

By Timothy Titus

Think for a moment about a pearl. Imagine the humble beginnings of this precious stone. It begins as an irritant, some foreign object that gets stuck inside the shell of a bottom-dwelling oyster. Over time, layers of calcium carbonate build around the irritating seed, forming a beautiful and mysterious jewel that is highly sought after by those on the surface. Only one oyster in a thousand creates a pearl, making these stones one of the rarest and most valuable objects on earth.

But then, think how many pearls exist at the depths of the sea that humanity never sees. The pearls are there, whether we see them or not. They are shrouded by dark waters and locked into mollusk shells, but they still exist, hidden forever from our eyes.

This was how Dorothy Clutterbuck lived her life. Famous for the expensive pearl necklace she always wore, "Old Dorothy" remains a mysterious jewel in Witchcraft's history. We know very little about who she was, but we have intriguing hints and subtle clues. The full truth may forever remain locked up inside the tight, strong shell she created for herself, but little pearls of her life offer a glimpse of this complex, fascinating woman who may (or may not) have been the final step in Witchcraft's slow and steady rise to public awareness.

In Witchcraft lore, Dorothy was responsible for the initiation of a strange retiree who was destined to lurch the Craft out of the murky water's shadow and into a glaring spotlight: Gerald Gardner. For years, Gardner referred to an "Aunt Agatha," then to "Old Dorothy." The last name of Clutterbuck did not appear publicly until 1984, when the Farrars published it in their book, *The Witches' Way* (Heselton, p. 179).

This led many to believe that it was Clutterbuck who initiated Gardner. However, what Gardner actually said was something different: that he was taken "to a big house in the neighborhood" that "belonged to 'Old Dorothy', "a woman who was wealthy, well known, always wore a pearl necklace." Gardner claimed to have been initiated "in this house" (Bracelin, quoted in Heselton, p. 177). By this account, despite the common belief that she initiated Gardner, all that the man actually claimed was that Dorothy owned the home in which his initiation ritual took place. While it is very different from actually initiating Gardner, it implies that Dorothy held some sympathy for the New Forest Witches.

The other feat that Dorothy is known for is the organization of the famous Lammas Ritual of 1940, also known as "Operation Cone of Power," in which she is said to have "called up covens right and left" and gathered them together for a huge, exhausting magickal working aimed at repelling a Nazi invasion of Britain. The gathering of power was so strenuous that a number of the Witches involved died within a few days of the working, giving their lives so that England might survive. Even Gardner claimed that his asthma, which he had not suffered from since childhood, returned to him severely following the ritual (Bracelin, quoted in Heselton, pp. 234, 236).

Indeed, Hitler's forces never succeeded in conquering Britain. They turned away in defeat on September 17, 1940, shortly after the famous ritual. From a magickal point of view, then, Dorothy Clutterbuck's crowning achievement was no less than saving the United Kingdom from Nazi invasion. That's a pretty valuable pearl.

Doreen and Dorothy

Up until the 1980s, historians and many witches doubted that Dorothy ever existed. It took the intrepid work of Doreen Valiente to prove that she indeed had been a real person. Her search was sparked by an internal discomfort she felt when reading that Clutterbuck may have been made up by Gardner. Knowing him as well as she did, Valiente had strong memories of Gardner's discussions about Dorothy. From these, she concluded that "she certainly sounded like a real person" (Valiente in Farrar and Farrar, 1984, p. 283). Seeking to resolve this conflict, the famous Witch set out on a quest to prove that Old Dorothy really had lived.

She succeeded. The first thing Valiente found was a record of Dorothy's residence in 1933 at Mill House in Highcliffe. The records noted that a man named Rupert Fordham arrived at Mill House in 1936. In 1940, a "Mrs. Fordham" is recorded at that address (p. 286). Valiente had found not only a Dorothy Clutterbuck who lived in the right place at the right time, but also an important record of her name change. She also may have found the fabled "big house" that hosted Gardner's initiation.

Later, an important clue pointed her toward Dorothy's death record. She chanced upon a guidebook for Gardner's Museum of Magic and Witchcraft on the Isle of Man. In it, she found an entry for an exhibit describing "A large number of objects belonging to a witch who died in 1951." Using this date, Valiente went right back to her research and quickly found the death record of "Dorothy St. Q Fordham," who passed away on January 12, 1951, at age 70 (p. 289).

Using this date and the age, Valiente was able to figure out that Old Dorothy must have been born in 1880 or 1881. But she could find no such record of birth. At her wit's end, Valiente followed a lead that took her to India House, where she had access to personal records from the time of British Colonial possession of India. Unfortunately, her parents had not filled out the proper paperwork upon her birth. Valiente's last chance was the baptismal records of the Anglican Church in India, which usually recorded a child's date of birth. It was here that she finally found her proof of birth:

Dorothy Clutterbuck had been born on 19 January 1880 and baptized in St. Paul's Church, Umbala, on 21 February 1880. Her parents were Thomas St. Q Clutterbuck, Captain in the 14th Sikhs and Ellen Anne Clutterbuck.

Thanks to Doreen Valiente's dogged research, we know for a fact that Dorothy St. Quintin Clutterbuck-Fordham did exist. She was born in India while her father served as a military captain for British Imperial forces. She moved to Highcliffe, England when she was nine years old (Heselton). She married (or at least took the name of) Rupert Fordham in the 1930s, and died of a stroke on January 12, 1951 as Dorothy St. Q Fordham. As Gardner described, she was indeed a woman of means who owned a large house near where he lived. Her death date matched the date shown on the museum guidebook. She died the very year that the Witchcraft Laws in England were repealed.

Doreen Valiente may have been the only person that ever could have taken on this research task. Only she had enough of a personal connection to Gerald Gardner to have some of the private information and documents that were vital to success of the project. Even then, Valiente is thankful that Dorothy had an unusual last name, quipping that, "had her name been Dorothy Smith or Dorothy Jones, my search would have been hopeless" (p. 287).

Valiente also obtained a copy of Clutterbuck's Will. In it, she found that Dorothy was the proud owner of some very expensive pearls.

The Little We Know

Thanks to Doreen Valiente, we know the basic statistics of Dorothy Clutterbuck's life. We know that she lived, which is more credit than most gave her before Valiente's evidence was published in Janet and Stewart Farrar's *The Witches' Way* in 1984.

That was about all we knew until Philip Heselton published his book *Wiccan Roots* in 2000. Heselton's research fleshes out the bare bones of Dorothy's life that Valiente had discovered.

Thomas St. Quintin Clutterbuck, Dorothy's father, was a Captain in the British Imperial Army, stationed in India when Dorothy was born in 1880. He eventually made it to the rank of Lieutenant Colonel before retiring sometime before 1893. Upon retirement, Heselton believes the Clutterbuck family returned to England and settled in Oxfordshire, in a home called Ditchley.

Dorothy would have been about nine when she moved to England. This would have been young enough to adapt to English society, as Heselton notes, but also old enough to have had exposure to Indian religious customs, beliefs, and rituals. Surrounded by local servants, as the daughter of a high-ranking British officer would have been in those days, she would have had plenty of opportunity to learn about Indian beliefs during these formative years.

It is certainly conceivable to believe that, like most privileged children of the time, Dorothy was taken care of by Indian nannies and servants, possibly seeing more of them than her own parents. If she were close enough to them, it is likely that they would have shared their own indigenous beliefs and practices with the little girl, practices which coexisted with the local Anglican Church, leaving the young girl with a background mixture of Christianity and possibly Hinduism, Sikhism, mysticism, and local folklore.

This is reminiscent of Gerald Gardner's fictional novel *High Magic's Aid*, published before Dorothy's death and – if Gardner's story is believed – by her permission, which features a group of servants who are nominally Christian but who secretly practice the "Old Religion." It is well known that *High Magic's Aid* was written to publicize Witchcraft under the disguise of fiction. Perhaps there is more to what Gardner was trying to expose than just the book's lengthy description of magical rituals.

Either way, the family moved into Mill House in 1908. Her father died in 1910. Ellen, her mother, lived with Dorothy at Mill House for another 10 years, dying in 1920. Significantly, Ellen Clutterbuck was a talented poet who, according to Heselton, wrote verses that were "full of love for and awareness of nature" (p. 138). Dorothy was to continue that tradition and, in so doing, supply one of the most intriguing clues about her beliefs.

As an adult, Dorothy was a lover of theater. After inheriting enough money from the death of her parents to sustain her for life, she organized and financed a performance troupe at her home called The Mill House Players. Dorothy financed, organized, and starred in the productions of the Mill House Players. More importantly, she used her considerable means to transport the cast, costumes, and props to performances in various locations around the area.

The Players are an overlooked but important facet of Dorothy's life. Her involvement demonstrates her love for theater, her ability to organize and pay for transportation, and her contact with many theaters outside of Highcliffe. Given later claims that she had personal access to covens from all over and financed their transportation to Highcliffe for the Lammas Ritual, Dorothy's experience with the Players provides a hint that these activities were within her reach.

Theater also was important to Gerald Gardner, who claimed to have made contact with Dorothy's coven at the Rosicrucian Theatre in Christchurch. Although Clutterbuck has no demonstrated connection with this theater, I have to wax personal for a moment. I grew up within the amateur theater community myself; actors know each other. They may specialize in specific theaters and have their personal preferences for play genres, but they are a small community who get to know each other well. I still get questioned at the oddest places whether I am Tom Titus' son.

All it would take to link Gardner to Clutterbuck would be one member of the Rosicrucian Theatre who was acquainted with Dorothy. Given Dorothy's prominence in the area, her well-known spending on theatrical activities, and the penchant for theater people to stick together, it seems more than likely that at least one Rosicrucian actor knew the venerable Mrs. Clutterbuck. There is, however, no proof.

All of these local contacts which Dorothy would have had through her work with the Mill House Players also demonstrates her organizational ability, especially as it pertains to getting large numbers of people to and from Highcliffe. Thinking back to the anti-Nazi Lammas ritual of 1940, these are exactly the kind of skills—and money—that would have been necessary to "call up covens right and left."

Further, on a purely speculative note, amateur theater would be the perfect cover story for a Witchcraft coven meeting at night at a time when Witchcraft was still against the law. Theatrical activities would give Witches an excuse to be out all night, in strange costumes, for an activity that was quite common and popular at the time (Heselton, p. 139).

The next stage in Old Dorothy's life was her marriage. Rupert Fordham was the heir to a brewery fortune. He had been married three times before he met Dorothy – and three times was the official number of Rupert's marriages. His third wife, Julia Blanche, was mentally ill and under the care of a nursing facility. On August 8, 1935, Rupert and Dorothy participated in a "marriage" ceremony that was completely illegal, for Julia was still alive and remained so until after Dorothy's death. Clearly, Old Dorothy was happy to break social convention when it suited her.

During her "marriage," the couple was the pillar of English conservative society. They hosted garden parties at their second home, called "Latimers," to raise money for the local conservative association and organized membership drives for the Tory Party. At the same time, however, they also took on an environmental cause, attempting to save the cliffs of Highcliffe for the continued use of the public (pp. 151-152).

On January 6, 1939, Dorothy and Rupert were involved in an automobile accident that eventually killed Rupert. He never regained his full strength and died on May 31 (pp. 152-153). Dorothy observed a mourning period, and then gradually re-emerged in the early 1940s. In late 1941, she officially changed her name to Dorothy St. Quintin-Fordham.

The culmination of her return to life was her diaries, which became objects of a debate that both reveal her true personality and obscure what was really going on within her spirit.

Controversy

So little was known about Old Dorothy for much of the history of modern witchcraft that, for a time, it was doubted that she even existed. Doreen Valiente proved that Dorothy did indeed exist – but that is all. However, controversy still rages as to her association, if any, with modern Witchcraft.

The major players in this debate are Professor Ronald Hutton and Gardnerian initiate Philip Heselton. Each has seen exactly the same evidence, but they have reached wildly different conclusions. Each has his own style of research. Hutton utilizes elements of the scientific method, doubting everything until empirical proof can be obtained. Heselton's style is more intuitive, drawing connections, asking questions, presenting copious amounts of evidence, and digging deeply into all facets of Dorothy's life. Neither can prove anything conclusively.

Hutton has reached the conclusion that Dorothy Clutterbuck had nothing at all to do with Witchcraft and that Gardner used her name to distract outsiders' attention from the New Forest Coven's real high priestess, Elizabeth Woodford –Grimes (AKA Dafo). He points out that Dorothy's activities consistently held the theme of social respectability and community service.

She was an Anglican churchgoer, for example. She also was a very active conservative, well known for recruiting members of the party.

He cites evidence that the social worlds of Gardner and Dorothy "never overlapped," because, while Dorothy was a "well-known and well-loved figure at the centre of the community's life," Gardner was shunned as an "exotic, mysterious, and rather sinister figure" (Hutton, 1999, p. 211).

Heselton counters that Walter Forder, a newspaper editor for the Christchurch Times "was definitely acquainted with both Gardner and his witch friends and with Dorothy" (Heselton, p. 248). Forder knew both of them and was interested in mysticism himself, having enjoyed Gardner's novel *A Goddess Arrives*. He attended Rupert Fordham's funeral. This establishes a possible connection between the upright Dorothy and the sinister Gardner.

Heselton agrees that Dorothy was a member of the Anglican Church, but "not a particularly enthusiastic or committed one." Delving into the society of the time, he points out that attending church was expected of everyone at the time; you just did it, and "one's personal beliefs really didn't enter into it" (Heselton, p. 193).

As evidence, Heselton searched the records of St. Mark's Church, Dorothy's parish. The only reference to her that he was able to find was a message that she would not be able to attend a general meeting of the congregation. According to church records, she was not on the Vestry, she did not hold any official position, and the only mention of her is for a time that she could not attend an all-church meeting (Heselton, p. 193).

Hutton points out that the gravestone Dorothy created for Rupert "bears one of the longest and most impassioned affirmations of faith in salvation through Jesus Christ" he has ever seen (Hutton, p. 211). Heselton found that the first two lines were handed down from the Clutterbuck family to Dorothy's mother, who included the same lines on her tombstone. The rest, Heselton claims, are directly from a common prayer that anyone who regularly attended services would know by heart. He also points out that the gravestone is decorated by a Celtic cross, not a typical Christian cross or crucifix.

And anyway, Heselton continues, gravestones should represent the beliefs of the deceased (Rupert), not the living (Dorothy).

Hutton points out that Dorothy bequeathed a large sum of money to the local Vicar. Heselton admits that Rev. Henry Brownlow received £1000 from Dorothy, but goes on to show that her doctor got £500, her bank manager £200, some of her staff received £2000, and others received £500.

There is no gravestone for Dorothy. Her ashes were supposed to be scattered at Rupert's gravesite, which probably occurred, but there is no monument for her- nothing that expresses a personal Christian belief as strongly as Hutton believes Rupert's stone to have expressed.

Hutton describes Dorothy as "simple, kindly, conventional, and pious" (Hutton, p. 211). Heselton questions this, citing the fact that Dorothy and Rupert were never truly married. Dorothy and Rupert went through a marriage ceremony in London on August 8, 1935. She changed her last name to Fordham. They lived together at Latimers until Rupert's death in 1939. All this time, Rupert was already married to Julia Blanche, who was under the care of a mental hospital. This does seem to cast doubt on Hutton's conclusion that Dorothy was a conventional and pious Christian.

The Diaries

The most complex pieces of evidence from Old Dorothy's life are her diaries. For the years 1942 and 1943, Dorothy wrote a detailed diary entry for each day of the year. Most of the entries were her own original poetry supplemented by watercolors by her friend Christine M. Wells. The books were intended to be left out for visitors to her home to look through. They provide the only vivid glimpse into the true personality of the mysterious figure that was Dorothy Clutterbuck-Fordham. Both Hutton and Heselton have experienced this window into Dorothy's soul, and, again, each man has reached a completely different conclusion.

Hutton finds that they reveal a simple, conventionally religious, conservative woman of society. He emphasizes that there are no references in Dorothy's poetry to Witchcraft, Paganism, or the occult in any portion of her works – including the entries that were "at the time of the four major witch festivals" of Imbolc, Beltane, Lammas, and Samhain (Hutton, p. 211). She says nothing about Witchcraft on the holidays of the Witch.

What is more interesting, though, is what they do not show. While there are no references to Paganism or Witchcraft at the four major sabbats, there also is not a single reference to Jesus in the entire two years for which the diaries were kept (Heselton, p. 162). This is the beginning of Heselton's argument that her diaries reveal a Dorothy Clutterbuck who found her most meaningful religious experience in the world of nature, not inside a church.

Even Christian holidays are completely devoid of orthodox religious sentiment. The entry for Christmas 1942 refers to Christmas as a "She," describes her as a "Radiant Creature," and discusses Christmas trees, bells, carols, and even "fairies, made of snow," but no discussion of Christ. Christmas 1943 is similar:

Once more a flash of scarlet
And there, in the frosted air
Shines the same Radiant vision
Christmas once more is Here
Her mantle made with Holly Leaves
Fringed round with Berries Red
And, her own Christmas Roses
Set like Stars around Her Head.
   (Quoted in Heselton, p. 163)

Not a single mention of the birth of Christ, mangers, Bethlehem, the Three Kings, or virgin birth. Again, Christmas is a "She." This entry focuses on the color red and the presence of "Holly Leaves." The capitalization of "Holly," "Roses," "Stars," and "Her" is interesting – usually you only capitalize proper nouns such as names of people and holidays...or deities.

The most sacred festival in the Christian calendar is Easter. In the Anglican Communion, the rebirth of Christ is a joyous event of song and praise. It marks the end of 40 days of Lenten fasting and caps off Holy Week, a time of intense spiritual reflection when Christians ritualize the betrayal, death, and rebirth of Christ. The Good Friday service is both extremely austere and extremely moving. Even the word "Alleluia" is banned from the sanctuary in the 40 days leading to Easter. Easter, then, is a welcome day of joy after a month and a half of sacrifice and a week of intense sorrow.

Dorothy mentions nothing of this in her entry for Easter 1943:

The Loveliest of Seasons Fair
Now Reigns once more on Earth
Easter, whose silver voice again
Sings to us of New Birth.
    (p. 163)

It definitely seems strange that, if Dorothy were the dedicated and conventional Christian that Hutton believes her to have been, she would not have mentioned Christ's resurrection at least once during Lent, Holy Week, or especially Easter over a span of two years. Instead, both Christmas and Easter are marked by passionate verses that praise the land, the stars, and the seasons.

Rather than focusing on the Christian holidays, she calls the Summer Solstice "Of all the days of the wonderful year, This is the day of all days most dear" (p. 164).

Heselton gives other examples of Pagan themes in Dorothy's writing. In this entry for June 28, 1942, Dorothy dreams about a religion that sounds a lot like modern Paganism:

And I will build an Altar to God in every field
And the fragrance of the flowers
The Incense of my Prayers
An open church, where everyone can roam
And the Sky, so blue above, shall be the Dome.
    (p. 168)

On June 21, 1943, she passionately describes her "Lady," encountered while she was asleep:

Of all the Ladies that I know
There's only one that can please me so
That all her Looks and Ways
Make Music for me all my Days
For Life, I love her, and adore
I only saw her once – not more
But once I saw her, as I can say

But once she crossed my Path, my Way
For Ever, She will be my Queen
Where did I see her? – in a Dream
    (pp. 170-171)

And Dorothy loved the moon, as shown by this passage on December 26, 1943:

The Forrest now is Silent
No Bird's voice sounds a note
A Hush is over Everything
The Snowflakes Downward Float
The Branche's Frozen Feathers
Like a Silver ostrich Plume
But the most Radiant Vision
Is the Bright December Moon
It Floods the Woods
With its Soft Light
And turns Them
To a Palace Bright
    (p. 171)

She even hints that her employees have joined her in the craft, calling her chauffer, Hudson a "wise man" and her gardener a "Wizard with a wand" (p. 157). Toward the end, she emphasizes the value she placed on keeping secrets in a way that sounds like good advice for any aspiring magick worker:

Words all have Wings
Once said, they fly for ever
And when they're spoken
We can recall them never
    (p. 161)

This general pattern, carried on throughout her two years of meticulous writing has led Heselton to conclude that "Dorothy was a pagan in all but name" (p. 176). The diaries reveal a woman who found her most profound spiritual experiences in the natural world and wished to express those feelings in a way that would be socially appropriate for a woman of her station at that time.

It is important to keep in mind that throughout Dorothy's entire life, Witchcraft was illegal in Britain. Even if Dorothy found deity in nature and wanted to share her experiences with the world, the threat of exposure through prosecution would have been powerful motivation to remain extremely secretive about it and to code her beliefs in nature-loving poetry.

To Keep Silent
Mind you keep your Promise, for it is a Trust
It must be just like a Rock, and not a bit of Crust

— Clutterbuck, quoted in Heselton, p. 161

Dorothy valued secrecy. She died in 1951, the same year the Witchcraft Laws in England were repealed, secrets intact. The date of 1951, given as the death date of an anonymous but important Witch, gave Doreen Valiente the clue she needed to uncover the life of Dorothy Clutterbuck-Fordham. Without it, Old Dorothy's involvement in the Craft—if it existed—would have remained an undiscovered pearl, a secret jewel cremated with her body and scattered upon the grave of her beloved Rupert. She hid her tracks extremely well.

If Dorothy truly was a Witch, that gem is hidden in an unseen oyster and lost in the waters of time.

References

Farrar, Janet and Farrar, Stewart. *A Witches' Bible*. Blaine, WA, Phoenix Publishing, 1984.

Gardner, Gerald B. *High Magic's Aid*. United Kingdom, Aurinia Books, 2010.

Heselton, Philip. *Wiccan Roots*. Freshfields, UK, Capall Bann Publishing, 2000.

Hutton, Ronald. *The Triumph of the Moon*. Oxford, Oxford University Press, 1999.

STEWART FARRAR
(1916-2000)

By Elizabeth Guerra

When one thinks of the pioneers of Wicca, thoughts turn to noted individuals such as Gerald Gardner, Doreen Valiente and Alex Sanders. And yet there is one other who has contributed greatly to the Wiccan movement world-wide and is worthy of our attention, and that individual is Stewart Farrar.

During World War I and shortly after Ireland's historic event, "The Easter Rising", Stewart was born on June 28, 1916, in Highams Park, Essex, which is now a part of greater London. His actual legal name was Frank Stewart Farrar, although he would be called Stewart.

His father, Frank Farrar, was serving in Salonika, in Northern Greece when Stewart was born and when he finally returned home from the war, Stewart was two years old. Frank was employed at the Hong Kong and Shanghai Bank's London office where he worked as head of current accounts. However, he never really had an interest in doing this. He was a gifted craftsman and made beautiful stained glass, woodworking and later, after retirement, became an expert at Scottish hand-woven tartans. He became an exceptional weaver and made the dyes from scratch using vegetables, herbs and berries. His work was so unique that his tartans were in high demand and were sold on Princes Street in Edinburgh.

Although Stewart was baptized Presbyterian, his parents would became Christian Scientists and raise both he and his younger sister as such. Stewart's mother, Agnes, was a teacher and taught at Claremont School, which was a Christian Science girl's school and Stewart's sister Jean attended it. During this time, at the age of 17, Stewart began to journal and wrote daily, although there was a period of time beginning in 1936 when he stopped journaling and did not resume this daily practice until 1979. He then continued until the end of his years.

Stewart came from a family of writers. In 1910, his paternal grandfather, Francis Albert Farrar, wrote *Old Greek Nature Stories*, which were stories and legends about the Greek Gods and Goddesses. Stewart's paternal grandmother, Isabella Jane Hornsby, authored a book entitled *Ruth Fielding*, a love story. His aunt, Kathleen Farrar wrote three novels and his cousin, James Farrar, who was killed during WWII, also wrote. However, his writings were not published until 1950, after his death.

Stewart's mother's family, the Pickens, were a sub-clan of the Ayreshire Stewarts, making Stewart half Scottish. Before he was born, the Picken name was part of the first sentence broadcast by Marconi's voice across the Atlantic by radio in 1912. The words, "can you hear me, Picken?" The Picken in question was Stewart's maternal Uncle Jim, who worked with the Marconi companies from their inception.

At 17 years of age, Stewart declared that he was a Communist or at the very least, a Socialist. He was an eternal optimist who hated class and racial discrimination and anything to do with Nazism. At the time, young people were drawn to Communism because they believed it brought the promise of a perfect society, a Utopia. The book *Utopia* by Thomas Moore, influenced these young minds who believed that this was possible. But of course history has proven this to not be the case and the horrors of Stalin's purges were not yet widely known to the world. Stewart would eventually change his political views.

Stewart really wanted to go to Oxford, but his parents couldn't afford it. So he attended the University College of London and enrolled in their two-year Journalist program (1935-1937). It was at this time that he left his parent's belief in Christian Science and considered himself to be an "interested Agnostic".

In December 1939, after Britain entered WWII, Stewart volunteered to serve and commanded a Machine Gun Platoon of the Lincolnshire Regiment, armed with Twin Vickers .303 machine guns in the anti-aircraft role. He was later transferred to the Royal Artillery Unit and eventually posted to a training camp as an instructor at the School of Anti-Aircraft Artillery (S.A.A.A.) in Wales. He completed a four-and-a-half month war gunnery course and learned how to use the 3.7 inch heavy anti-aircraft guns as well as the Bofors. Stewart was discharged from the Army with the rank of

Major in early 1946. After serving, he began working in the Allied Control Commission for Germany as a civilian officer. He would later take a British trade union delegation for a tour of Poland. On the trip, Stewart had the opportunity to visit the notorious concentration camp Auschwitz. The group was led through the site by former inmates still bearing tattooed numbers on their arms. Seeing the remnants of the inhumanity was an event that would affect Stewart for many years to come.

Later in his career, Stewart would become an accomplished script writer and a journalist working for many prominent and respected media companies such as Reuters and the newspaper Reveille. As a world traveler and prior to discovering Wicca, Stewart had the opportunity to meet and work with many fascinating people and noted celebrities during his profession. He was also a gifted photographer and by the time he was in his early 50s, he had already written four novels: a crime trilogy and a romance novel.

As a documentary scriptwriter for British-Pathe News, Stewart was able to travel all over the world scripting films that Pathe was producing. He visited Jordan, Saudi Arabia and was even invited on a VIP cruise organized by the Turkish government where he met the famous British comic, Leslie Phillips, and the well-known British journalist and novelist, Penelope Mortimer. At this point, he was really at the height of his career, meeting and working with celebrities, and even scripted a feature film, *It's All over Town* featuring the British rock group, The Hollies and starring Frankie Vaughan. In 1965, Stewart was asked to jointly write a 90-minute play with John Betjeman called *Pity About the Abbey*, which was very successful. John Betjeman would later be knighted and become the British Poet Laureate, he and Stewart were great friends.

One of Stewart's highest accomplishments was winning the Writer's Guild Award in 1968 for the best British radio drama serial script series for the BBC. The honor was bestowed upon him for writing a six-part radio serial called *Watch the Wall My Darling*.

Although Stewart considered himself to be an Agnostic, that soon would change and in 1969, at the age of 53, he met Alex Sanders—the infamous "King of the Witches"—and his wife Maxine while interviewing the couple for Reveille. The encounter introduced him to a world of Witchcraft and magic and changed the course of his life. He wrote his first of many books on Witchcraft, *What Witches Do*, and while researching material for the book, Stewart was initiated on February 21, 1970, First Degree by Alex and Maxine. It was at this time that he met a young and beautiful 19 year old woman, Janet Owen, who was later to become his sixth wife.

Although a romance did not occur right away, the two began working ritually together. After receiving their Second Degree on October 17, 1970, the couple began their own coven as a hive-off of Alex and Maxine's. On April 24, 1971, Janet and Stewart received their Third Degree at Alex and Maxine's flat, in the presence of their coven. They legally married on July 19, 1975.

The Republic of Ireland does not charge income tax on writer's royalties so the couple made the decision to leave England and on May 15, 1976, they moved to Ireland making it their permanent home. During his years in Ireland, Stewart authored many books on Witchcraft, together with Janet, becoming the most widely read and respected works on the topic. Stewart wrote a total of thirteen books as a sole author, which included seven science fiction novels. The books that he jointly wrote with Janet totaled seven and the couple jointly wrote three books on paganism with Gavin Bone. Gavin joined forces with Stewart and Janet and moved from England to their home in Ireland in March of 1993, where they wrote and lectured often together. Gavin, a nurse by profession, would also become Stewart's caregiver when his health began to fail.

Stewart was a kind and gentle soul who loved the Goddess and devoted his life to honoring her and the Horned God. He did not fear death, he embraced it, knowing that the soul's journey does not stop with death, but continues. The very last journal entry he wrote was logged on Monday, January 10, 2000: "Home at last, and ready for it. Janet had two tarot customers". The entry, "home at last" is noteworthy because Stewart had not gone anywhere for quite some time due to his poor health, and furthermore, he was already home in Ireland. The "home" to which Stewart referred may have been his spiritual home. Though he was very ill and could barely communicate, he must have known he would soon leave this world and return "home." He was prepared, ready for it, and expressed this in his journal. Even at the very end if his life, he was able to communicate through the means in which he loved. Writing was his chosen vehicle of expression, and he had done so quite beautifully from the earliest age until the very end.

Stewart passed from this world on February 7, 2000, at the age of 83.

Stewart Farrar found Witchcraft by accident but devoted the rest of his life to it and became one of the most prolific writers on the subject. He helped to make Wicca a viable and accessible path for many and, as a pioneer, has done more for the Craft on educating and spreading the spirit of this religion. In doing so, he touched many lives. Artistic and sensitive, he was an amazing man who led an amazing life.

THE ROEBUCK WITHIN:
EVAN JOHN JONES
(1937-2003)

By Shani Oates

"When the shadow faces from the past draw close, and claim you for their own, You drift through past lives and places my friend, to seek the Castle and the Rose."

My first impression of John was one I'll never forget. Stepping off the train onto the station platform at Brighton Station, a fierce wall of heat winded me, causing me to stop dead in my tracks. It was very much a scorching hot and dusty day typical of our August fugue; somewhat jaded therefore, I wearily ambled out into the main foyer teeming with holiday-makers, shoppers and travelers. Peering around I spotted John's unmistakable presence – it was quite uncanny, despite never having seen a photograph. He lifted his head to catch my gaze in an eerie moment of mutual recognition. A faded cream panama hat emphasised his mannered persona that belonged to another gentler, simpler era.

Supported by his rather stout walking stick, he slowly hoisted himself up from the wooden bench and began walking purposefully towards me. Upon reaching me, he slowly lowered himself to his knees, took hold of my hand and raising it to his lips, kissed it, utterly oblivious of the extreme bustle around us. Aiding him to his feet, I was speechless, and excruciatingly embarrassed. John did not speak for quite a while, but when he did some time later his gruff voice was quite intimidating.

A couple of hours were spent mindfully as John executed his authority in seeking quite specific information in a most bizarre manner. After a morning's adventures involving further pressing questions within a graveyard concerning life and death, followed by hot tea and chocolate, we finally returned to his home where he introduced me firstly to his wife, then his family. Upon passing their threshold, his tie was deftly unwrapped and thrown across the room, "catch," he barked!

"What do you make of that?"

Feeling his gaze bearing down upon me, I drew in a long breath and as I exhaled, I opened my senses up to whatever impressions were resident within the rather innocuous tie within my hands. Images rapidly formed and I gasped at the realisation of whom the tie's previous owner had been. Throwing it back to John, I said:

"This was Roy's and he left it here just before that fateful day; it must have been his last visit?"

Unruffled, John responded positively, nodding his head as he put the tie down, slowly and deliberately. During that first encounter there were many similar questions and probings as he sought to test me in terms of what I knew, who I knew, and what I had learned along the way. Later that night I lay dazed, contemplating the fantastic and unbelievable situation I'd found myself in, mulling over and over in my mind all the threads that had led me to that moment. The next chapter, I was totally unprepared for. John had suggested a proposition that was to change my life irrevocably. My mind raced as I rationalised the many pros and cons of acceptance or withdrawal. I had no choice. There was never really any choice.

It had all begun two years previous to that day, when after reading John's provocative article "The Roebuck in the Thicket" in the pages of *The Cauldron*, I impulsively decided to write to the editor Mike Howard to thank him for publishing such an inspiring article. This comment was passed onto Evan John Jones who wrote to me in the summer of 1996 beginning a two year flurry of correspondence that developed into a strong friendship. Then, mentioning that I was visiting a friend in Hastings, and would not be far from him, he responded with an invitation to visit his home in Brighton.

Thus began, on that searingly hot day in August 1998, my descent into another dimension of reality regarding my magical argosy. Despite being absolutely overwhelmed on that 'fateful' day when Evan John Jones asked me to take up the Mantle of Virtue Holder as Maid and heir to the Clan of Tubal Cain, I could never have foreseen the enormity of the responsibility or involvement required. Seeing me safely onto the bus back to the station this irascible old trickster pronounced his parting shot:

"*...if I were you Lady, I'd hitch up my shirts and run!*"

Of course I did not, and I returned one month later on the 26th September after considerable preparation to perform the 'Rite of Actuation.' This effectively began my official 'training' and John's delegation as 'consort' to 'Year King' after which time, he would pass over the Hand-staff and position of 'Magister' to my own partner, Robin-the-dart. By the time of John's death in August 2003, we had shared seven fruitful years, during which his invaluable friendship was a constant boon and source of frustration to both me and Robin. Many times we visited his home, and subject to his austere guidance were able to grasp the basic rudiments of a Craft I felt born to.

John's Socratic mentorship proved to be exacting, bewildering and enormously beneficent as he deftly juggled the roles of tutor, friend and guide, joking frequently that Robert Cochrane had named him – 'the worst witch in the world.' Seven intense years later, attending his funeral on yet another blindingly bright and sunny day, I pondered over this man who had become so dear to us and whose physical presence has been sorely missed ever since that final farewell. His easy manner filled a room. Blustering, blunt, candid yet also secretive, short-tempered, yet compassionate, this belligerent devotee to the Pale Faced Goddess or 'Diana' as he liked to refer to Her, was utterly at peace with his lot. Having surrendered himself to Her, he cautioned us that:

"*Once you embrace a dedicated magical path, you must live within its bounds; to forget that mundane and profane are one, to step out from its boundaries, is to invite chaos.*"

Formerly retired from the army due to injuries sustained in the Sudan, he'd compounded his health with heavy smoking which no doubt contributed to his emphysema contracted in later years. During those early years of the 1960s – 1970s, he had smoked to excess his favourite brand of French cigarettes, [Gauloises] without filters! Though it has to be said, this in no way diminished his obstinate insistence on smoking continual roll-ups, even as this occasionally forced him to grasp his Ventolin inhaler, ever ready within his other hand. Nonetheless, the medication did spoil his taste buds forcing him to cease indulgence of his favourite tipple – 'London's Pride'. Nonetheless, in abject defiance, he would rarely treat himself to a sparing glass of Calvados, straight from the nearby docks.

His inordinate lack of sentimentality again had no bearing on the bond he held for his wife and family, all of whom he loved dearly. His pride in them was touching to behold. When visiting us here in Derbyshire, one of his favourite pastimes was to attend our local flea market, where he would rummage for micro relics of the Second World War and stylish costume broaches that his good lady avidly collected. Given to lapses in his otherwise strict diet, he indulged in the odd MacDonald's, Fish & Chips or Pie and Peas at the 'Templar' Pub in Chesterfield, and of course, Mr Kipling's Bakewell Tarts, which were a constant source of amusement between ourselves; being purists for the 'real' pudding from Bakewell itself, we were bound to tease him about his lack of taste in cakes.

Gregarious and astute, this man was not one easily fooled, although he loved to play that role himself; one minute he could be grinning broadly, the next barking his displeasure. Having mastered his ego, he was quite at ease with how others perceived him. His greatest pleasure though was his gun collection, several of which he'd acquired over the years as rare models. And I remember him telling me of his hunting trip to Canada, in whose stark beauty he'd gloriously relished a vital, raw and uncompromising element, pitting his wits against the landscape and the beasts upon it. In fact it was very probably one of the few places he'd been able to utilise his gun collection satisfactorily. Unusually perhaps for most, army discipline wherein John served as an engineer, was most agreeable and he discovered a lifestyle that suited him to such an extent his subsequent release had devastated him. Talking to him about my planned trip to Egypt in 1998, he'd jovially asked me to 'look out for his left kneecap, tragically lost to a landmine there.'

Such information as this concerning his ordinary life would be cunningly woven into contrary conversation, where, in keeping me awake until the early hours of the morning, he would then suddenly release a precious pearl before moving rapidly on, fully expecting it to have been noted and retained. The next morning over breakfast, I would invariably be questioned about it and woe unto me if I'd not understood it or remembered it correctly. Being 'Old School' he was an exacting task master, tough and unstinting in his expectations. He saw 'glamour' and 'grey magic' as unnecessary distractions, a hangover from a more superstitious time, preferring instead a more direct and uncompromising expression of belief and practise. In fact, when we once asked his advice on a problem we were experiencing, he responded with:

> "No sense in wasting time and energy on spell craft or magic when a punch in the mouth works just as well."

This was indeed his perennial philosophy; if it could be dealt with easily then it should be. Matters of the mundane and of this realm should be dealt with in an appropriate and relative manner; he asserted that magic belonged only to the realms of spirit. His wisdoms regarding detachment have stayed with me and there isn't a day passes that I am not aware of his voice guiding me in my thoughts or actions. But what of the man himself, what story may we tell of him?

Tracing his ancestry right back, it was John's impression that his line of blood lay with either the 'silures' or the 'Demetae;' both tribes had in fact been based across the border in Wales close to his family village. Importantly, I feel that John's early or private life is his own and has no place here, so I shall leave it there and move onto his entry in the Craft arena. This had been a gradual process, beginning in his youth where a deep friendship with another whose family held considerable farmland in West Wycombe [Buckinghamshire] led to his adoption into their tradition centred around a Horned Deity. During his valuable time with them he absorbed a not inconsiderable amount of lore that later became acutely significant to the volatile and impressionable Roy Bowers. This was however, one of the most unlikely friendships that often saw them in a bout of fisticuffs, due in no small part to a conflict of interest in politics. Roy had been an active anarchist in stark contrast to John whose beam swung to the right; although he did humorously assert the view that even Tony Blair was far too right wing for his taste.

Before that momentous meeting though with Roy Bowers, his yearning to join Her Majesty's Forces induced him to look afar to distant shores and cultures. Taking up 'the monarch's shilling,' he found himself in active duty fighting communists in Malaya acquiring his life-long hearing impediment. More injuries were sustained when he suffered his irreparable hip and knee injury as a paratrooper in the 1956 Suez Crisis. When speaking of such sites as Stonehenge, John would reminisce that they were for him the areas of military training. Curiously, as a veteran war geek, he stated that Edgehill was the spookiest battle site of all those he'd ever visited. He'd once been terribly disappointed though when he attempted to visit his old army barracks in Portsmouth, only to discover a modern housing estate raised on their former premises. All that remained of their former glory were military styled road names. The military life pulled strong and hard in John's family, for his elder brother Bill had been a navy man.

Nonetheless, being retired early due to his debilitating leg injuries, John's engineering skills found him employment with two people who were to influence his life, as he in turn influenced my own. With Jane and Roy Bowers he formed a firm and lasting friendship, enduring many issues of ego, pride, folly and sorrow. Forming a secure nucleus of the 'Clan of Tubal Cain' other crafters quickly became attracted to its core. These were mainly George 'Winter,' [Stannard] and Ronald 'Chalky' White [now both deceased]. This was around 1964 and others of note soon followed. Among those who later became close friends, Willam Gray, his wife Bobbie and Doreen Valiente, regular 'guests' including the editor of one of the first Occult Magazines – Gerard Noel, the cunning-man Norman Gill, and several others who remained only distant associates.

The Craft scene, though one he purposely steered clear of, was at that time very small and almost everyone knew or knew of everyone else in it. Despite his familiarity amongst a rich variety of occultists from diverse practises, John firmly believed that there was common ground between all of them. John had borne the role of 'Man in Black' within the 'Clan of Tubal Cain,' assuming only later the

Magisterial post when Roy's own widow and Maid bequeathed John the mantle along with its Virtue and full responsibility following the tragic death of Roy Bowers in 1966, its former Magister and founder of the Tradition in this form.

Holding the tradition for many years after, John continued to work its mysteries alongside those of other traditions he encountered among his friends and acquaintances, especially William Gray and Doreen Valiente, with whom he developed a considerable Craft relationship. Tutor and mentor to numerous correspondents, his advice and opinion were much sought after from such notable heavy weights, including Nigel Jackson, Andrew Chumbley, Joseph 'bear walker' Wilson, Stuart Inman, Tony Steel, Iain Steele and Caroline Tully, drawing enquiries from as far afield as North and South America, Australia, Africa and Eurasia. Many other anonymous names and faces consulted and received advice from this gregarious bear of a man. Though unlike his predecessor, Roy Bowers, John believed that the Craft could be of value to those Roy would not have considered as being "of the blood."

Perhaps somewhat ironically, John is best known for his adoption into the Clan of Tubal Cain, of certain people from America, well known personages from another offshoot of the '1734' Tradition seeking advancement within the original flux that generated it. In that regard, he exposed himself to a pointless controversy, eventually seeking a means of correction via familiar media open to him. His private papers refute utterly their contra claims and his final interview with Mike Howard editor of the occult magazine, *The Cauldron* just weeks before his death, cleared all concerns and doubts of those uncertain of his direction and motivations. This was very much clarified and supported by facts asserted within his final book: *The Robert Cochrane Letters* co-authored by Mike Howard. He was up to his last breath a devoted child of the goddess, 'plucked by Diana as one of her darling crew' as oft he would say, somewhat wistfully. Every Full Moon he would raise a cup to Her where again he strongly believed that one could satisfactorily work alone and in his very first letter to me he advised me that:

"The hardest thing of all for people to grasp is that no-one actually needs a group to become a 'witch,' witch is only a name, there are no degrees of initiation to go through or anything like that. You find what you want and develop it yourself and this will have as much validity in the eyes of the goddess as any formal gathering."

In fact this neatly sums up his nature in embracing his Craft, which was his life – fluid, adaptable, flexible, dedicated, earnest, sincere and versatile. He was also pragmatic and headstrong, broken only by his outrageous humour bordered on the cheeky, being full of 'schoolboy' fun. If there was a 'dark' side to John, it was his absolute uncompromising brevity in his approach to the 'work'...he was all for fun before and after the event – but the work was deadly serious. He did not suffer fools easily and hid his contempt well from those he considered unworthy; being a gentleman, his manners overrode much his instinct yelled out to acknowledge. He added in a later letter:

"In fact, in the beginning, when working with Cochrane, we were actually practising a rather basic form of the old shamanistic witchcraft without realising it; at the same time, no-one had ever thought of putting it into a more formal footing...the deeper you go into this, the more you realise that the craft is not the be all and end all, so that in the end, you stop being a witch and become a magus, a magician in the old sense of the word."

Right from the beginning recorded in his next letter was his absolute conviction that we;

"...all, sooner or later find what we need rather than what we want."

And yet he would also refer to himself as 'Od's man'; he was particularly thrilled when at Lammastide he activated a new working site near an old mill. Fortunately for John, this private land was owned by a local farmer known to him, being long-standing and close friend. The site had been discovered when John went shooting up there by the farmer's permission. A keen gun collector, John amassed an enviable cache that included a Brown Bess musket, a Winchester and a Baker Rifle. Due to his former military background, he would often joke that he would one day write a treatise on the social history of the Vickers M1 machine gun. In point of fact, his knowledge was extremely broad-ranging, not that he gave much away, especially concerning himself or his private life.

For example, his small garden was a veritable Garden of Eden, packed to the gills with all manner of splayed fruit trees, vines, strawberries in hanging baskets, tomatoes, potatoes and other vegetables, flowers and roses. Unless you had seen it though, it was not something he would mention, and yet he not only loved his garden, but held a treasure trove of gardening lore. He was certainly a man of complex and seeming contradiction. One of the most valuable things he taught me was how:

"Anger can be a good magical tool used correctly. Directed calmly in a 'circle' anger can be the clinching key to a successful working – a valuable tool, save it for when you really need it."

Despite the numerous setbacks in his life, John was certainly an optimist, harbouring no regrets. Many long nights we would burn the midnight oil, philosophising over all manner of topics, both related to the mundane and sacred worlds. When speaking once of Fate and its importance within the Clan's Mythos, I proffered how we have no 'free will' as the 'Three Ladies' have long woven their weft of time and space. To which he simply assured me: "we have to live out our Fate/Doom." That was my first lesson in the "Web of Wyrd." Countless others followed; one of these included my first visit to the Sutton Hoo exhibition at the British Museum at his behest, where I was specifically instructed to ponder upon the ceremonial whetstone there. It was sometime however, before I came to realise the significance of this easily overlooked and modest item amongst this glittering horde. When John finally presented his own 'hand staff,' bedecked with similar attributes and used in cognate fashion, I was agog.

Most intriguing of all was the Stag, mounted at the top, a symbol of Kingship, divine authority, and psychopomp – a true leader of his kin. Being John's totem, it had become represented through his own Stag mask. He poignantly removed this small metal icon from between the tangs of the staff in passing it over to me, so that the Magister that followed him could place his own totem where his had previously reigned. He told me of Roy's, and I remember thinking what a profound thread this had spun, a legacy as told through totems, particularly as Roy had made John his spiritual heir long before his tragic death in 1966. What made this even more poignant was the realisation that the shaft of the Magister's Hand staff had been formed from the haft section of Roy's own staff.

The Stang was referred to by John as 'the child of wisdom' and the middle pillar or Yggdrassil, the World Tree upon which Odhin hangs entranced, listening to the wind whispering Her wisdoms there even as the Mother embraces him in Her thrall. Thus She bears him upon Herself, the Stang, symbol of the divine 'Tree of Life.' She is both Serpent and Eve, He is both Adam and Cain. This is why John was so insistent that the Maid and no other 'holds' the Stang, for whosoever wields it, raises Cain. There was an old occult maxim John was rather fond of concerning 'truth' where:

"The male head of the Clan reflects the occult truth that this world is a mirror image of the inner plane, in which this world is his [as Her representative] and the other world is Hers."

Moreover, John believed that a Magister should and must therefore be in full accord with that role as just and true guardian, especially in the sense of one untainted by error. His extreme sense of honour and justice permeated his view that only by embracing these principles into oneself could one generate evolutionary growth and progression onto a higher path:

"He who wields Odhin's spear never fails to hit the mark."

During the Autumn of 1998, an article he'd written was published in the *Pomegranate* a notable, academic American esoteric magazine. He was notably thrilled exclaiming his delight at making it into such a prestigious publication in the absence of any academic qualifications. This was of course yet another example of his humility. He was pleased that I was beginning to write although he was quite taken aback with my original use of a pseudonym, stressing that no-one should be unable to place their name to their work, if it was presented with integrity as the truth and accepted as it. Of course he used Roy as a negative example of this and Doreen as a positive example. After that he suggested that I meet Doreen Valiente, a lady of great significance to both streams that had molded me. We eventually managed to achieve this the following year, when I had the pleasure and delight of meeting such an influential figure within the Craft a couple of times before her own death.

Unlike Doreen, however, John did not share her passion for folk music, Morris Men or pagan celebration. In fact he found them 'an abhorrence to the senses,' somewhat tongue in cheek, however. Nonetheless local folk custom fascinated him; laughing widely he related curious tales of 'Wurzles and 'Mackerel Bashing;' all so very odd, but oh so true. Neither did he share Doreen's passion for curios and esoterica, finding them an unnecessary clutter. As I do share that same collector's drive, I became subject to his merciless teasing, where once he advised Robin to 'tip' all my 'unnecessary paraphernalia' into a skip when I was next away from home, jesting that it is what he would do with Doreen's 'treasures,' given half a chance. Despite his jokes, he respectfully attended Doreen's cremation, honouring that great lady and life-long friend. There he met Prof. Ronald Hutton for the first time in person and wrote to me of his admiration for him, especially with regard to the sincerity of his work. When speaking of curses and cursing, ethics in that regard and certain myths and fables, he'd responded somewhat perplexedly:

"The curse of Ol Tubal lies in the management of the Clan itself. You are stuck with it until you feel the need to download it on someone else and when you do, you'll get a tremendous feeling of lightness and relief. In the end you find if you let it, it will rule your entire life and that quite simply is, the 'curse.'"

This comment was his response to a question I'd asked him concerning the well-known "curse of Cain." He did add the remark that though the mantle was heavy, it could also be a blessing at best. Usually it was simply a paradox. His philosophy of life is one many might consider harsh, even brutal; in fact his pragmatic minimalism cut through all aspects of his life. In fact he strongly believed that we must all bear our conviction inwardly asserting that:

"You don't have to justify your work to anyone – this is how we work, and this is what we believe in, and it is no-one else's business. They either accept that or they don't, as must you."

Being no idealist, he suffered no illusions, a quality I found wonderfully refreshing. Sadly it is a virtue in short supply in this rather self-indulgent and over materialistic world of the 21st century. Another significant lesson and a harsh one occurred when another of his old craft friends died. John discussed how that person had amassed a considerable hoard of magical grimoires, manuscripts and diaries, yet had them burned upon his death. At that time I was horrified and could not understand John's insistence that this was the correct thing to do. As his mentoring continued, the logic and purpose of this apparently savage action began to dawn upon me. John was keen to promote the Gnostic premise that asserts each person must tread their own path and not walk in the steps of another. No journey may be duplicated, no information relevant, irrespective of who they are. So this man's work, being his own and relevant only to his process of gnosis would not best serve another, and must be destroyed lest it present an impediment to another's process of gnosis. Having forged my own path, I am obliged to concur with this principle; no-one may grasp another's insights.

The last two years of his life witnessed many changes, chiefly, major surgery for a hip replacement in December 2001 and the death of an old rescue tom cat, his long and faithful companion of over two decades in October 2002. Sadly he did not acquire his much sought after Mk1 Bren for his collection, nor did he purchase and sail his dream boat into retirement in the Spanish sunshine. But he did sustain, enflesh and honour the priceless legacy he enriched for those who follow him; and in this, for readers of *The White Goddess* by Robert Graves,' he played his part as the 'Roebuck' to the very end.

His books are listed chronologically as follows:

Witchcraft a Tradition Renewed with Doreen Valiente 1990 Phoenix Publishing, Washington USA

Sacred Mask Sacred Dance with Chas Clifton 1997 Llewellyn St Paul, USA

Roebuck in the Thicket with Michael Howard 2001 Capall Bann. UK

The Robert Cochrane Letters with Michael Howard 2002 Capall Bann UK

The First Family of Feri: Victor Anderson (1917-2001), Cora Anderson (1915-2008) & Gwydion Pendderwen (1946-1982)

By Storm Faerywolf

"Anything I can tell you, I would be glad to share with you, because the secrets of the Craft are like the secrets of science. How in the world can you learn if you don't ask, if you don't try to learn?"

– Victor Anderson

To speak of the elders of one's tradition is both a tremendous honor, and a great responsibility. To tell their stories; of how they dedicated their lives to the betterment of the Craft, and to the people within it, is a humbling experience for me. To me, these stories are something like legends; special tales of our people and how we came to be; a "family saga" that we each can share in to give us a sense of belonging, and of community. To retell these tales that were first told to me at the feet of my teachers and mentors is to assume a particular role within the community of the Craft; the bard or storyteller who is entrusted with keeping the history alive within our memory. It is with this particular purpose that I recall these stories.

The recorded personal accounts of the individuals involved are unfortunately not accompanied by much in the form of physical evidence, making verification of many of the spiritual claims quite impossible. Additionally, some of the details cited in those accounts are thought by some to be visionary rather than physical experiences.[1] It has, however, been recounted by those who studied directly with

---

[1] During my training I was exposed to this idea from multiple sources within the Bloodrose line of Feri.

directly with the founders, that these incidents were reported as actual physical occurrences.[2]

No account of Feri can be told without speaking first of the blind shaman and poet Victor Anderson (1917-2001) who is widely considered to be the "founder" of what has come to be called the Feri tradition of witchcraft. Though he himself denied that he founded the tradition, and spoke instead of a mystical lineage tracing back to the earliest humans in ancient Africa, in terms of verifiable history the origins of Feri undisputedly begin with him and his wife Cora, and to a lesser extent, their adopted foster-son, the shaman and bard Gwydion Pendderwen.

Victor was born May 21, 1917 in New Mexico. When he was two years old he suffered a fall that left him nearly blind[3], a condition that would reportedly strengthen his mystical vision in years to come. At the age of nine it is said that he followed the sound of drums to the forest near his home where he found a small dark woman sitting in a circle surrounded by brass bowls filled with herbs and teas. She informed him that she was a faerie and that he was a witch[4]. She then initiated him into witchcraft which caused him to have a vision in which he was able to see clearly in spite of his physical blindness. In this vision, the forest became a lush jungle and the woman became the Goddess; he had an experience with the Horned God and when the ecstatic communion with divinity subsided, the woman instructed him in the ritual use of the various herbs, washed him in butter, salt, and oil and told him to be patient, adding that his people would find him one day.

Years passed...and because of his disability he was sent to study at a school for the blind in Oregon. It was in this state that in his mid-teens he met a group of people who were involved in traditional witchcraft, a coven that went by the name of "Harpy". During the

---

[2] Private correspondence with SoulFire, a student and initiate of Victor and Cora Anderson, and member of the Anderson's final coven. 2011.

[3] SoulFire.

[4] *Victor & Cora Anderson*, by George Knowles, http://www.controverscial.com/Victor%20Henry%20Anderson.htm (accessed 3/3/2011)

1930s the Harpies practiced a type of witchcraft quite unlike that which is commonly spoken of in terms of a modern practice. Being pre-Gardnerian, it did not possess some of the more elaborate theological and ceremonial elements so common to Wicca and Western magic, instead utilizing spontaneous ritual observances and ecstatic celebrations geared toward harmonizing with nature, "The Old Gods", and the working of magic. They met regularly until they disbanded in the early 1940s at the onset of World War II.

In 1944 Victor met Cora Ann Cremeans (Later, Cora Anderson, 1915-2008). Upon meeting for the first time they both recognized each other from the previous experiences that they had shared together on the astral plane. In these encounters their astral selves would meet and travel. They grew connected, and in this state even made love. When meeting physically for the first time their attraction was instant, and they were married three days later. They were together until his death in 2001.

Cora too, had a magical background. Growing up in rural Alabama, she was surrounded by the folk magic inherent in the culture. Herbal remedies and healing charms, some of which relied on passages from the Bible, were commonly employed as she grew up. A woman of Romani descent, she was raised with the stories and traditions of both sides of her family...of her maternal grandfather, who emigrated from Ireland where he was reputed to be a druid and 'root (or herb) doctor'[5]...of her maternal aunt, a midwife and healer.[6]

Soon after they were married, Victor initiated Cora into witchcraft and together they blended their knowledge and magic, achieving a type of synthesis most often cited in their teaching; he the power of fire and air, the sheer power of the sorcerous shaman, and she the power of water and earth, the compassionate and ample presence of the Goddess. Where he often taught with trance or

---

5 Memorial for Cora Ann Anderson, ©2008, SoulFire. *http://www.lilithslantern.com/cora.htm* (accessed 3/3/2011). This is described in detail in Cora's book *Kitchen Witch* in which she recounts her childhood upbringing and gives examples of the folk magic and healing remedies that were a part of her everyday life.

6 SoulFire.

poetry, she most often would teach in the kitchen, together offering what was needed to nourish those around them, body, mind, and soul.

In 1948 they relocated to California and eventually settled in San Leandro where they would live the rest of their lives. In the mid '50s Victor read Gerald Gardner's *Witchcraft Today*, the first book written by a self-avowed witch, which introduced the concept of witchcraft as a legitimate religion for modern times. Victor decided that if this much was already known then perhaps it was time for the Craft to go public. A letter written to Victor in 1960 from Dr. Leo Martello, a prominent witch of Sicilian descent, urged him to start teaching the Craft in California, so Victor and Cora formed a coven, "Mahealani", the Hawaiian word for "Full Moon".

Most accounts say that the Andersons met the next player in this story when they broke up a fistfight between him and their son, but most are incorrect in this regard. Though it makes for a poetic story, the Andersons had already known Tom Delong (later changed to, Gwydion Pendderwen, 1946-1982) as he was on the chess team with their son.[7] Victor tutored Gwydion and eventually initiated him into the Craft and together began a journey to further develop the Craft into a more robust system of religious magic.

Gwydion brought certain insights into the work and drew from multiple sources. Much beloved to him were the old Irish and Welsh tales of the old gods and little people, with which both he and Victor had a special affinity, and it is because of this association that the name "Faery" (or "Faerie", "Fairy" and later quasi-standardized by some as "Feri") became accidentally attached to our tradition, when before it was most often simply referred to as "the Craft".

Gwydion became an influential leader of the modern neo-Pagan movement and brought an awareness of Feri to many outside the (then) small, family tradition. His involvement with the Church of All Worlds, Nemeton, and Forever Forests are important achievements that allowed an awareness of Feri to begin to spread, and with that piquing interest the small tradition began to grow.

Far from being a system of overly complicated rituals and artificially constructed theologies, the Feri tradition that Victor

---

[7] SoulFire.

espoused was more of a devotional science.[8] One of the driving elements of the Feri tradition as it was practiced and taught at the time was the idea of the *Hidden Kingdom;* the unseen spiritual world that intersects our own, from which we can derive inspiration, power, and gnosis. This Hidden Kingdom could be found in various places: in the works of an author...the words of a poet...on the canvas of an artist. Regardless of whether or not the artist themselves proclaimed such knowledge or affiliations, certain core truths about the magical world were observed in such works as those by Robert Graves, H.P. Lovecraft, Leland, Herbert, and Tolkein, to name but a few. The early days of Feri saw much borrowing from published sources as a means to further illustrate this Hidden Kingdom and its impact on the lives of those who strived to live in harmony with it. Students of the Andersons are well known to have drawn from these external sources combined with the Andersons' teachings and formed schools and lineages of the tradition, which bear fruit to this day. Victor himself was quite well-read, despite his visual impairment, and might speak to his students using the language of whatever his reading material consisted of at the time; such was his desire to include approaches from a wide spectrum of cultural influence.

Where specific witchcraft material was being published, they saw no issue with adopting certain elements that seemed in line with their own work; a practice that has lead to the blurring of the boundaries that separate Feri (a uniquely American phenomenon) from Wicca (a British one). For example, the act of "Casting a Circle", while common in Feri rituals today, is not considered to be a "core" element of our practice, and is often forgone in favor of other observances designed for the observance of ritual space. While the early days of Feri may not have stressed the importance of the circle, after the published materials of Wicca became available and influenced the modern Pagan movement, the idea of a ritual circle was so firmly entrenched in the mind of the modern practitioner that most people adopted its use anyway until finally it became a part of Feri practice, if only because of convenience or universal familiarity.

---

8 *The Feri Tradition: Vicia Line,* ©2003 Corvia Blackthorn. *http://www.witchvox.com/va/dt_va.html?a=ukgb2&c=trads&id=7737* (accessed 3/4/2011).

Unlike the teachers who would set themselves behind a velvet rope of exclusivity, Victor and Cora would teach anyone who would show up at their suburban home. Victor would reportedly sit in his rocking chair, talking about myths...about poetry...about magic... about any particular topic that he felt was of importance to the development of the students who often scribbled furiously to capture notes of their experience with him. Victor would speak of rites and rituals learned in past lives in which he was a Polynesian Kahuna, or a Voudon priest. He claimed racial connection to nearly every indigenous people on the planet and spoke of the Craft in terms of art and poetry, as well as science and religion. He taught mysticism, but also magic; practical sorcery for the betterment of one's earthly conditions, as well as techniques to speak to spirits and to develop one's soul. Cora would also be present for these discussions, but was most often remembered making her magic in the kitchen, infusing the food she cooked with *mana*, life force for the betterment and healing of those to whom she served the meal. She would weave spells into her cooking as well as her sewing, embodying a kind of domestic magic that was part of her own family tradition before informing that of Feri. Together they formed a perfect unit and bestowed their teachings upon the world, one story and food filled visit at a time.

Victor was often consulted for matters of personal development. In her book *Fifty Years in the Feri Tradition,* Cora recalls how Victor reportedly cured a man from a severe cocaine addiction by performing for the man the *Kala Rite,* a simple ritual involving the energetic charging of a glass of water for the purpose of spiritual purification. In this account Victor charged the water with *mana* and after taking a sip, offered it to the man to drink. When he did he felt an electric shock and became temporarily paralyzed, but the addiction was no longer an issue for him from that day forward.

Victor trained and initiated several of the American Crafts' early luminaries (such as Gwydion, Starhawk, and Alison Harlow) but he always was clear that the lineage of our magic came from the earliest of humans; those primitive African peoples who rose up and into their power before the dawn of recorded civilization. In doing so he effectively dispelled any ideas of racism that might otherwise arise within our Craft; by connecting the origins of our path to the origins of humanity, *all* humans could lay claim to a genetic connection to our path; we need only look through the lens of Feri in order to see resonate threads of the magic in the various cultures across the globe. Victor used the language of those cultures in order to further illustrate his points when speaking to various students. Because of this some have said that Victor "taught different things to different people". While technically true, this statement oversimplifies the issue; Victor spoke in terms that he felt were most effective for the individual in question. For someone of African descent he may have stressed African practices...for someone of Scottish descent, he might stress those cultural trappings. The undercurrent of what he taught, however, always remained the same, regardless of the particular cultural form that he might use in the moment to drive his point home.

To some he was seen as "making it up as he went along", an accusation that he famously met with the response that he was "keeping the tradition authentic!" This I understand to mean that he was constantly striving to learn new ways of working magic and was adept at the inclusion of these ways as a counterbalance to the human tendency to descend into dogmatic practice; by approaching the core practices in different ways, he effectively kept the practice fresh as well as simple.

While some teachers went on to form their own lineages and styles of working, Victor and Cora remained at home, teaching those who would show up and do the work. Victor published a collection of his liturgical poems under the title *Thorns of the Blood Rose,* and would often use his poetry as a kind of "test" to see if his students could grasp the deeper meanings.

One description of his teaching style remarked at how skilled he was at grasping the essence of a person's soul[9]; an excellent skill to possess for a spiritual teacher. In my one and only conversation with Victor[10] he impressed me in this regard to the degree of being almost uncanny. At the time I was not known outside my local circle of

---

9 Brian Dragon. *What is Draconian Pictish-Elven Witchcraft? http://www.pictdom.org/WhatIs.html* (accessed 3/31/2011).

10 Via telephone, circa 1994.

students and peers, and I had not yet adopted my current *nom de plume,* so when he began the conversation by extolling the virtues of the spirit of the wolf, I was dumbfounded. After asking me why I was interested in Faerie tradition, he shared with me some personal stories about some of the Craft luminaries whom he had taught and initiated, and then he discussed theology, science, the Goddess, all the while expressing the importance of aligning one's triple soul. But strange to me at the time was his caution to keep an open mind in regards to religious study, emphasizing the importance of Biblical stories and lore. He said, "Pagans today are throwing the baby out with the bathwater; there's a lot of good stuff in that Bible if they only knew where to look." Admittedly, at the time I was surprised that this renowned witch of impressive traditional background and experience would be talking so positively about Christian lore, as most neo-Pagans rebelled against an oppressive Christian society. But Victor was more interest in a genuine connection to the unknowable mystery that feeds all religions and magical systems. He drew spiritual wisdom from many sources. In the Bible he saw just another set of stories of the divine and how it manifests on earth, taking inspiration and spiritual meaning from those stories and allowing them to fuel his magic. At the end of our conversation he offered to teach me Feri, suggesting that I send him a series of questions via cassette tape, which he would then respond to in the same manner.[11]

While I only gave bewildered acknowledgment to his statements at the time, years later I find myself in a better position to accept his wisdom, which has proved indispensable for me in my own spiritual development.

While Victor was widely regarded as a shaman and priest, he also embodied the frailty which all human beings must endure. Many stories float around between initiates and students about Victor relishing in casting hexes at his enemies or even taking delight were they to fall. He was a powerful man in the occult world. But as powerful as was, he could do little for his beloved wife after she suffered a debilitating stroke. Magic and prayer proved to be almost

---

[11] I considered his offer, but then soon afterward found a Feri teacher with whom I was able to meet with in-person, which was preferable to me at the time.

useless, rendering him powerless, a state that he was largely unaccustomed to.

On September 21, 2001 Victor died. He was 84. The night of his memorial service was unusual in that there was a spectacular lightning storm in the skies over the San Francisco Bay Area; an event that very rarely occurs in our climate. I have lived in this area my entire life and up until that night I had never seen anything even remotely resembling it likeness. Visitors or those who migrated from the Midwest compared it to the spectacular storms often seen in those areas, but the most that California will see is a flash or two of light, and maybe an arc, if we are lucky. This was an entire light show; numerous brilliant arcs of lightning flashing and dancing across the sky in almost kaleidoscopic fashion. Add to this that much of the lightning appeared *pink*, a phenomenon that has been said to occur to mark the death of a Kahuna. Standing underneath the raging and beautiful sky, we said prayers for Victor and made offerings, using this time to charge our tools and commune with the hidden forces of nature.

When Samhain came little over a month later there was a huge gathering from across the family tree of the tradition. What had started so small had become so much bigger…and much more diverse. Individuals and groups who had bad histories together put aside feuds and past hurts to celebrate the passing of our beloved Grandmaster. It was a beautiful event, and one that was worthy of such an influential man.

I was introduced to Cora in 2004. At that time she spent most of her time in bed, but still wanted to receive visitors. Birthday parties, holidays, and even book releases were causes for celebration in which friends and family would converge upon her small suburban home. Outside of these larger affairs I was fortunate enough to have had the opportunity to visit with her more intimately; sitting with her and talking about the Craft, listening to stories about her life. When asked, she had many opinions about what she saw and heard about in our community, and not all of it favorable. But she always came from a place of love; even when she felt strongly about how some might be conducting themselves she could never deny them because they were family. She would remind us that our initiation was a marriage to the Goddess, and that there was no divorce.

I had several more opportunities to visit and talk with her before she died. I was even blessed to have been able to share magical space with her, and from her receive gifts of power and blessing. From her I was exposed to very different perspectives about our religion than I had from the culture surrounding my own initiatory lineage; my eyes were further opened to the role that individuals have had in the adaptations that our tradition has undergone and just how different individual lineages of the tradition have become, when compared to the simple and down-to-earth approach espoused by the Andersons themselves.

Cora Anderson passed away on May 1, 2008. She was 93. She had looked so frail when I had last seen her that the news came as a sad relief. Now she was free to travel the astral with Victor, looking over and assisting us from beyond the veil, an activity with which her late husband has been much accredited.

Many people –initiates, students, and even others –have reported experiences with Victor appearing to them in dreams and visions, providing advice, insight, and in some cases, blessings and magical power. I myself have experienced this in ways that were exceptionally vivid, leaving me with absolute certainty that both he and Cora are operating as the Mighty Dead; the souls of departed witches and warlocks who gained enough power in life to now oversee the Craft and assist in magical workings from the other side. Even in death they continue to teach and to guide us.

While they were adamant that certain aspects of our Craft were to be held in secret by the initiates, Victor & Cora were both quite open about much of our practices and lore. This is a theme that has been carried on by those who studied directly with them in the latter years of their lives.[12] In 2005 I asked Cora about secrecy in Feri. She responded that there were very few secrets in the Craft, and that much of the secrecy as it was practiced in the past had more to do

---

[12] Of the four members of the Anderson's final coven with whom I am acquainted, two formed a publishing house that keeps the Andersons' works in print, and the other two have taught Feri publicly throughout the U.S.

with practical concerns than with religious observance; explaining that even just a generation or two ago it would have been placing oneself and their immediate family in danger to reveal themselves as a witch...but because now we did not live in quite the same world the secrecy that was once almost compulsory, was now largely obsolete.

The Andersons' generally open approach to the Craft is further evidenced by the fact that they collectively wrote numerous articles and gave several interviews for publication in books and periodicals, as well as lectured at public pan-Pagan events. In each of these mediums they described many elements of Feri in detail, even discussing material that later lines of the tradition would consider to be secret.

Among these public offerings there are several worthy of note. Cora's book, *Fifty Years in the Feri Tradition* was the first attempt at publicly detailing Feri spirituality. Written as a 50th anniversary present for Victor, it addressed the Feri community as it existed at the time and made clear some aspects of our faith, explaining in simple terms a core theology, and describing a practice to assist the seeker in cultivating their etheric sight.

Etheric Anatomy was originally an article written by Victor for the now defunct *Nemeton* magazine that was posthumously published as a book with additional material from Cora. This detailed their experiences with astral travel as well as the three souls, a concept at the heart of Feri tradition witchcraft.

Perhaps one of the most important books by the Andersons was also published posthumously; *The Heart of the Initiate* was a limited edition collection of recorded talks and "teaching letters"; actual correspondences written by the Andersons to their students which detailed various aspects of Feri Craft. The material presented in this thin volume is a veritable feast of wisdom and lore; an indispensable guide to understanding some of the more esoteric aspects of Feri spirituality. This work in particular stands out as it reveals some lesser-known details about how the Andersons viewed the Feri Craft, which is at times in stark contrast to how some lineages of the tradition later evolved.

No matter what branch of the tradition we may practice...no matter our personal views on secrecy...or magic...or the Gods...we all trace the core teachings of our tradition back to Victor and Cora. Together they helped to usher in a new awareness of the Craft by preserving an ancient lineage and by adapting what they were taught to apply to a modern world. Steeped in rich tradition, theirs was an approach of a living path, that continues to live and thrive today, bearing many branches and many different fruits. While some branches reach for the light in different ways, let us remember what we share in common, however small; a lineage and a responsibility that we each receive through the legacy of our elders. May we prove worthy of it.

Gwen Thompson
(1928-1986)

By Andrew Theitic

In September of 1928, Gwen Thompson was born Phyllis Ruth Healy. Gwen had a magical inheritance. Her father was a Rosicrucian, her paternal grandmother – a "witch." Through the years, she also spoke of other witches in her family, including a cousin Netta, Uncle Jim, a cousin in Rhode Island and two aunts in Nova Scotia. Gwen initiated at least one of her numerous husbands, as well as her son, daughter, daughter-in-law and two grandchildren. She claimed that her family witchcraft dated back to her relatives in Somerset England in the 13th century.

Not just a local figure

Gwen's family came over on the Mayflower. A member of the Mayflower Society and the Daughters of the American Revolution, Gwen was also in the Navy, and this might have spurred her love for travel; in one year I received postcards from Georgia, North Dakota, Texas, England, Tennessee, Nova Scotia, Connecticut, and back to North Dakota again. She was a hard one to keep track of, but, you could always send mail to her mother's address and eventually it was answered. During the 1970s, Gwen was an authority to many members of the Craft. A prolific writer, her teachings, transmitted through her letters and other writings, strongly influenced the works of George Patterson, Bonnie Sherlock, Kitty Lessing, Leo Martello, Roy Diamond and Jill Johns. Other "pen pals" were Theos & Phoenix, Ray Buckland, Gavin & Yvonne Frost, Tim & Morning Glory Zell, and every other popular witch from the 70s. Morning Glory used to call her "the grandmother of East coast witchcraft."

Magick first, religion second

I was fortunate enough to have known Gwen from 1974 until her death in 1986. During that time, I was given the opportunity to study with her for an uninterrupted two and a half years. She was a remarkable woman. Her sensitivity to all things magical was the driving force in her life. Despite the complications and obstacles that affect all our lives, she never turned away from Craft, but instead, turned to her true convictions as a source of strength to overcome the hardships of life. Gwen cared for children, pets and nature. She was a fighter, politically natured, and a powerfully opinionated woman. Some described her as a formidable force and not someone to be reckoned with. She was deeply loved, but she did make enemies. Magic came naturally to Gwen. She worshipped the old Pagan gods, but she always had one hand on a nearby box of candles. Magic flowed through her blood.

A rolling stone ...

This story came to me some years ago from a woman who lived near Gwen when she was living in Tennessee. Gwen was in the midst of a feud with a neighbor. The neighbor lived on one side of a running stream and Gwen on the other. Apparently, some yelling and name calling began this feud. Gwen summoned a word of power and threw a rock across the stream. It rolled toward the neighbor's house, and when it struck the outside wall, the rock and wall burst into flame. When talking to those who knew her well, you come to find out that this is just one of many stories that tell the tale of Gwen and her magic.

The New England Coven of Traditionalist Witches

Gwen Thompson founded the New England Coven of Traditionalist Witches. Her Coven boasted of having well known witches as members or frequent guests, some coming to New Haven for meetings from as far as Maryland on a regular basis. The title of New England Coven of Traditionalist Witches was passed down by Gwen through two generations of initiates to its present incarnation, and is currently based in Providence, Rhode Island. As the historian for the N.E.C.T.W., I am frequently in contact with people that have great "Gwen stories."

A close encounter of the Gwen kind

Over dinner one night, Gwen told me that she was doing battle with aliens. She made it clear that some aliens were friendly to humans, but others were not. "Aliens have been here for centuries. They are all around us," she would say. I wasn't sure what to think of this, but some years later I was talking to Ayeisha from Keepers of the Ancient Mysteries in Maryland and she told me that during one of her visits to see Gwen, she was shocked to find Gwen didn't have even one hair on her head! Ayeisha asked what happened, and Gwen replied that the night before, she was on the rooftop battling aliens and she had lost all of her hair in the process. Until the day she died, Gwen would teach her students that there were forces of darkness and forces of light, and that we should all be conscious of the ongoing battle between the two. This battle was a heavenly battle that raged in the skies. We were to take sword with the forces of light (wisdom) and drive back the forces of darkness (ignorance). It was our duty to spread the Light.

Man's best friends

Gwen loved animals and nature. She was always taking in stray cats; at one time she had as many as 13. We were driving around New Haven one day and we came across a dead dog by the side of the highway. She insisted that I stop the car for her to get out and say a prayer over the dog's body. In addition to caring for pets, other forms of nature were Gwen's companions. "The trees are our friends" was a common phrase for Gwen to use with her students. We were strolling through a park, when she stopped to teach me a tree blessing ritual from her family Tradition. The energy that she exuded during the rite was so strong that the bond between her and the tree during this blessing rite was almost visual.

Rain, rain go away ...

Gwen's last working partner, Owen, tells the story of a ritual evening in North Haven, CT. It had been raining all day and the ground was muddy. No one wanted to do Circle in the rain, barefoot in the mud. But, Gwen was determined that the rain should stop and they should have Circle outside. Once she decided and made her decree, it was only a few minutes before the rain stopped. Because of the objections of the Coveners to work in the mud, Gwen said the mud would not linger. No one believed her, but within 10 minutes the ground was completely dry. Circle carried on at precisely the time Gwen said it should. Immediately after Circle was completed, the sky opened and the rain resumed.

Enamored by the concept of Wicca

Gwen, like many other Witches of her generation, became enamored by Wicca. As a Tradition, her practices were a complete system of magic. But, like so many U.K. traditional witches, she would alter her handed-down material to come in line with contemporary Craft practices and beliefs. In the public's mind, Wicca was a legitimate religion, whereas some forms of Traditional or hereditary Craft were perceived as just a hoax, thought to be made up by thrill seekers. Thus, many true and authentic Craft practitioners hid their practices and beliefs from the public and went underground. Ultimately, Gwen's Tradition was handed down in the late 1960s as a Traditional system of Witchcraft and magic with a veneer of Wicca and Paganism laid over it.

The Rede of the Wiccae

There is almost no way of talking about Gwen Thompson without talking about *The Rede of the Wiccae*. This poem was handed down to her by her grandmother, Adriana Porter. A great deal of research went into the book entitled *The Rede of the Wiccae* by Professor Robert Mathiesen and myself, published by Olympian Press. Professor Mathiesen, who had done most of the research, drew some fascinating conclusions regarding the Rede poem. Here, I have chosen to reprint an article by Gwen Thompson which is the first time the Rede was put into print for the public. This article débuted in the *Green Egg* Magazine.

A Fundamentalist Christian recently said to me: "Satan rules this planet!" I replied: "I know it." My answer was unnerving to the person making the statement due to the fact that Fundamentalists, along with numerous other Christian "demon-inations," firmly believe that Witches and Pagans are "devil-worshippers." I did not elaborate upon the fact that we do not believe in a "devil" as such, but we do believe in a *controlling force* that is anathema to our way of life as we would like to live it, and should be able to live it, upon this planet. Our ancient lore tells us that thousands of years ago there were two forces seeking control of the mode of life upon this planet; one group wishing to teach mankind the "facts of life" and the other to exploit mankind. There were many names applied to these beings: Gods, Angels, Watchers, sons of God, etc. The leaders of these two opposing forces, for want of a better term or name, were referred to as The Lord of Light and The Lord of Darkness. There is no need to be specific about which of them wanted what. Oh yes, and lest we forget, their "hosts" (in modern terminology, armies).

The Christian Bible, garbled as it currently is, speaks of a battle in the "heavens". Well, we know there was one, although the Christians have their time-space continuum a bit mixed up, to the point where it is all done and over with, according to them. But, we know that as it was in the beginning so it will be in the end, giving us the Alpha and Omega of history. When Christians speak of "fallen angels" and "salvation," I merely reply: "Ummm...of course." Then they are gently felled with the statement, "If the Lord of Light lost the battle for control of Earth, who won?" They were taught that the Lord of Light was Lucifer, a very naughty angel who went against God and got his. Along with his followers, naturally it is clear that a large number of the followers of the Lord of Light were confined to Earth, bred with Earth people, and produced what we now have as a breed of "different" beings, classified as people who "have the POWER" or "KNOWING ONES." Thus, we have an admixture upon this planet of Light and Darkness. The demarcation line becomes more obvious daily. Shall we call it "The Omega Caper?"

When it comes down to the nitty gritty of hassles and bickering and the rest of the fertilizer, consider the fact that antagonistic elements of Darkness infiltrate for the express purpose of dimming the LIGHT. The sad tales of recorded history are replete with data on thousands of enlightened ones who brought forth progress upon the Earth as new inventions and new ways of Thought in order to ADVANCE mankind. Were they not all ridiculed at one time or another? Was there not an element among mankind hat continually sought to prevent progress? We have had our "Mighty Ones" who overcame the opposing and controlling forces to progress our people in spite of any obstacle, often at great personal sacrifice.

We are all well aware of the people who have been continually opposed to our space program...they give various and sundry reasons: "expensive" (so what?); "we need the money for the poor and needy;" or "we should not mess around with God's Universe," etc. etc.... blah, blah, blah. The numerous wars, inspired by Darkness, were also "expensive," very expensive. The "poor and needy" wouldn't be about to get any of the lucre, and as for "God's universe"...it belongs to everyone to share equally. There is no need to be imprisoned upon the giant spaceship Earth if one wishes to go elsewhere. For those who are not already well aware of it, the battle is once more raging. This time, however, the thumb-screws are on the other pinkies.

Old Religionists who allow themselves to be photographed by the news media in the "altogether" (sky-clad), and often in positions that suggest obscene practices, aren't doing the Old Religion any service whatsoever, but rather giving it a very black eye. Worship in such a case, if it is worship, should be sacred to the Goddess and God alone and not for the eyes of cowans to see and misinterpret. We live in a clothed society which is not all that ready to accept what some Witches or Pagans do. If we wish to get across the message that we are intelligent, dignified and worthy of respect just as much as the controlling religions of Earth...then we should not use back-door tactics, but utilize some of the Wisdom our forebears bestowed upon us to give the proper impression of what and who we really are. Many Witches ignore the age-old counsel of the Wise Ones as given in the Rede.

Many different traditions have different redes. That is understandable, considering the time involved from Alpha to Omega. Our own particular Rede, however, has appeared within the past year in a perverted form. That is to say, the wording has been changed. This is sad for those who are seeking the Light of the Old Religion because it confuses them. The same thing was done to the ancient seals of Solomon, and thus we do not have his great wisdom as it was meant to be in the original form. Some would-be artists thought to "improve" upon the drawings of the seals, not realizing it was not artwork, but sacred symbolism...not to be tampered with. Thus, many wonder why the current seals so often bring them undesired results or no results at all.

We are not "into" Cabalistic magic, as such, but do not deny its relationship to our way of life. We have all received our lore from the same root source. As a Traditionalist, versed in lore taken from certain Witches of the British Isles, I can say that our own particular tradition consists of the practices and beliefs of folk Witches and not those people who were generally wealthy enough to be formally educated. Country people were simple people and had simple rituals in practice and wording. Many never knew how to read or write, but they were not without their share of "nobles" who did know how. Many Old Religion dances and songs became the nursery rhymes and dances of children, following the centuries-old "witch" trials. Thus, many legends and songs are almost childlike in their context because this was the level of basic understanding of folk Witches at that time. Unable to openly express what they knew to be truth in actual "university" terms, they resorted to simple symbolism in ritual, legend, and drawings, and preserved their sacred heritage in the most comprehensive manner, and in a manner that would be ignored by their adversaries, for the most part. Our own particular form of the Wiccan Rede is that which was passed on to her heirs by Adriana Porter, who was well into her nineties when she crossed over into the Summerland in the year 1946. This Rede in its original form is as follows:

Rede of the Wiccae
(Being knowne as the counsel of the Wise Ones)

1. Bide the Wiccan laws ye must in perfect love an perfect trust.
2. Live an let live -fairly take an fairly give.
3. Cast the Circle thrice about to keep all evil spirits out.
4. To bind the spell every time, let the spell be spake in rhyme.
5. Soft of eye an light of touch – speak little, listen much.
6. Deosil go by the waxing Moon -sing an dance the Wiccan rune.
7. Widdershins go when the Moon doth wane, an' the Werewolf howls by the dread Wolfsbane.
8. When the Lady's Moon is new, kiss the hand to her times two.
9. When the Moon rides at her peak, then your heart's desire seek.

10. Heed the Northwind's mighty gale – lock the door and drop the sail.
11. When the wind comes from the South, love will kiss thee on the mouth.
12. When the wind blows from the East, expect the new and set the feast.
13. When the West wind blows o'er thee, departed spirits restless be.
14. Nine woods in the Cauldron go – burn them quick an' burn them slow.
15. Elder be ye Lady's tree – burn it not or cursed ye'll be.
16. When the Wheel begins to turn – let the Beltane fires burn.
17. When the Wheel has turned a Yule, light the Log an let Pan rule.
18. Heed ye flower, bush an tree – by the Lady blessed be.
19. Where the rippling waters go, cast a stone an truth ye'll know.
20. When ye have need, hearken not to other's greed.
21. With the fool no season spend or be counted as his friend.
22. Merry meet an merry part – bright the cheeks an warm the heart.
23. Mind the Threefold Law ye should – three times bad an three times good.
24. When misfortune is enow, wear the blue star on thy brow.
25. True in love ever be unless thy lover's false to thee.
26. Eight words the Wiccan Rede fulfill – an' it harm none, do what ye will.

The foregoing is explained fully to the initiated Witch. The contents of the Book of Shadows (our public name for it) must be orally taught as well as copied. All wording has its special meaning which the Wise can often quickly discern. Meditation is a most important adjunct to the learning of the Mysteries of the Old Religion. The number of Old Religionists currently abiding by counsel of the Wise can be counted on fingers of one hand and the thumb would left over.

There is only one form of wisdom that time alone can bestow, and that is lessons learned from experience. Our children were taught to respect the old ones, even though they were often people of little formal education or very simple in their ways. They had lived long and had, therefore, experienced much of life and its ways. Their advice through their own lessons learned was considered invaluable, and thus they were held in deep respect for those things in which they had learned Wisdom. Children were not taught to strive for perfection, but for Wisdom. Perfection is a broad concept with different meanings for different people. It actually does not exist. The caution was: "Do not seek perfection in others unless you yourself can give it." Therefore "we have the counsel to 'live an let live.' "

When anyone refers to a particular Old Religion tradition as a "sect" it brings to mind bug spray. It is a poor term to apply to a sacred way of life, and the word "cult" is enough to set one's teeth on edge. Although Webster's now gives it a more dignified connotation, the general public and Webster do not necessarily agree on all points of definition. There was originally just a Single tradition of Witchcraft and many traditions within Paganism due to country, customs, etc. When certain priests of the early Christian church became bored with their celibate life they perverted their own religion by reversing their rituals and brought forth Satanism. Why they insisted upon calling themselves Witches is anyone's guess, for the majority of them still do it. Unless, perhaps, they are so guilt-ridden about their practices and beliefs that they wish to place the blame elsewhere. Genuine Witches and Pagans are not running around cutting off the heads of black chickens, nor are they offering up babies and virgins to some obscure demon. We have too much respect for life. It is almost useless to try getting the truth across to those who do not and will not understand our ways due to a messed-up news media and the general Christian-Judeo clamor for titillating reading...such as evidenced in the book, *The Devil on Lammas Night* by Susan Howatch, whoever that is. It is a cross-continent version of what the adversary imagines Witchcraft to be or would like the reading public to think it is. A quite exciting and well-written book, to be sure. An accursed lie, however. How unlike the beautiful writing of Mary Stewart, author of the much read and beloved book, *The Crystal Cave*, and its sequel, *The Hollow Hills*. Mary Stewart is to Susan Howatch what diamonds are to coal.

At this point I should like to quote from a very learned patriarch of the Old Religion, one whom we would refer to as a "Wizen Elder" in our tradition. (Wizen being pronounced as "whizzen." It is derived from the title Wizard, one highly skilled in the arts of the Craft.) I feel he would not mind my including his comments on book authors at this point. They are simply stated: "The Craft view is that a book is only a man talking on paper and is no more accurate than the spoken word by the same man. Any man who talks for an extended length of time must make a few mistakes. No book, therefore, not even a college text, is 100% accurate. Also, no man has all the facts about any particular subject. There is always something more to be told, something the author did not know." I might only add that this applies to female authors as well. "...speak little, listen much."

Many in the Old Religion are now finding it wise to shun the limelight and keep their activities secret from the public on all levels. One might even say they are going "underground." This includes many High Priestesses and High Priests who are either choosing to take their entire Covens "underground" or to practice their religion quietly by themselves. This is logical and sane at this time in history. It does not mean a creeping away into some hidden corner for fear of the foe, but a carefully calculated plan to keep the foe guessing. Considering the apparent IQ level of many of our critics the cerebral exercise will do them good. Our forebears did not go about thumping their chests and proclaiming to the world at large "I am a Witch!" simply because it was the "in" thing or the current social "fad." They did not wish to raise eyebrows or attract the adversary or the ever-increasing horde of misfits. In discretion and Wisdom they preserved the old truths, else we would not have them today.

Food for thought: I don't care what anyone does just so long as they do not interfere with Life, this planet, or me. Surprising how limiting that can be. "As you sow so shall you reap" is not a Christian original...it is the Threefold Law simply expressed in farm language. Disharmony begets disharmony and time travels in a *circle*, not a straight line. The Serpent eating his own tail. Perversions of ancient Traditions often bring ancient curses as well. The invisible becomes manifest. Twin Earths exchanging bric-a-brac. The insatiable guru-chasers, book collectors, coven hoppers, name-droppers, and ego-trippers; we've all had our share of them. Monsters roam the planet in various guises. People who seldom make anyone happy, feigning

Wisdom. Nobody can hear a whisper while they're talking. Wiccan-Pagan teachings are not for everyone.

© 2011 Andrew Theitic

Elizabeth Pepper Da Costa
(1923-2005)

by Andrew Theitic

Elizabeth was born into a family of "metaphysicians," as her mother use to say. She was raised by her close family, including her four maternal aunts – Katherine (Kitty), Mable, Elizabeth and Mary. As a child, school mates would frequently poke fun at Elizabeth, or Betty, as some friends called her. Children would taunt her and say "You're a Witch." One day, Betty went home and asked her mother, "Mother, are we witches?" Her mother replied with a smile, "We study metaphysics, dear." Elizabeth never heard the word "witch" being used to describe anyone in the family or any of their practices, but indeed, Witchcraft is what they did.

Elizabeth recalled her experiences as a child, when she frequently sat around the living room, with other family members and their friends, asking who might have a problem that the group would be able to work for. From meeting to meeting, each in turn might or might not share a problem with the other members of the "coven." But, when an issue was discussed, the method of working was determined and all would hold hands and work for the success of the magic. These people didn't mix religion with magic. Magic was considered to be a way of life. It was just something you did. Once a Dominican Catholic priest asked to join their group, and was immediately accepted in. He practiced, wished, chanted, and worked as the other members did and remained a loyal member for many years.

I met Elizabeth in 1975. I owned and operated a metaphysical shop in East Greenwich, Rhode Island called The Flaming Cauldron. Elizabeth owned and operated a small company in New York State called Images. I wrote to her looking to buy some of the printed cards that she had for sale in her catalog. Elizabeth wrote back, saying that the mail-order business had been closed. She offered to sell me the remains of her print overruns. I agreed to this and we soon made plans to meet and discuss the purchase. Once we met, we were both enthralled with the conversation. I was living on a street that she had often visited as a child. It was her favorite place to go sledding in the winter. Potter road was a winding street with a continuous downward slope for almost a mile. Over the 30 years that I knew Elizabeth, we shared many stories over a cup of tea. Here are a few stories and experiences to share.

A Walk along the Beach

One sunny Sunday afternoon, I was visiting with Elizabeth and her five cats and two dogs at her home in Newport, RI. We sat drinking tea for several hours, solving the problems of the metaphysical universe, when she suddenly said to me, "Let's take a walk along the beach." Knowing Elizabeth as I did, I knew there was a plan involved. We drove to Crescent Beach in Newport. There, we got out and she immediately began telling me about how her aunt—I believe this was Mable—would instruct her to pick up three items at the beach, after which you would hand them to a gifted friend to psychically "read" them for you. She explained that you could always put one back and choose another, but after the walk was completed, you needed to have just three items in your hand. We walked the beach, or should I say Elizabeth very briskly walked the beach. Fortunately for me, she was already in her seventies, or I would not have been able to catch up to her. Elizabeth was an enthusiastic walker. Over rocks and across the beach sand, it was a task for me to keep up with her pace. After about 1 hour of walking, picking up, putting down, and picking up again…we both had three items that we were satisfied with and were ready to go home to read for each other. As I recall, I had one shell and two pebbles. We got to Elizabeth's home and she began preparing the tea cart. We had a plate of lemon cookies, tea, honey, sugar and cream. Once we settled down, we each held our own three objects, focused our desire for clarity into them, and concentrated. After which, we traded objects and I began first. I gave her impressions as they came to me. Calling off objects, describing situations, repeating the words that came to me and recounting everything I saw. Elizabeth was pleased. She used to frequently call me her "young apprentice." This brought her joy. After I was done with my prophecy, Elizabeth began. She went on to describe many things happening in my future. Most of these came to pass over the next couple of years.

Aunt Kitty's love spells

Elizabeth carried one family trait forward from her mother's sister, Kitty. Elizabeth was a meddler! She loved to match folks up. On more than one occasion, I found her doing it with me. There were times when I would go to visit, usually on a Sunday, and she would have someone there for me to meet. After the person left, she would question me – did I like them, wasn't so-and-so funny, did I know that this person was not married, etc. Aunt Kitty's magic played an important part in Elizabeth's life. Much of what we would call a "Book of Shadows," in Elizabeth's case, was a book of love spells handed down from her aunt. Many of these appear in the book, *Love Spells* by Elizabeth Pepper.

The Witches' Almanac

Elizabeth's life-long project and love was *The Witches' Almanac*. She began the *Almanac* in 1971 as a small private publication, but soon after she looked for a distributor to make the *Almanac* available to the public. In a short time, the book was doing wonderfully and had been picked up by Grosset & Dunlap publishers/distributors. The book was an immediate success and sold 93,000 copies that year. Elizabeth wanted to put out a handsome book that gave the reader just enough information on a subject to inspire him or her to go out and learn more. No topic was covered in any great depth, as this was not her goal. She wanted to interest the reader just enough to inspire personal research on the subjects they felt drawn to. The short and teasing articles became a hit with her readership. *The Witches' Almanac* was published annually by Elizabeth until she passed away in 2005 and entrusted it to me. I have continued its publication each year since, knowing that she is behind me watching my every move.

And Mother reads the cards

Elizabeth's mother, who was called Dove, as all the witches of the family had bird names, was very famous for her card reading. She would read for family, friends, and clients. Dove had a small room off the front hall in their home in Providence, Rhode Island. This room was her reading room. When Elizabeth came home from school, if the door was open, she could call out and be greeted by her mother. But, if the door was closed, she was to tip-toe about and keep busy until the door opened and the person left. Her mother was a card reader, but never called a witch. She was responsible for teaching Elizabeth how to read the cards and encouraged her to explore her skills with other divinatory methods.

The Witches come a knocking

Primarily as a result of *The Witches' Almanac*, Elizabeth was always a popular BNW (big name witch). Despite the popularity, she never entertained publicity. She turned down interviews, book signings, radio shows, and even visitors. Although she liked a good gossipy visit over a cup of hot tea, Elizabeth liked being to herself as well, and frequently turned down visiting witch dignitaries, preferring to walk on the beach, or work in her garden, instead.

Being in the moment

I often think of how Elizabeth spoke of simply being in the moment and accepting and celebrating whatever that moment held. She talked about walking outdoors on a rainy day and how instead of hunching over and running for cover, one should hold their head high or even look up with a smile. She accepted life as it was given to her – for good or for ill. Many years ago, while visiting Elizabeth, I began to suffer from a headache. She explained that much of the discomfort was due to the struggle of trying to defeat the headache. Instead, she explained how the pain would be reduced, if I just allowed it to pass over and through me, and that I should accept this as a part of life.

Southernwood in the garden

The garden by the house in Newport was a favorite place for Elizabeth to spend her time. She kept a beautiful garden – sage, thyme, southernwood (a favorite of hers), aconite, comfrey, violets, rue, and many other beloved plants, came together to help Elizabeth celebrate. This rich garden was a pool of life. By the side of the garden door, Elizabeth kept a cement Buddha. A tranquil and peaceful place, she often preferred to spend time talking in the garden. For several years, she had a daily visitor at her back door—a neighboring red fox, for whom grapes and other food would be left outside to feast upon.

She frequently said, "A true witch loves animals...and it doesn't hurt to have a garden either."

Happily reunited with Martin

Elizabeth lost her husband, Martin, in the fall of 2004. She and Martin were very much in love until the day he died, and beyond. The bond they had was something special. When Elizabeth took sick, I drove from Providence to Newport Hospital every day to be with her. She was in the hospital on and off for some time – probably about 4-5 months. I would sit with her and listen to her tell stories about Martin. In the end, when she passed away, her close friends took her ashes aboard a small boat and sailed through Narragansett Bay to the open Atlantic Sea. Here I said a few words, and we mixed her ashes with Martin's, and then poured them into the Atlantic Ocean, as she had wished.

© 2011 Andrew Theitic

Lady Sheba (Jessie Wicker Bell): Witch Queen (1920-2002)

By Virginia Villarreal

Jessie Wicker Bell was born on July 18, 1920 in the mountains of Kentucky. Jessie was born into a family that had lots of magick and spiritual beliefs in it. On her maternal side of the family came the Fairy lore of the Irish Isle and from her paternal side the Native American Spirit Guides of her Cherokee great grandfather. When she was 6 years old her grandmother began to teach her the craft and taught her Fairy lore and Cherokee Magick. Her family had many psychics throughout the generations and she believed that she inherited what they called, "Hand of Power" so that she could protect people from evil. She claimed that her family were traditional witches and had practiced witchcraft for 7 generations. She also believed that she lived several lives so she believed in reincarnation. She claimed to be traditional by birth and a "Gardnerian Witch by choice."

Lady Sheba was the name that Jessie took when she was initiated into a local coven of witches in the late 1930s. She was said to believe that Lady Sheba was a name that she had from another life. It was something she knew to be true because she felt it with all her being. She got married in 1940 and had 8 children, four boys and four girls. She divided her time between being mother to her eight children and practicing witchcraft. In 1950, she and her family moved to Michigan and she began her first coven there. This coven later evolved to be the 'American Celtic Wicca Tradition', which was based on the beliefs of her own Celtic family. She became so popular that covens began to spring up all across the country and then it crossed the ocean to Europe where some covens began taking on influences of other traditions which later would birth covens with unique practices. Lady Sheba started new traditions where all the different covens could join and work in unity for the same cause. This tradition was called the "American Order of the Brotherhood of the Wicca".

Lady Sheba claimed that the Goddess had directed her to publish her "Book of Shadows", so that it could be helpful to the public and benefit those seekers who were seeking to know the work of the Wise. It was in 1970 that the Goddess was said to have directed her to publish it and in 1971, with the help of Carl Weschcke of Llewellyn Publishing Co., her first book was published under the name, *Book of Shadows.*

Lady Sheba was the first person to register Wicca as a religion in the United States. She registered Wicca in the state of Michigan which began a nationwide registration of Wicca as a religion. Wicca was "out of the broom closet" and has grown into a major religion because of Lady Sheba's *Book of Shadows*. But it hasn't been a bed of roses for Lady Sheba because after the book was published, she was accused of violating the "oath of secrecy" and that some of the material was not her own. She later replied that secrecy was in the past and that she never told anyone that she was the author of any of it, only that this was her Book of Shadows as it was passed on to her. She also played an active part in the organization of the Council of American Witches in 1973. As the founder of two growing traditions, Lady Sheba took on a self-proclaimed title, "American Witch Queen". With this name she became the ridicule of the community. The most serious criticism against Lady Sheba was and still is the publication of her *Book of Shadows*. Many in the community felt she had violated a sacred oath which was unforgivable.

Such animosity toward Lady Sheba continued for several years and by the late 1970s she had withdrawn from public life altogether. Everyone she knew in the community had lost touch with her and didn't even know if she was still alive. She was in her eighties by then.

Despite all the ridicule and criticism she had suffered over her book, Lady Sheba always defended the publication of her *Book of Shadows,* and was proud of the way her book had helped to change the secretive and selective attitudes of the Craft.

On March 20, 2002 Lady Sheba died in her birth city of Knotts County, Kentucky, and her final wishes were that she be cremated along with a copy of her Book of Shadows and the ashes scattered about the graveyard of the Wicker family cemetery in Kentucky. Her last wishes were carried out as she had wanted. Little more is known of the life and times of Lady Sheba A.K.A. Jessie Wicker Bell, but the impact that she had on the New Age and Pagan community will live on as long as there are those who seek the Path of the Goddess and the life of a witch.

References

The Encyclopedia of Witches &Witchcraft – By Rosemary Ellen Guiley

The Encyclopedia of Modern Witchcraft and Neo-paganism – By Shelley Rabinovitch

HANS HOLZER
(1920-2009)

by Andrew Theitic

Hans Holzer, the world-famous parapsychologist, ghost hunter, and author, was born in Vienna in 1920. Tales he heard from his Uncle Henry inspired young Hans to fascinate his kindergarten classmates —and shock their mothers— with ghost stories of his own creation. They also created a fascination with the supernatural, which was to last his entire life.

Hans wrote one hundred and thirty-eight books, as well as plays, musicals, and episodes of television shows. Most of his work deals extensively with the occult. In pop culture, perhaps his most well-known works are those surrounding the house in Amityville, Long Island, which was the basis for *The Amityville Horror*. However, he also wrote several books that are immensely important to witchcraft in the 20th century, including *Witches: True Encounters with Wicca, Wizards, Covens, Cults and Magick; Wicca: The Way of the Witches;* and *Powers of the New Age*.

I met Hans through a mutual friend. For fifteen years, I was lucky enough to enjoy Hans' friendship and knowledge. I was frequently a guest at his apartment on Manhattan's Upper West Side, where he would talk with me about his books, his life, and his outlook on the world. While it would take several books to describe the full extent of his rich and eventful life, the following are some stories that illustrate our friendship and the character of this remarkable gentleman.

Searching the Flea Markets

Hans loved his apartment, where he lived for forty-seven years, from 1962 to 2009. He filled it with incredible objects, whose ultimate origins ranged from India and Egypt to Western Europe. Ironically, Hans found most of these artifacts much closer to home — at the New York City flea markets where he was a regular browser. Whenever he and I were making plans for me to visit, Hans would not be available on Sunday. That was his day for going to the flea market.

Hans had an excellent memory for each and every one of the beautiful things he owned. If I asked about something I saw in his apartment, he would be able to tell me a detailed history: where and how he found the object in question, what it was and what it meant, how much he paid for it, and even how the process of haggling went! Everything had a story and a meaning behind it.

From Vienna to Manhattan—and Beyond

In 1938, Hans came to America, where his father had lived for several years at the beginning of the century. His grandmother's brothers owned a garage in the Bronx and provided a connection with which to start life in America. The political climate of Europe had prompted Hans and his brother to make the journey: Hans could see that war was coming, and he wanted to get himself and his brother away from an increasingly aggressive Germany.

When war did break out, the U.S. Army draft board turned Hans down because he suffered anxiety in closed rooms. The OSS, precursor to the CIA, however, did offer him a position, but Hans refused, because he had to take care of his parents and he wanted to continue his studies at Columbia University. After the war, he did become a foreign correspondent, a job which took him all across Europe.

By the time I knew Hans, he didn't talk much about his days as a correspondent. He seemed mostly to have moved on from that part of his life. Witnessing the damage that war left on countries and people clearly had an impact on him. Even near the end of his life, in interviews with both *The Witches' Almanac* and *GhostVillage*, he mentioned disliking violence and war. Hans was very concerned by "mankind's continuing preoccupation" with such things. *(http://www.ghostvillage.com/legends/2005/legends35_02072005.shtml)*.

A Cat Person

When I was first getting to know Hans, we were sitting in his apartment talking and his cat came up and sat down next to me, so I said hello and petted her.

"Do you like Isis?" Hans asked.

"Of course!" I said.

Hans laughed. "That's my cat—Isis," he said. "She likes you too."

Isis and I got along very well over the years. She always enjoyed sitting next to me and would come out and say hello to friends that I brought over for a visit.

Hans always described himself as a cat person, not a dog person. He owned two cats before Isis: Silvy and Stripes. The latter became the subject of his book, *Confessions of a House Cat as Told*.

The Amityville Horror

When George and Kathleen Lutz began to talk about their supernatural experiences in an Amityville, New York house, the public grew interested—and so did Hans. In 1977, he took Ethel Meyers, a spiritual medium, to investigate. After viewing the house, Meyers claimed that an angry Native American chief had possessed Ronald DeFeo, the man who had occupied the house before the Lutzes and had murdered his family.

The house in Amityville and its history fascinated Hans. He spent a great deal of time walking around the property and talking to the Lutzes about their experiences. Ultimately, he wrote three books on the subject—*Murder in Amityville*, *The Secret of Amityville*, and *The Amityville Curse*—and gave interviews devoted to it to TV and film crews. *Murder in Amityville* and *The Amityville Curse* became the basis for the first two sequels to *The Amityville Horror* film.

Despite the grimness of the subject, Hans loved working on projects about Amityville. When we were talking about it, he often used to say that everything had some reason for happening and that what we called magic was really just science that hadn't been discovered yet. Maybe the amount of attention that the Amityville incident received was a sign to him that we were getting closer to making some of those discoveries.

The United Kingdom and the Craft

In the 1960s, Hans went to the United Kingdom to meet and interview prominent witches there. During this period, Witchcraft was just beginning to get public attention and Hans met some of the most important figures of the time, such as Alex and Maxine Sanders and Sybil Leek. He recorded many of those interviews on film, as well as some ceremonies that he was able to witness. The footage has since come to me and I am currently working on a project involving this film. The recordings show, among other things, images of group prayer during rituals, people riding on brooms, and an initiation ritual. It's fascinating material and I'm very excited to be working with it.

Hans himself was initiated during his time in the UK. During his work with Alex Sanders, "King of the Witches" and founder of the Alexandrian tradition, Hans became involved in the Craft, eventually receiving his Alexandrian degrees from Maxine Sanders, Alex's wife. Hans would go on to write four books specifically about Witchcraft, in addition to his numerous works on general spirituality and parapsychology.

A Man of Many Languages

As a young man entering the University of Vienna, Hans had already learned Latin in addition to other modern languages. However, when he decided to study ancient history and archaeology, Hans found out that the program required him to know Greek—a language he'd never learned—so he found a teacher and began to study. In six months, Hans had learned enough Greek to enter the program; more than half a century later, he still knew Ancient Greek.

When impending war in Europe brought him to America, Hans enrolled in Columbia University, where he studied Japanese for three and a half years. He also studied music—composition in Europe and conducting at Julliard—and ended up conducting musical comedies and writing a number of songs. In an interview with *The Witches' Almanac,* Hans said that "you never know when you can use it."

Hans seemed to apply that attitude toward knowledge of all sorts. Perhaps his study of different forms of communication—both spoken language and music—is one of the things that led to both his interest in and his success at investigating the paranormal.

Books and Stories, More Books and More Stories

For a while, every time I visited Hans in New York, I'd bring up one or two of his books so that he could sign them. He always did so very nicely, but he was such a prolific writer that, by taking up a book or two at a time, I wasn't really making much of a dent in my collection of his works. Eventually, I packed up all the unsigned copies of his books that I owned and took them up to Hans's apartment: the packing itself was quite a process, as my suitcase ended up containing more than a hundred books.

I had thought the process of signing would take the better part of an hour or two. Every time I gave Hans a book, though, it inspired a whole chain of reminiscences. He would talk about how he'd come to write that particular book, what had happened during the writing itself, and why that book was his favorite. I ended up spending a whole afternoon in Hans's apartment, listening to him tell all the stories that each book made him remember and coming to find out that every book was his favorite book!

Hollywood in Manhattan

Between his work in Amityville, particularly his role as a consultant for the films and the wide-ranging subjects of his books, Hans became quite familiar with many people in the film industry. I remember going into his office and seeing dozens of photos hanging from the walls, all people who were popular at the time — everyone from movie stars to talk show celebrities. Many of those photos were autographed headshots, with personal messages to Hans from the star in question. Others were pictures of Hans and one famous person or another together. He had countless friends in Hollywood. For example, as a consultant on the TV show *In Search Of*, he got to know one of my favorite people – Leonard Nimoy of *Star Trek* fame.

Naturally, Hans and I talked about all of the interesting and colorful people he'd met during his work on films and TV shows. He told me who in Hollywood had been initiated into the Craft and actually showed me one very recognizable celebrity signature on a list of initiates in Alex Sanders's Book of Shadows. Of course, I can't name any names, but there were a good number of celebrities involved in Witchcraft and many of them were not at all who you'd expect.

A Family Legacy

Hans married Countess Catherine Buxhoeveden in 1962. The two divorced in 1986, but Hans stated in a 2009 interview with The Witches' Almanac that he and Catherine were still friendly and that he looked back fondly on the time that they had spent together. They had two daughters, Nadine and Alexandra, and five grandchildren.

Hans's daughter Alexandra continued her father's tradition of spiritual investigation, as well as involvement with the Lutz house in Amityville. She appeared in the third installment of Shattered Hopes, a documentary film exploring the murders that took place in the house and served as a psychic consultant for the film. Alexandra has also written *Growing Up Haunted,* a memoir, and a science fiction trilogy called *Lady Ambrosia: Secret Past Revealed.* The UK's *Daily Telegraph*, when printing Hans's obituary, mentioned that he had sent his posthumous thanks for their interest through one of his daughters and Alexandra seems like the likely candidate.

Life as a Vegan

When Hans was eleven years old, he stopped eating meat; when he was forty, he adopted a completely vegan diet. At the time, such eating habits were highly unusual, and there were almost no restaurants where you could be sure you weren't eating any animal products. It took a great deal of commitment and willpower to be vegetarian, much less vegan. Nonetheless, Hans remained a vegan from the age of forty until he died at age eighty-nine. Toward the end of his life, when he was no longer able to cook for himself, he still had his caretaker prepare vegan food for him daily.

Aware of how rare vegan food was and how unpleasant many people found it—especially the forms available in the seventies and eighties—Hans would generally have his meals on his own. When I went to New York to see him, he always made sure that I visited early in the afternoon, after lunch and with plenty of time before dinner; he knew that I probably wouldn't like what he was going to eat.

Hans credited a lot of his good health to his diet. In a 2005 interview with GhostVillage, he said that he hadn't even had a cold in 15 years and also that he never took prescription drugs or had any kind of injection. In fact, at eighty-four years old, he still went to bed at midnight and remained active in swing dancing.

Knowledge Conquers Fear

Hans dedicated his life to scholarship and the pursuit of knowledge. He applied a very scientific, fact-based approach to the work he did with the occult and used to say that he didn't believe in the supernatural, only in natural laws that humanity hadn't figured out yet. He rejected the idea of using technology, such as Geiger counters and instruments to measure cold spots, when investigating hauntings. Ghosts to him were nothing more or less than human beings, best dealt with by talking to them through a good trance medium.

Likewise, Hans didn't believe in the devil, monsters, or other supernatural races. "There is nothing out there," he said, "that isn't one way or the other human."

And, although his quest for knowledge took him to places with grisly pasts, Hans said that he was never frightened. "Fear is created by not understanding something. You bring on the fear. There is no object to fear," he said.

A Natural Storyteller

Over the years that I knew Hans, I got to hear many of his stories, which he always loved to tell. Sitting in a big armchair in his Manhattan apartment, he'd start a tale about his experiences, always keeping an eye on his audience to see their reactions. When he knew that something in one of his stories was going to be funny, he'd lead up to it and tease it out: he'd drop a few hints, spin off to a related subject, come back and work up to the funny part a little more, then dance around it again, drawing out the story while you waited on the edge of your seat. Then he'd drop the punch line, look you straight in the eye, and wait to see your reaction.

Hans had a great sense of timing and content, of what worked in a story and what didn't and he could really apply that knowledge on the fly. His writing process showed it: he dictated many of his books onto tapes; he used a typewriter for his whole life even though he was writing well into the computer age and he never edited or rewrote his book. "I write it correctly the first time," he told *The Witches' Almanac*.

A Path to Happiness

Throughout his life, Hans believed that he had a very definite purpose: to investigate what most people think of as the "supernatural" and, through the entertainment industry, to let the world know what he had found. He saw patterns in his career and the people he'd gotten to know that all pointed to this mission. He decided early on to let those signs guide him. The path he found brought him great happiness. At 85, he said that he was doing what he loved to do and that he felt no need to retire.

Hans's life was a rich and exciting one. He could talk for hours about all of the places he had been and the people he had met: I found it fascinating just to sit and listen to him reminisce. It would really make you envious to hear about all of his adventures and the joy he took in remembering them.

Meeting Hans and listening to him always reminded me how many amazing things a person could do in his or her lifetime. He had an incredibly full life and left an extremely important and enduring legacy in both the Craft and the wider world. Anyone who talked with him would think that, if they could have the kind of life he did, they would feel like they had accomplished a great deal. Certainly Hans's accomplishments will live on with all of us.

© 2013 Andrew Theitic

Scott Cunningham
(1956-1993)

By Christine Ashworth

I have the great good fortune to be Scott Cunningham's sister as well as a friend/follower of Christopher Penzcak. When Christopher asked if I would be willing to write a bio-sketch of Scott, a part of me resisted – surely I had said everything I could think of, as eloquently as I could, for the *Book of Shadows* that Llewellyn had put out in 2009?

Apparently not. Here are memories of the brother I sometimes loved, sometimes hated as siblings often do, but who always fascinated me. Our older brother Greg, my parents, and my husband also appear in these memories, as they were there "in real time" and were part of the fabric of Scott's life.

Early Days

Greg, Scott and I got along about as well as most siblings. Meaning, when it mattered we were fine; when nothing really serious was happening, we bickered and sniped at each other like typical siblings. Greg was two years older than Scott, and Scott was four years older than me.

While none of us were sports-mad, we did enjoy playing a game of pickup baseball in the front yard. The home plate stood right in front of the house, between my dad's office window and the boys' bedroom window, thus lowering the possibility of broken windows considerably. I believe the garage window was a casualty at least once, though.

First base was the electrical wiring that came down to the ground between lawns. Second base was the Carrotwood tree that stood in the parking strip. Third base was the Chinese Elm tree that still rules the front yard. Whenever we brought out the bats and the gloves, the neighbor kids came out in droves.

Our peak baseball years were from 1967 to 1971. By '71, Greg was 17 and already more away from home than at home. Scott was 15, and just discovering Wicca and witchcraft. At 11, I was book-mad and just months away from diving back into the world of ballet. It was during this summer that Scott came up with a new nickname for me – "Legs". He even put it in my autograph album that year. I remember being slightly astonished that he paid me such a compliment, and it's one of the memories I treasure the most.

I don't remember many day-to-day details of those years. There were the big things, like swimming lessons and piano lessons; and there was the summer my parents had a wood-burning fireplace built into the house. Another summer, my parents decided to convert the garage for more living space. My grandparents, Hazel and Merle Cunningham, came down for that venture, and Grandpa and my Dad did all the work while Grandma and Mom made sure the men ate well.

Then there were the summers we took car vacations. We went most often up to Oregon to see my dad's parents, but one year we actually went to Glacier National Park in Montana, which also included a stop to see my Dad's sister and family in Livingston, Montana. In 1969 we drove around the country for six weeks, hauling a trailer and exploring the great big U.S.A. But over all, ours was a normal, easy-going life marked by family dinners filled with laughter, much exploring of the dictionary, and storytelling.

We had a safe, normal, boring childhood. Only later did we find out how much our house had been a beacon of safety for so many kids. Our parents didn't drink or smoke, and they were always around; a big deal in the late Sixties and early Seventies. Mom would pass out snacks and Dad would show his face to keep the boys in line, but we rarely needed his intervention. It is this very normalcy and sense of safety that allowed Scott, in his teens, to follow his newly awakened interest in witchcraft and natural magics.

(He was also mischievous. He showed me all the good hiding places for Christmas presents that my parents used, and for several years after we would ooh and ahh and poke at the wrapped presents. One year I looked by myself. Unfortunately, some presents were unwrapped and I felt so ashamed that I never peeked at the hiding places again.)

I became aware of his interests slowly, as he felt more comfortable within himself. Some nights, fabulous scents would drift from his window and into mine. I had some amazing dreams, spurred on no doubt by the incenses he'd been exploring. At other times, his enthusiasm would almost force him to show me how to make hand-dipped candles, or divine the future using candlewax in a pot of water. He also showed me how to ask yes/no questions using a crystal on the end of a chain. Very beginner stuff, but fascinating for me to get this hint of what went on in his life. (I actually have some of the last candles he ever hand-dipped. They hang in my office, a pale blue, the wicks tangled now and the wax showing signs of heat and cold.) Years later, he gave me my first Tarot card deck.

The Cabin

The love for the cabin in the Laguna Mountains acted as a unifying force within our family. My parents bought it the year I turned six and due to circumstances, ended up selling it the year I turned sixteen. The place was magical. The original structure was an octagon; at some point, a sleeping porch, a bathroom, and a kitchen had all been attached.

Whether it was the thunderstorms in summer, walking in 85 degree heat the two miles on an unpaved road to buy candy and other treats at the general store, or being surrounded by the peaceful hush of a landscape buried under a blanket of snow, the cabin in the mountains was our retreat. There, we could be who we truly were.

Dad wrote, of course; but he also chopped wood. He took us on hikes and arrowhead hunts, and made us clear brush for the fire season. He shimmied up an old oak tree and hung a rope down for a swing. We also cleared a parcel of land not far from the patio and set up a volleyball net for games, something that came in handy whenever we had a lot of guests.

Mom lazed. She read (well, we *all* read!) She wrote, a little. Studied her bible. Unsteady on her feet, she didn't go for many walks, but she watched the birds and the squirrels. She cooked some amazing meals, and was there for all the board games or puzzles we chose to do at night.

In later years, Greg always seemed to be on the sleeping porch, playing guitar. Most frequently, the dulcet notes of "GLORIA" would come wafting out on the summer breeze.

I'd either read on one of the comfy couches inside or I'd be outside playing solitaire. We have a photo of at least five of us playing solitaire on the huge outdoor table my dad had made. During summers, this is also where we ate most of our meals.

Scott, however, was a different story. By the time he'd turned fifteen, he'd often grab an apple or something and be off by midday, on a ramble over the hill behind the cabin. The few times I tried to follow him, he'd give me the slip and I'd have to turn back before I got hopelessly lost. I never knew if he knew he was being followed, but I never did find him. He would come back from these hours sunburnt and dusty and glowing with energy. It wasn't until much later that I realized he was learning his herbal craft, soaking it up in the wilds of the mountains.

Adults Now

Even though Scott and I became roommates in early 1978, I can honestly say I spent maybe a total of a full week of nights at the apartment on Orange Avenue during my six or seven months there. I used it as a place to go change, or maybe pick up some clothes. I spent almost all my time over at my boyfriend, Tom Ashworth's, apartment or at the ballet studio, where I was working under an arts grant. (I graduated from high school in January, a half-year early.) Scott was glad that I had managed to contain my stuff to only my room – he could shut the door and no one would ever know his sister lived there, as there was literally nothing of myself in the rest of the apartment. I don't ever remember hanging up posters or artwork or photos. It was a way-station for me, and we both knew it. We just didn't expect my leaving to happen so soon.

In the summer of 1978 I auditioned for a dancer position at the Arizona Ballet Theatre, and was hired. They took three or four of us from San Diego that year. Even though I was in love with Tom, I felt I had to spread my wings. When that company folded a mere three months later, I moved back home with Mom and Dad and rejoined the California Ballet Company in time to perform The Nutcracker. Scott had a roommate that he liked (Don Kraig) and would even see on a daily basis, so there wasn't any reason to let me come back to the apartment. While disappointed, I totally understood – especially since I was, for all intents and purposes, unemployed.

The 1980s

The Eighties were both trying and wonderful. Tom and I had married and moved up to Los Angeles. Scott had his first fiction book published, *The Shadow of Love,* in 1980. The first Llewellyn Publications book came out in 1982, called *Magical Herbalism.* Scott was on his way. He published nine more books through Llewellyn during the Eighties, and thirteen novels for Carousel Books. Being the private person he was, he rarely mentioned these triumphs to me. My dad kept me informed of my big brother's successes.

In September of 1983 he was diagnosed with lymphoma, a particularly nasty form of cancer. Our relationship was such that we'd talk on the phone briefly, but he never urged me to come down and see him. I guess maybe a part of him knew he would beat the cancer. We'd have our time to spend with each other, later perhaps, when it would mean more. So while I knew he was sick, and at times very sick, he kept me isolated from most of the worry.

1990

Early in 1990 two things happened that rocked my world and forever changed my life. I became pregnant with my first son and Scott, on a long book tour, was found unconscious in his hotel room in Salem, Massachusetts. His hosts took him, via taxi, from Salem to Massachusetts General Hospital in Boston. That was quite a long taxi ride, but they wanted only the best for him. (This could be family legend, but it is what was told to me and I've never been told a different story of how he got to Boston from Salem.) It turned out to be a solid call; Scott was diagnosed with cryptococcal meningitis and some other opportunistic infections, typical of a compromised immune system. It was weeks before he was allowed to return to San Diego, and when he did, it was to check in to the University of California, San Diego Medical Center.

When my dad first broke the news to me, again it was with a cushioning of love. He told me I couldn't risk seeing Scott, and though I was ready to fly back East to help take care of him, being in my first trimester of pregnancy there were too many things that could go wrong. As my dad said, healthy people had no place in a hospital. My husband, too, asked me to stay home.

The next time I saw Scott I had to be well into my seventh month of pregnancy, probably around the time of his birthday. He looked good if thin; and he told me then that he didn't have much time. By now, the family knew he was dying. The date was not set, but the clock had been started. Scott had much that he felt compelled to do, to write, before he left this world for the next.

Last Days

In January of 1993, Scott and I had lunch together one day in Hillcrest, a hip part of San Diego. While it was one of his better days, overall he was very ill and had reluctantly made plans to move back into my parents' house.

His vision was going, and as we moved from my car to the restaurant he held my arm. I gave him direction – "curb in two paces." "Three steps going down." We made it to our table, and sat facing each other, both of us just reveling in being together. We hadn't seen each other in months, not since his birthday celebration in June of '92. As we'd grown older, we'd grown more comfortable together; four years' difference means a lot between 11 and 15; not so much between 32 and 36.

Scott talked a lot that day. Lunch lasted well over two hours and ranged across a wide variety of topics. I wish now I had taken notes, but who takes notes when you're just living life?

He wanted first of all to be sure that I was happy, that my marriage was strong and I loved being a mother. He and Tom had always gotten along; their sly banter and sexual innuendo made me blush whenever I could follow it. Tom had long ago gotten his approval, but still he pressed. Was I happy with my life? I assured him I was happy with my husband and son, and that I was hoping to conceive another child soon. He smiled and told me I wouldn't have much longer to wait. I didn't realize it at the time, but I was already pregnant with my second son. I have no doubt at all that he knew. He voiced concerns about our brother's current relationship, and concern for our parents, and I told him then that I'd keep an eye out.

Everything would either work out, or it wouldn't, and there wasn't much he could do about that. He didn't exactly appreciate the sentiment.

We talked about his moving back home, and he apologized for taking my room. I told him it didn't matter, as it had stopped being my room years before. We talked about our childhood, how lucky we'd been. He scolded me about not spending more time with Mom, told me I should make time for her. Scott had always been the one to protect Mom, to surprise her with flowers or thoughtful gifts. His care of her was very sweet, and their relationship very close. While I knew my mother would welcome a more intimate relationship with me, it wasn't something I could give her at the time and I knew it. But I didn't say much to Scott about it, not wanting to upset him. Sometimes he hit nerves that were too close to home, and it was easier to tune out the message than to take it to heart.

Soon enough, though, our conversation turned to the silent partner at our table – the specter of death. Scott wasn't afraid of dying, but he was irritated that there were still so many projects he wanted to complete, projects that would take years. He had a perfectionist streak that came out only in his writing, but that included everything that went into his writing – his research, his own understanding, and his craft, both of the written word and of his Wiccan beliefs. His main concern about moving back home and dying was that he'd be too cranky, too difficult a patient for our parents.

Over dessert I asked Scott the big question...did he believe in reincarnation? That he'd be reincarnated? When, and how, and why?

He smiled at me. He did believe in reincarnation. As to the when and how, he didn't know and couldn't care, as he was too busy living his best life. The next life would just have to wait. When I pushed the point, he paused and his eyes got a far-away look. Finally, he told me not to look for him, as there wouldn't be any point. Foreknowledge? I don't know.

At some point during our lunch, I asked him what his regrets were, aside from the obvious. He laughed at me and told me some weren't for his baby sister's ears. When I persisted, he changed the subject. Oh well, so much for that! He had always been a private person. Preparing for the next world hadn't changed that aspect of him. I told him my regret for him was that he'd never found a lasting love, a steady partner to share his life with. He smiled and changed the subject again.

I know we discussed other topics at lunch, but many have slipped through my memory during the past decades. These are the most vital ones, the ones that live on with me.

Two months later, he passed away.

Aftermath

Grief is a funny thing. I thought I'd prepared for it. Time would pass and I'd think well, I've gone through all the stages and have come out the other side. Then, weeks later, I'd be driving along and catch sight of someone in another car that I would *swear* was Scott, and the tears would start. Being pregnant at this point in time was interesting, to say the least.

In June, I went to a massage therapist to have a pregnancy massage, and she told me that unless I allowed myself to truly grieve, the baby I was carrying would be affected. It was my first, and last, time at that particular massage therapist's office. I left without having the massage and played hooky from work by fleeing to the ocean an hour away. I sat on the sand and ranted and cried and poured my heart out to Scott on that empty stretch of beach.

It wasn't until two full summers later that I realized the impact Scott had on the Magickal community. At the time, my husband Tom was Artistic Director and co-founder of Nevada Shakespeare in the Park in Henderson, Nevada. We were there in September doing a production of MacBeth that Tom directed. 5-year-old Chet played Fleance in that production, but 2-year-old Tim wanted nothing to do with the stage. Tom and both kids painted the sets in our back yard, and Tom figured a prominent pentagram with a circle around it was a fine thing to put on the raked stage floor for a play that had witches.

The production was fabulous – we were an Equity company, and were able to offer union contracts to L.A. actors to participate. We garnered a lot of support and a huge audience in the eight years we'd been acting in the outdoor venue in Foxridge Park.

One night after the show, a few college kids came back to talk to Tom and some of the actors. I'm not sure how it came about, but Tom told them that I was Scott Cunningham's sister. Pretty soon I found myself surrounded – and a couple of the boys were kneeling at my feet. They all hugged me, thanked me, told me that Scott had opened doors for them that otherwise might have remained shut. Word spread, and I shook more hands that night as Scott Cunningham's sister than I ever have as an Assistant Director of a play.

This reaction has remained true, even to this day – though perhaps more subdued. (No one else, in my memory, has knelt at my feet. I suspect those boys had been enjoying some wine with their picnic on the lawns.) As more books on Wicca and other traditions come out, not everyone has been as excited to hear of the sibling bond between Scott and I; but if or when they hear of the connection, all are usually respectful to my face.

Scott opened the dialog with *Magical Herbalism* in 1982, and published five more books on magic and Wicca between 1982 and 1988 through Llewellyn Publications. He fed the fires of those who felt he shouldn't be divulging "secrets" when he wrote *Wicca: A Guide for the Solitary Practitioner* in 1988. For quite a few years thereafter, he told me, he received threats of punishment and death. None of them apparently serious enough to get the authorities involved, but scary enough that he guarded his personal information closely and was particular about home and car safety.

I look back at his life and can only marvel at the courage it must have taken to share his gifts with the world. Many more authors are out there now who have written on being a "solitary practitioner," and there are herbal books that discuss secrets that used to be the wise woman's milieu; but Scott paved the way, and for that many are grateful.

I still miss him. I miss his sarcasm, his wit, and his love of puns. His ever-thoughtful gifts. I miss thinking about him, and getting a phone call from him minutes later. I miss his hugs. He would have loved today, bemoaned his age, and owned the latest i-Whatever going. And his Yule decorations would have been over the top, as usual.

This is hard to end, but I must. As I have mentioned elsewhere, Scott was a giver. His greatest gifts to those who didn't get to know the man himself have been his books; my wish is that they may survive in perpetuity, in one form or another, for all who want, need, and desire the information offered.

Bright Blessings,
Christine Ashworth
Simi Valley, California
January, 2013

Edmund "Eddie" Buczynski, Jr. (1947-1989)
American Neo-Pagan Witch, occult shop owner, author, and archaeologist

By Michael Lloyd

Eddie Buczynski grew up nominally Catholic, though his family was not what one would consider devout. After losing his father at age eleven, Buczynski grew more religious and had seriously considered taking vows in the Catholic priesthood. But after being repeatedly gay-bashed in both Catholic and public high schools, he chose instead to rebel against the establishment. Dropping out of school in 1964 at age seventeen, Buczynski moved to Manhattan and immersed himself in the Hippie subculture of Greenwich Village. Eddie stumbled across a copy of Gerald Gardner's book *Witchcraft Today* in 1971 and soon after sought out and became friends with occult author and activist Leo Louis Martello. Leo was a well-known figure in the New York gay scene due both to his activism in the months immediately following the 1969 Stonewall riots and through his "Gay Witch" column that ran in a local newspaper.

Martello introduced Buczynski to Herman Slater in 1971, and the two men quickly formed a romantic and business partnership which would last for several years. It was Buczynski's close relationship with Slater that would propel both men to prominence in the occult community of New York City. Together in 1972 they opened the Warlock Shop, an occult supplies store in Brooklyn Heights. The Warlock Shop published a newspaper, the *Earth Religion News*, which Buczynski edited for a brief time. The shop would eventually move to the Manhattan neighborhood of Chelsea and be renamed the Magickal Childe, thereafter becoming one of the most famous occult stores in the world.

Before meeting Leo Martello, Buczynski had only been superficially aware of the Neo-Pagan movement that was sweeping the country. Martello introduced him to Gwen Thompson, who headed the New England Covens of Celtic Traditionalist Witchcraft

(NECTW). Thompson brought Buczynski (as Hermes) into her North Haven, CT coven in early 1972, quickly making him her High Priest. Uncomfortable with the expectations being placed upon him by Thompson, and tiring of the long train trips between Brooklyn and North Haven, Buczynski took the writings Thompson had given him and combined them with other materials to craft a new tradition of Welsh Witchcraft called the Traditionalist Gwyddoniaid. After informing Thompson of his intentions to operate a Welsh coven from closer to home, Buczynski was banished from her coven in September 1972. The following month, Buczynski (as Gwydion) founded the first coven of the Traditionalist Gwyddoniaid with Kay Smith (as Vivienne). This Welsh tradition had the distinction of mentoring the first known coven mainly comprising teenagers, and was also one of the first fully-integrated Witchcraft traditions on the basis of race and sexual orientation.

Buczynski and Slater were initiated into Gardnerian Wica in 1973, although their standing in that tradition was ultimately disputed by others during a period characterized by many at the time as one of "power-over politics." In response to his ill treatment, he founded a neo-Gardnerian tradition called "The Wica" in 1974. Based on a revised Gardnerian book of shadows, The Wica book incorporated concepts communicated to Eddie by Raymond Buckland, who at the time was working on the manuscript for his book on Seax-Wica (The Tree, 1974). These included a more egalitarian coven structure where the Priest and Priestess were co-equals and elected to their positions. Buczynski also abrogated the wording in the Gardnerian book of shadows which had long been interpreted as prohibiting homosexuals from the practice of Witchcraft.

Eddie participated in other Neo-Pagan groups during the mid-1970s, including Leo Martello's coven of Continental Witchcraft, the Church of the Eternal Source (an Egyptian reconstructionist order), and another neo-Gardnerian group of his own devising. Buczynski was also named as a respected elder in the Georgian tradition for the advice and friendship he gave to its founders. Inspired by the sexual revolution taking place within the gay community, Buczynski founded the Minoan Brotherhood in 1977 with the specific goal of making Witchcraft more accessible and spiritually meaningful to gay and bisexual men. In crafting the Minoan book of shadows, Buczynski incorporated concepts he had previously learned and perfected during his practice with other spiritual groups, as well as the research he had conducted on early Aegean religious traditions. Using the guidance supplied by Buczynski as a template, Ria Farnham (as Rhea) and Carol Bulzone (as Miw) founded the Minoan Sisterhood, a sibling path celebrating the women's Mysteries. Together, the Brotherhood and Sisterhood comprise the Minoan Tradition. Eddie Buczynski firmly believed that members of the Minoan Brotherhood should be priests to the gay community and not just to themselves, reflecting both the activist spirit of the 1970s and the need for visible alternatives to what he saw as the abusive relationship the Christian church generally had with regard to homosexuals.

Buczynski withdrew from the public face of Witchcraft in 1981. After receiving his GED, he earned a BA with a triple major in Special Honors, Classical Studies and History from Hunter College SUNY in 1985, consequently securing a Mellon Fellowship. Eddie subsequently graduated with an MA in Classical and Near Eastern Archaeology from Bryn Mawr College in 1988 before succumbing from complications associated with AIDS in early 1989. He is the author of *Witchcraft Fact Book* (Earth Religions Supplies, 1974 and Magickal Childe, 1984) and, posthumously, *Pagan Rituals III* (Magickal Childe, 1989). All three Witchcraft traditions founded by Buczynski continue to this day.

Source: Lloyd, Michael. *Bull of Heaven: The Mythic Life of Eddie Buczynski and the Rise of the New York Pagan* (Hubbardston: Asphodel Press). 2012.

HERMAN SLATER
(1938-1992)
American Neo-Pagan and Witch, author, publisher, broadcaster and occult shop owner.

By Michael Lloyd

Herman Slater was arguably one of the most famous occult shop owners in the history of modern Neo-Paganism. Although of Jewish heritage, Slater was not an observant Jew. In the early 1960s, he had become interested in the occult and began attending spiritualist meetings facilitated by Clifford Bias, a notable clairvoyant living in New York City. In the latter half of the 1960s, Slater became friends with Leo Louis Martello, a New York City author and Witch. Martello introduced Slater to Edmund "Eddie" Buczynski in 1971.

It was Slater's close relationship with Buczynski that would propel both men to prominence in the occult community of New York. Together, they opened an occult supplies store – the Warlock Shop – in Brooklyn Heights, New York in 1972. The Warlock Shop became one of the first such stores to offer catalogue sales of a wide variety of occult-related goods to a national audience. The shop also sponsored classes and, for a short time, published a newspaper called the *Earth Religion News*. In late 1975, the shop was moved to the Manhattan neighborhood of Chelsea, where its name was changed to Magickal Childe in 1976. In 1980, the shop branched out into publishing and, under the Magickal Childe imprint, became a successful small press for occult works by Gerald Gardner, Janet and Stewart Farrar, Aleister Crowley and others.

Herman and Eddie were initiated into Gardnerian Wica in 1973, although their standing in that tradition was ultimately disputed by others during a period characterized by many at the time as one of "power-over politics." During this same period, the status of homosexuals in Witchcraft was being challenged by conservative elements that were reacting in opposition to the push for gay civil rights that was taking place in America and Great Britain. It isn't clear that homophobia was the main driver for Buczynski and Slater's treatment. However, Slater was particularly concerned about the pressure being exerted to discriminate against homosexuals within Gardnerian Wica and its Craft offshoots, which then comprised a majority within the Neo-Pagan movement. He and others such as Leo Martello, who had himself been involved early in the post-Stonewall gay rights movement, worked to ensure that Witchcraft as a spiritual pursuit was available to all who felt called to it. These efforts culminated in the approval of a resolution introduced by Slater at the Minneapolis Witchmeet of April 1974 which affirmed the right of homosexuals to practice Witchcraft – a first for the Craft in the US. Ironically, Slater was also viscerally opposed to the formation of same-sex covens and spiritual paths, believing instead that Neo-Pagan worship should be blind to the variations of human sexuality rather than either celebrating or opposing them.

In 1972, Slater (as Govannon) was initiated into a tradition of Welsh Witchcraft founded by Buczynski called the Traditionalist Gwyddoniaid. Slater's role as a High Priest in this Welsh tradition would last for the next 20 years via covens and Pagan Way groups which met in or were associated with his shop. Every spiritual tradition was welcomed at both incarnations of the store, and this outreach was credited for helping to facilitate the rebirth of the Ordo Templi Orientis (O.T.O.) on the east coast of the US through the support of local chapters and the national organization. The Magickal Childe was the setting for several films and documentaries, and Slater often used the Magickal Childe's annual Witches Ball to raise money for charity. The store closed in 1999, seven years after Slater's passing from complications associated with AIDS.

While Herman Slater's often confrontational manner, in combination with his sometimes questionable business ethics, have served to color his reputation in the greater Neo-Pagan community, he is nevertheless remembered as a tireless promoter of alternative sources of spirituality and esoteric knowledge, and a strong advocate for the rights of gay and lesbian practitioners of the occult.

Source: Lloyd, Michael. *Bull of Heaven: The Mythic Life of Eddie Buczynski and the Rise of the New York Pagan* (Hubbardston: Asphodel Press). 2012.

PHILIP EMMONS ISAAC BONEWITS
(1949-2010)

by Deborah Lipp

Let's play the Isaac Bonewits drinking game. Every time I name something that Isaac did that was a first, or was unique, or is recognizable by the whole Pagan community, you take a shot. Most people will be seeing double before we're done.

First (and only) person to receive an accredited university degree in Magic (drink). Author of *Real Magic,* considered one of the classic texts of modern occultism (drink). Founder of the first anti-discrimination organization for Pagans and occultists, the Aquarian Anti-Defamation League (drink). Author of *The Aquarian Manifesto*, which closes with the well-known rallying cry, "Never again the Burning!" (drink). Founder of the largest Neopagan Druid organization in North America (drink). Author of the "Advanced Bonewits Cult Danger Evaluation Frame," used to analyze the harmfulness of organizations, and widely translated and re-published all over the world (drink). Coined the terms "Paleopagan" and "Mesopagan" to contribute to the discussion of kinds of Paganism opened up by the use of the term "Neopagan" (drink). Coined the term "Fam-Trad" Witchcraft (drink).

By my count you have had eight shots and are now seeing double, and I could continue.

Philip Emmons Isaac Bonewits was born on October 1, 1949 in Royal Oak, Michigan, the fourth of five children. He graduated from San Clemente (California) High School at the age of fifteen, attended one year of junior college, and subsequently graduated from the University of California at Berkeley in 1970 with a degree in Magic and Thaumaturgy (signed, he was proud to point out, by then-governor Ronald Reagan). His unusual degree garnered some media attention, which led to a book contract. *Real Magic: An Introductory Treatise on the Basic Principles of Yellow Magic* was published in 1971 and is still considered a classic. In 2003, *PanGaia Magazine* did a special issue on "best books." *Real Magic* was listed as #3 of the top ten "Classics:"

> *"Groundbreaking and thought-provoking, this seminal work of magical theory was perhaps the first logical, rigorously sensible look at magic: how it works, why it works, and how you can use it. No serious student should miss the chance to enjoy Bonewits' precise and dryly amusing prose. Special attention should be paid to how Real Magic handles the interplay of magic and morality, as well as the clear, concise, and brilliant simplification of the universal laws of magic."*

Isaac Bonewits wrote seven books and co-authored one. He recorded two albums (and part of a third) of mostly original Pagan music, published magazines, wrote innumerable essays, founded several organizations, married five times, fathered one child, and died far, far too young.

He had a questing, constantly active mind. Whether arguing theology or forming elaborate puns, Isaac was always thinking, always "on," always fully engaged. He was funny, brilliant, obnoxious, and absolutely committed to saving the world.

His life was always about religion, from his youthful goal of becoming a Catholic priest, to his brief foray in the Church of Satan at the age of 17 (documented in Isaac's essay "My Satanic Adventure"), to becoming a member of the Reformed Druids of North America a year later. Druidism became his true calling and his life's passion. Although a Wiccan High Priest in multiple traditions and a member of other paths as well, it was as a Druid that he was most himself.

They say Libras are the marrying sign. A double Libra, Isaac married five times. I was his fourth wife (from 1988-1998), and we had a son, Arthur Lipp-Bonewits, born in 1990. When Steve Jobs died, I said to Arthur, "I think I know now how to describe your father." Like Jobs, Isaac Bonewits was a *thought leader*. He was creative, inventive, and a leader of Pagan groups, but most importantly, he was a thinker. Isaac was among the handful of people responsible for shaping and reshaping the nature of the modern Pagan community. Since he was a leader of ideas, it is impossible for me to say if Isaac was first or foremost in any number of areas, but that doesn't matter. He was out there, ahead of the curve, speaking, writing, thinking, shaping, demanding. We can be better, he said, we can be our best selves.

It is fitting that the motto he chose for Ár nDraíocht Féin: A Druid Fellowship (ADF), the Druid organization he formed in 1983, was a question: *Why Not Excellence?* It was Isaac's nature to question: What is this? What more is there? What more can we do? What more can we be? Why are things this way? What value does this express? Is this the value we *want* to express? He stood in front of the Pagan community and asked these questions and demanded answers, or demanded, at least, that you ask too.

He asked if the Pagan community really needed "grandmother stories" and fake paleolithic roots in order to be valid and vital. He asked if the rules normally applied to magic made sense. He asked why we weren't researching paleopaganism more, and he did the research, and wrote about his results. There were many scholars more learned than Isaac, but his greatness was in holding up the scholarship in front of the Pagan community and asking "Have you seen this? Does it impact your Paganism? How?"

The ADF study program was a shining example of Isaac's creative output and of his vision for the Pagan community. Rigorous, diverse, and difficult, its very existence asked a question: What do we say when we say "Priest" or "Priestess" in Paganism, and is it enough?

The ADF study program has changed over the years, and I am not familiar with its current structure. As originally designed, it demanded study in ritual design, performance, comparative religion, meditation, psychology, counseling, and physical well-being, among other things. In his vision statement for ADF, Isaac wrote:

"In ADF we believe that excellence in clergy training and practice is vital for any healthy, growing religion. To that end we are attempting to create a professional clergy training program equal in difficulty and superior in results to anything done by the world's other religions. Unlike many alternate religions, we will never have 'instant initiations' into our clergy."

Isaac was a ladies man, a punster, and the life of the party. He had a loud, barking laugh. He had no sense of time and was incapable of punctuality. He loved science fiction, Irish whiskey, Victorian novels, loud colors, and sushi. He made a terrific chicken soup. He knew needlepoint, played the Irish harp, and liked t-shirts with silly sayings.

He had no appreciation for rock and roll. Deeply countercultural, and proud to bear the label "aging hippie," he may well have been the only person in Berkeley in the late 1960s who didn't see a relationship between the counterculture and rock music.

Despite being very cerebral (he used to say he had his feet planted firmly in mid-air) he was also a sensualist: He loved food, drink, sex, laughter, and sensory experience of all kinds. He spoke with a Midwestern twang, had a California mindset, and lived the last twenty-two years of his life in the New York metropolitan area. He loved aging; he was a curmudgeon when he was too young to pull it off, so the premature gray (a wide stripe down the middle of his head by the time he was twenty) suited him.

I miss him.

Isaac Bonewits died on August 12, 2010, after a short battle with cancer. He loved life and wanted every last minute of it. Upon his death, the Gods opened Their arms and embraced one of Their own.

Ted Andrews
(1952-2009)

by Shea Morgan

Animal-Speak. That is one of the first books I was repeatedly told to read. I wondered why. What is it that is so special about this book? Who is this Ted Andrews? A trip to a local bookstore, and I had my own copy.

I had started on the path of the witch, but as everyone knows, there are many different paths that converge even within witchcraft. Like many who come to this path, I spent years doing comparative religious study before I became a witch. Once I started in earnest as a witch, I began with my own solitary study and practice. Then, I started taking classes on intuition, psychic development and more – though from teachers who would describe themselves as something other than a witch, and I did not tell them the word I used to identify myself. Along the way, I read *Animal-Speak: The Spiritual and Magical Powers of Creatures Great and Small*, and started to watch the way of the animals. I had not yet learned that I was hearing their voices and messages already – I just needed to stop, be silent and truly listen to their story.

I met Ted Andrews during the two years that I spent with a small group solely dedicated to shamanism. He did a book signing and taught an afternoon program that spring on animals at a pagan shop in St. Louis. Before this, though I had teachers, none of them were witches or really on the pagan path. I had never really spent time talking with a witch or someone identifying as a pagan, though I already was a frequent visitor to this shop, and had met witches in Salem, MA where I bought my first witchcraft books years before. Everything comes in its own time.

Ted Andrews was approachable, as was his writing, which is part of what makes him so attractive to so many. His books are readable and easy to understand, yet contain amazing insights on so many shamanic, magickal and witchcraft related subjects. Yet, he is the first author that many read, because *Animal-Speak* is more main stream, more known and acceptable to the general public. It is less scary and intimidating. It is safe. You can tell people that you just bought this great book on animals, and it is somehow okay. You can also recommend it to others who have a need, but have not yet quite realized their path. I believe Ted Andrews has been responsible for gently bringing many onto the path of the witch and to the pagan community at large with his messages and the messages of those spirits and guides whose stories he so gracefully told.

He was a magickal speaker. In both my experience in the class with him, and in his CDs, it was clear that he could weave a yarn with the beauty that the spider weaves its web. His love for animals – and their love of him – shone through his words in such a way that had the power to move you and help you reach understanding. You felt the presence of the animals and their spirits. He helped you find and realize those "ah-ha" moments that we prize so greatly on this path. He was present – simply present in the moment, and you could see it in his eyes.

One of the things that struck me the most was his love for and description of animals at which most would turn up their noses. I mean, Skunk? Vultures? Spiders? Really? But he made their stories into a thing of beauty – because it is about their medicine and their own unique skills and abilities to heal. What a gift in this he gave me and the world.

He made the story of the opossum beautiful as well – this little, persistent and quiet creature who teaches us of the wisdom in stillness and silence. He made you want to have this creature as your animal ally, what he called an animal totem. Opossum has come to me over the years, and it has been an ally, though it was not until years later that I truly understood its message, and its message is profound.

One of the things he said about opossums that was surprising to me, was that if you see an opossum dead on the side of the road, to get out and check it as it may have babies still alive somehow in a pocket inside of it. He told stories of saving these baby opossums. I never looked the same at an opossum again. Each time I drove by an animal's sacrifice on the road, I did what he recommended and sent a blessing of peace to it. Ted Andrews said that it was an honor for an animal to feel safe on your property to come onto your land and chose to die there.

Ted Andrew's message was to honor the animal by studying it in all ways, developing a relationship with it, bringing its qualities into your life, and then it will truly become medicine for you. Another message that stuck with me over the years, tied into this, was that the animals you are most afraid of have the most to teach you.

He had several key messages on how to study and honor the animals. Study its biological rhythm. Study its natural characteristics and qualities. Look at how the animal adapts to survive. Consider the environment where it is found and how it relates to other animals. Try to connect with the animal by studying its movements and imitate it.

In my first shamanic journey that I ever did, in the autumn six months prior to meeting Ted Andrews, the Black Panther and Hawk came to me. As I sat in his class that spring, literally his first message in this talk, though he was speaking about no animal being more spiritual than another, was about the Black Panther. I knew what I had read about the panther, but was just beginning to truly know it. Ted Andrews described the Black Panther as a healer, but one that has trauma before healing takes place and said that it was not as gentle of a healer as the Vulture. Vulture again? I later learned to understand the beauty of Vulture's medicine as an ally as well.

He also said that Black Panther teaches how we come into our own power. Much of my journey since meeting Ted Andrews has been along those lines, and I have made great strides. Ted Andrews is the first teacher that I spoke to about my black panther, which was still at the point where I was still trying to figure it all out – what is this animal? What is this relationship? What does it mean in my life? I asked him about my black panther and described my journey. He said that as the Black Panther was taking me to other animals, that it was what he called my watcher. His words and his kindness helped me to begin to develop my relationship with the Black Panther. Where Ted Andrews left off, Christopher Penczak appeared to help me on my journey, and the Black Panther became my Fetch Beast. Today, we do not have Ted Andrews here with us for everyone to hear these messages directly, but we have his books and the messages of the animals shine through the words on the page.

Ted Andrews also introduced me to Hawk, one of my allies. He said that many times students would come to him and then later would see Hawk everywhere, and Hawk would become an ally for them. He would open the door that Hawk was already waiting for you to walk through. In my case, it was the Black Panther, Hawk and Vulture. He shared his current with me to awaken all of that which was just beneath the surface, and he showed up at just the right time in my life given my recent journey experiences with these animals.

After I met Ted Andrews, the visits from Hawk and Vulture accelerated. Every time I drove anywhere, particularly to our family farm, there was Hawk and Vulture. He was right.

He had us do a journey that he called an "exercise" – yes, definitely approachable. He said it would bring about encounters with animals and a response in our normal, everyday life. When he took us into the journey, there was Hawk, Oak, the Black Panther, Horse, Deer, and before I left the journey, I took Black Panther into myself. These have all become strong allies for me over the years.

Ted Andrews had a profound impact on my spiritual path and practice. He died on October 24, 2009, the day before my birthday. I felt his death strongly. Our circle, soon to become a coven, included him in our Samhain ritual that fall and honored his presence in our lives and the gifts he gave us. There were many changes in my life at that time, and the Morrighan was just beginning the process where she would eventually become my Matron. I felt his presence a great deal that fall, and he still continued to give me his gifts and markers on my path after his death.

I found and started to use his *Animal Wise Tarot* deck around that time, and I found such wisdom in it. For years, I had not been able to really understand the tarot. I had practiced with it, studied it on my own, but it just would not click for me. Tarot would not speak to me. When I picked up this deck, the animals on its cards and their messages in his pages really helped me to bridge the gap between the animals and the tarot. It was another "ah-ha" moment that he helped me to find along my path. I now have many tarot decks and use them regularly in many different ways. Each time, I think of his gift at making the tarot accessible in a way that I could truly begin to understand its wisdom.

Another thing struck me after he left this earth. I had several of his books, but mostly the ones related to animals. As I looked into it more, and studied him more as a way of honoring his presence on this earth and the gifts he gave me, I found a breadth of writings on so many topics – trees, plants, elements, Faery, Tree of Life/Qabala, magick and more. I have quite a collection of his books in my mystical library and feel I have still barely scratched the surface of the wisdom they contain.

What a legacy and gift he has left generations to come. I only wish they could hear his voice, but now it will be whispers on the winds and from the animals and spirits who greatly loved him.

ANDREW CHUMBLEY
(1967-2004)

By Dan Fox

Andrew Chumbley (September 15, 1967 – September 15, 2004), practitioner of the East Anglia tradition of witchcraft, Magister of the UK-based Cultus Sabbati from 1991 until his death, succeeded by Daniel A. Schulke, member of Peter Carroll's Illuminates of Thanateros, member, from 1993 through 1999, of Kenneth Grant's O.T.O., was a writer, poet and artist.

Chumbley defined what he called the `Sabbatic Craft', a way to describe elements of witch-lore, Sabbath mythology, and imagery, employed into the craft into which he was inducted. Founded upon two lineages of traditional witchcraft, the Sabbatic Craft pre-dated the modern revivalist forms of witchcraft, classified today as Wicca.

An unknown member of the Sabbatic Craft described their tradition:

In a historic sense, the Sabbatic Craft is usefully set against a background of both rural folk-magic, the so-called Cunning-craft, and the learned practices of European high ritual magic...It is a body of magical initiates who practice both solitary and collective rituals, whose lineal tradition descends, in both oral and textual forms, from surviving 19th century cunning-folk and ritual magic practice. It is not claimed that they practice the very same rites, spells and so forth of the 16/17th century cunning-folk, for it is the very nature of things to change their form and manner.

Entrance into the Sabbatic Craft was through invitation only—those that ask must be refused. If invited, the Sabbatic tradition is first taught with a nine-month probationary period while the character of the initiate is judged, followed by a rite of initiation leading to a year and a day tutelage, in which the candidate is "led around the circle in a complete circumambulation of mind, body and spirit," along with the passing down of artifacts from master to apprentice.

Michael Howard, publisher of the UK-based occult magazine, The Cauldron, described Chumbley as:

...a man of the land, rural in both birth and character. He fitted totally within the traditional archetypal parameters of the English (and specifically Essex) cunning man...To outsiders Andrew could sometimes appear to be aloof, intense and serious to the point of obsession...However, if he met kindred spirits of sincerity and honor, who shared his interests and serious intent, he would willingly go out of his way to offer them help and guidance on the Path...In fact he was a natural teacher and, like all good occult teachers, acted as a catalyst in the lives of his students.

Chumbley promoted what he called "Transcendental Sorcery", the doctrine that all forms of magick arose from a single point or source, a singularity he called "Magical Quintessence." He defined magick as "the transmutability of the Quintessence of all nature" and sorcery as "the knowledge of the universal points of transmutation. Its art is to cultivate the ability to manipulate these foci of power in accordance with Will, Desire and Belief."

Chumbley described "willed dreaming", probably a combination of lucid dreaming and shamanic journeying, as a means of interacting directly with "the High Sabbat", loosely defined as spiritual dimensions. He said:

Every word, deed and thought can empower, magnetise, and establish points of receptivity for a magical dream, likewise any of these means can do the opposite – fixating perception in a manner that is not receptive – that seals the soul in the body instead of enabling it to go forth at will.

Chumbley also used trance, automatic writing, and automatic drawing to gain magickal knowledge. He said:

Dreaming and the mutual translation of dreamt ritual and ritual-as-dreamt form the basic rationale and context for our work. The active discourse between initiates and our spirit-patrons inspires and motivates this dreaming. This is demonstrably manifest in the magical artistry of individual initiates, whether through text, ritual performance, song, tapestry, craftsmanship, or image.

Within the witchcraft tradition, Chumbley's influences appear to be: the Qabalah; Enochian Magick; the Hermetic Order of the

Golden Dawn; Crowley's Thelemic School; as well as the works of Austin Osman Spare and Grant. Outside of the witchcraft tradition, he was influenced by Sufish, left-hand Tantra, and Petro Voodoo. The neo-Sufi Idries Shah was cited in Qutub, particulary his theories concerning possible connections between witchcraft and various cults such as the Yezidi, Mandaeans, Sufis and Zoroastrians.

Chumbley spoke out strongly about the Left vs. Right-hand-path:

In scholarly terms...(LHP and RHP) are theoretical constructs...which—via a metaphor of cheirality (hands)—are...used...to distinguish between differing forms and interpretive levels of magical practice...they have become 'loaded terms' which may be considered collations of assorted polarised associations: good/bad, black/white...symbolic/literal, diurnal/nocturnal...all of which are adaptable in the personal worldview of an occultist and thus without definitive objectivity...LHP/RHP describe the magical forms...under the auspices of one's opposing but mutually complementary hands, literally... both are deemed differing means to potentially identical ends, though symbolically the right hand governs the beneifc method and the left malefic... we are each a body with two hands, and though one hand may not know well the deeds of the other, both serve one master.

Chumbley's thoughts on initiatory practice is as follows:

If you call upon the Gods and they answer, who is there to oppose or to challenge the integrity of your Path?

Concealed within the myth (of the Fall, Lucifer, and the children of Cain) there is an initiated doctrine regarding the secret nature of Divinity and the evolution of man.

...it is deemed needful for the Seeker to cast himself into the battleground of attainment—to willfully enter situations of adversity and therein confront all and aught which will necessitate the honing of intent...the practicioner consciously draws himself into that which conflicts with the direction and nature of his intent. Embracing greater and greater circumstances of adversity the practicioner is forced to exert himself to greater and greater degrees in discipline.

Chumbley's writings were extremely inaccessible, as hard to understand and digest as the works of Aleister Crowley, perhaps in response to peer pressure that he should not reveal such information to the general public.

Chumbley published his first book in 1992, *The Azoëtia*, a grimoire, the core text for the study and practice of the Sabbatic Craft, with a second edition published on Samhain in 2002, labeled the Sethos Edition. Relating the Three Great Rites of Ingress, Congress, and Egress, including a description of the 22 Letters of the Sorcerers Alphabet, Chumbley presents "Will, Desire, and Belief" as a threefold unity, an idea coming from Grant's writings, ultimately derived from Spare. Sigils and magickal glyphs abound in the work, presumably a result from automatic writing and drawing.

Chumbley published his second book in 1995, *Qutub: The Point*. Michael Staley, editor of Starfire Magazine, described the work thus:

> *Qutub is the Point. Its root, QTB, enumerates as 111. We have immediately the essence of the matter, since 'The Point' suggests Kether and 111 suggests Aleph, the Fool, Atu 0, etc. 'The Point' is the deliciously-sharp point of insight into the reality beyond and underlying its expression in terms of duality. The idea called forth by the correspondence with Atu 0 is that of the illumined adept who has experienced this Point, realised its immanence in everything and at all times, and who is thereby liberated whilst yet living. It is this delicious insight which is conveyed by the very best of 'mystical poetry'.*

Chumbley published his third book in 2000, *ONE: The Grimoire of the Golden Toad*, a personal account of the traditional East Anglian ritual called "The Waters of the Moon."

Chumbley had more works that were not published for public consumption. One of these was *The Draconian Grimoire: The Dragon-Book of Essex*, which is reported to be a follow-up to *Azoëtia*, of which only 10 copies were published for initiates. Chumbley referred to another follow-up called *The Auraeon*, for solitary initiation, which may or may not have been published. Another reported work was *The Greene Gospel*, privately published. Chumbley also authored a series of hand-written and illustrated books known as the "Unique Transmission Series".

Chumbley died on September 15, 2004, on his 37th birthday, of an asthma-induced heart attack.

Dave Evans said that "...his book values at second hand resales, which were already high, increased in an exponential and quite insane fashion within hours of his death becoming known."

Passing the Rattle: The Goddess Magic of Shekhinah Mountainwater (1939-2007)

By Silvermoone

It all started with *Ariadne's Thread: A Workbook of Goddess Magic*. My exposure to woman-centered magick, to the flow of going deeper within the Mysteries of the Goddess, all began with Shekhinah Mountainwater, a woman who embodied the beauty of the storyteller. Shekhinah described herself as a *muse-ical mystical woman*, and it was from her poetry that I embraced a calling...

A foremother of the Womanspirit Movement, Shekhinah Mountainwater was born Ellen Adler on October 24, 1939, raised in New York by her Atheist/Marxist parents, she didn't experience the kind of spiritual conditioning in her youth the way many who came to her for teachings and healings had experienced. She went on a spiritual quest in search of the deeper spirituality of understanding the affirmation of herself as woman.

Her path led her from Judaism, Hinduism, Buddhism, Kaballah, Jungianism and Christianity (to name a few), finding gems in each of the journeys that would allow her to go deeper within her path. It wasn't until she entered, what she called, the Goddess Gate, that she recognized the relationship between her and the Goddess, from there her devotion to Her began.

Much like Shekhinah, I grew up without spiritual conditioning as others I knew had. Though I was thirsty for a clearer understanding of Self and of life, my purpose, I didn't know where to begin, though I remember beginning with nature Herself. The Goddess Gate revealed itself to me, through the works of many wonderful Pagan authors, but it wasn't until I "met" Shekhinah that I would understand the beauty of Goddess Magic.

As a member of her Moonspells group online, Shekhinah embraced each syster there, whether you were on the path for 10 years or 10 minutes, she opened her heart and was willing to share her knowledge and experience of the Goddess, and was eager to hear your own experiences. Never interested in monetary wealth, her work was about Service for the Greater Good...she exemplified that to her very last breath, and beyond.

A Priestess of Aphrodite, Shekhinah has shared stories of how as a feminist lesbian witch she saw her love dwindle over the years in comparison to her younger, heterosexual years, which prompted her to focus more of her energy on her devotion to Aphrodite, both in Her guise of Goddess of Love as well as facing Her dark side of the death and rebirth of love. Through her lessons learned from working with Aphrodite on spells of love, she described herself as the "wounded healer", hoping that systers of the next generation would benefit and learn from the pains she experienced, though grateful for.

In 1991 Shekhinah published *Ariadne's Thread: A Workbook of Goddess Magic*, which became an inspiration to a great movement. It inspired me. It continues to inspire me. Shekhinah didn't need to talk about lineage or who she was connected to; *Ariadne's Thread* brought women together in magick. Her book was a travel guide to explore yourself deeply, and to come to the entrance of your own Goddess Gate. 13 Cycles, Three Passages, from Gathering, Spinning to Weaving, her book became a guide to women that took us through creating the journey and meeting the Triple Goddess, through the holydays of the Craft, to deepening our magickal skills of ritual, spellwork and divination. It became the start of a movement that would only continue to grow.

Shekhinah created her own divination system, *Womanrunes*, on the Summer Solstice in 1987. She had been looking for a woman-identified divination system, and after creating her *Shekhinah Tarot*, a friend urged her to do the same for the runes. Years later she added several runes to the final creation and completed a *Womanrunes* booklet devoted to teaching this system of divination. She always graciously encouraged anyone to use this system and to share its wisdom with others. That's who Shekhinah was...the magick she experienced was the magick she shared, without hesitation.

Over the years of service, Shekhinah offered a new way of approaching magick, whether it be her divination system of tarot or runes, or the creation of her *Moonwheels* calendar, and for me personally, her permissive nature of exploring magick, ritual and the Mysteries of the Goddess was something I resonated deeply with. She lived actively with the Five Keys of Magic: To See, To Know, To Will, To Dare, and To Keep Silent, and with that magic she inspired and laid the ground work for the Goddess Movement to grow stronger.

In the Afterward of *Ariadne's Thread* (pg 302), she says, "*So our movement grows, and I feel satisfied that I am doing my part.*" The role she played and the generations of women who connected to her work, to her teachings, to her, we are a better movement for it. Below is my offer of gratitude and honor to the work she has done, how her work so greatly affected me (and continues to), and her teaching of how the ultimate beauty of loving the Goddess is loving the Self. I wrote this in May 2009 for a woman's circle I was facilitating, though this ritual could easily be done solitary and is encouraged.

This ritual is both inspired and adapted from the works of Shekhinah Mountainwater.

Awakening the Inner Lover

Create sacred space and cast the circle:

The circle is cast
The spell is made fast
Only the good
Can enter herein
The magic is made
So let it begin!

Call to the Seven Directions with sacred sound

Invocation to Aphrodite (lighting a pink/red or white colored candle):

Aphrodite!
From our hearts and from our blood, we call to You.
May Your beauty be our beauty;
May Your love be our love;

May Your strength be our strength;
And may we align ourselves and awaken to the Spiral of Creation You weave,
from the blossoming Earth to the rainbowed Sky.
We honor Your presence with us.
Welcome Sweet Maiden!

This time is now given to each woman to share her own experiences of love; of self-love, of honored or neglected/rejected love...how do we love ourselves? This is the time and this is the place to free ourselves from our own personal binds.

After sharing our stories we begin the healing and awakening of Aphrodite's love within ourselves:

Aphrodite's Lover's Blessing: Awakening the Goddess of Love within.

Items needed: Bowl/chalice/vessel of spring water charged with rose quartz chips (one for each woman) and rose petals floating in the water.

Take the rose quartz chip and place at each power point (physically or energetically), saying:

Third-eye – *May Aphrodite bless you with Her love.*
Lips – *Your lips that speak in love*
Heart – drawing the *Rune of Love* (see *Ariadne's Thread*) – *Your heart that beats with desire*
Breasts – *Your breasts that give life and beauty*
Stomach – *Your womb and yoni that nurtures and gives pleasure*
Feet – *Your feet that walk in Her ways.*

Each woman offers the blessing to another, taking the rose quartz with them back to the circle. Sit in circle, tightly together, focusing on Aphrodite's blessing and love. Empower yourselves and open your heart chakra.

Sit cross-legged and let the tips of your index finger and thumb touch, placing the rose quartz chip in between these fingers. Put your left hand on your left knee and your right hand in front of the lower part of your breast bone (a bit above the solar plexus). Concentrate on the heart chakra, feeling the rose quartz at your fingertips stir an awakening within you, and visualize pink mist surrounding you. Chant these three words as you envision sealing in the vibrations of love into your being:

YAM MAAA AH

YAM = Opening the heart
MAAA = Honoring the Goddess within and without
AH = Generating compassion

Continue to chant, raising the energy and raising the vibration so that the circle is flowing in love. Flow with the chant, be the words, be the love.

When complete, look at your systers, at these women in circle with you, those who have shared their heart-felt stories of love, who have blessed you as you have blessed them. Honor them, looking deeply into their eyes, saying:

You are a Goddess of Love.

When complete, breathe in that love and ground yourself.
Thank Aphrodite for Her presence and blessings.
Release the 7 Directions.
Close circle, saying:

May the circle never be broken
May the earth always be whole
May the rattle ever be shaken
May the Goddess live in our souls.
Blessed Be!

Shawn Poirier
(1967-2007)

By Leanne Marrama

He stood out like a sore thumb prancing around Pagan Pride. He looked like Rob Zombie breaking into Woodstock. He was towering over six feet tall, with black eyeliner and a long black trench coat.

I stood before him, a meager five-foot-one with my colorful green cape and plastic flowers in my hair. I was horrified when he took me by the hand and pranced me around the circle. He defied everything I ever read about Wicca and Paganism. When we parted he called me magical and a witch. It made no sense to me. But he left me thinking.... Yes, I thought. See I was an unhappy soccer mom who just wanted to worship the goddess and find joy. How could I be magical when I felt so terribly alone; so useless.

After several random meetings in Salem, I discovered that this was Shawn Poirier, witch, psychic and my future best friend and High Priest.

Shawn Louis Poirier was originally from New Bedford Massachusetts and moved to Salem Mass when he was in his early 20s. Shawn always attributed his magic to his Irish grandmother. He often told the tale of the day he learned how to fly a broom. Fly a broom you say? Oh yes we flew brooms when we were with Shawn. He, like his grandmother, handed me a broom and told me to fly. Unlike a six year old Shawn, I laughed, while the young boy listened to his grandmother and ran with that besom till he nearly collapsed. Feeling defeated, Shawn laid his head on his Nana's lap and listened to her teach him how to "relax and feel your body soar". This was the start of his astral travel. When this was taught to me, this was the start of my path, faith and career I still follow today.

Magic was part of Shawn's every day existence. He never doubted. He saw magic and witchcraft as a fact, a science and a way of life. The first time I entered his home I was slightly scared when I met Claudia and Robert. They were sitting on his kitchen table as he was drinking and eating. You see Claudia and Robert are human skulls.

He saw my reservations and said, "are you a witch or not." Of course he made me hold them, because that was Shawn. Shawn felt witchcraft and magic were not taught in a classroom. Witchcraft was only glanced at in a book. True magic was discovered by living it and being it and apparently, at this moment, touching it. The minute I held these skulls something opened up in me. Let's call it my third eye. Let's call it knowledge. He got me thinking again. I realized these were not just magical tools; these were members of the family. These were his friends and soon became mine.

Over the years I watched this man do so many amazing things. His desire to help people was often overshadowed by his overwhelming desire to break rules and create controversy. In 1989, Shawn attained status as a legally ordained minister of the craft. Soon after this time he was among the Witches who founded W.A.R.D. (Witches Against Religious Discrimination), an anti-defamation organization aimed at correcting the many misconceptions about Witchcraft, and assisted in his role as Massachusetts chapter head.

Much like his business partner and best friend Christian Day, no one remembered that their world class event, the Festival of the Dead and Witches' Ball, provided acceptance and joy for so many who visited Salem. Shawn's Annual Séance was a beautiful memorial done in honor of his first teacher, Dottie, who had passed many years ago. He had been able to reach out to the dead and give messages to comfort those in grief. Not an easy task I learned.

Shawn taught under the title of Salem Tradition of Witchcraft. He said, "The Salem Tradition of Witchcraft is both an old way and a new way. While in keeping with my old world Witch training, I have managed to combine my skills with the type of glittering magic found only in Salem." Our coven, Raven Moon, was a family coven. We didn't have esbats; we had monthly coven dinner. There were no rules or laws I had ever seen in any witchcraft book. Once, part of my training was to speak in rhyme all day to learn how to present myself in circle. Every ritual was done with an element of surprise, yet our traditions were strong and true. I was proud to be initiated on Halloween night on the dark of the moon, signing my promise into the Book of Blood, only months later to be elevated to High Priestess because he wanted to...Yes, Shawn worked with his gut, his magical soul and no one was going tell him any different. He taught us how to work with the element of Air by riding roller coasters and yelling out intentions. He had us connect with Fire by walking on it. We ran around in graveyards at 2 A.M. to understand Earth and we swam in the ocean to see the gifts in Water.

March 18, 2007 Shawn left this world to fly on brooms with his nana. He left behind one of his greatest gifts; us, His Coven, His family. Shawn's greatest magical lesson was teaching us to believe in our own powers and magic. He taught us "eat the chicken and spit out the bones". Since his passing so many of my coven mates have changed and grown. Christian Day still runs the Festival of the Dead as well as Hex and Omen, shops in Salem, MA. Coven members have been seen on *Ghost Adventures,* some have had babies and others have got married and have amazing jobs and own homes. I, Leanne Marrama, now host his séance in honor of him, teach students of my own and on my kitchen table when my students come to visit me, they may be frightened too by a human skull named Claudia that I met so long ago.

Part Four: Personal Guides on the Path

Bragi and the Dead

By Galina Krasskova

Honoring the dead, paying homage to one's ancestors, is a very important part of the Northern Tradition. It took me years and years to realize exactly how important it truly is and even longer to 'get my ancestral house in order,' as certain of my colleagues might put it, but once I did, it transformed my spiritual practice. There is very little more important than properly honoring the dead. Those who have come before us, whose struggles and failures, victories and sacrifices, joys and sorrows paved the way for our own being, and for the survival of our line, are owed our respect and remembrance. Moreover, they have a vested and very personal interest in helping us succeed. To have one's ancestral house in order is to have a well spring of assistance, strength, protection, and power at one's back. That is no small thing. I have also found that if one has a deep, reciprocal relationship with one's own ancestors, they can teach a person how to get one's relationship with the Gods right. They can teach us how to do this thing called living rightly, honorably, and well.

Because we as 21st century Americans are living in a dominant culture radically cut off from its own ancestral traditions; because few of us grew up in households where honoring the dead was consciously practiced as a religious act, and because we have so few public models for how to get this "right," it can be difficult at first to really ground oneself in the wholeness of these practices. Of course the ancestors will do their best to help, but in addition, I have found help from an unexpected source: the God Bragi.

I had never considered a connection between Bragi and honoring the ancestors until I was working on an article about Him as part of the Deity of the Month series that I run on my blog (*http://krasskova.weebly.com/blog.html*). I was formatting a ritual to Bragi that a colleague had submitted to me and upon reading through his ritual, I had a moment of enlightenment. While not a God of the dead per se, Bragi, as Skald of the Gods is perfectly positioned to teach us how to enhance our relationships with our ancestors. Skalds are, in their own way, liminal figures. They are truth speakers, tale weavers, and through the power of their gifts, they weave the threads of the past into a cohesive tapestry for the present. They navigate those often misty channels between the living and the dead, between all that has passed before, and all that will be given to the future.

Part of a Skald or Bard's job was to facilitate remembrance of the dead. Through the telling of their stories, the singing of songs, the speaking and sharing forth of their names and deeds, the dead, our honored ancestors, are able to draw near and live again and we are able to learn from their stories. The most sacred duty a Skald has is the duty of remembrance. He or she is able to teach the rest of us how to connect to our ancestors, how to honor them, how to maintain that most sacred connection. Moreover, Skalds are our tradition keepers, vessels of living memory.

Our ancestors had predominantly oral traditions. While they may have possessed writing, the dominant means of cultural transmission was not through the written word. This means that remembrance, values, connections to the ancestors, to the past, to the Holy Powers, and to the future was all woven together and maintained through the sharing of stories and songs. This is how the tradition thrived. There is a saying in Lukumi: 'when an elder dies, a whole world dies with him.' This is all the more so of a Bard or Skald, who would have spent years and years studying the traditions of his or her people. They are, by the very nature of what they do and know, bridges between the world of the living and the world of the dead. The knowledge they bear and transform through the act of performing is a knowledge of culture told through the deeds of the dead, and that knowledge is transmitted through the creative synergy between listener and performer, just as the skills of a Bard would be transmitted from master to student through the process of training.

When a master Skald passes on a song or intricate musical passage to a student, he or she is not just teaching technique; he is initiating that student into a world of tradition stretching back to the very beginnings of the craft itself, a craft that was born out of the deeds and longings, joys and sorrows of our ancestors. The teacher is the living conduit for a tradition that passed through him from his teacher, to his teacher from his teacher's teacher, and so forth. It is transmission through the body of those actually performing the craft.

Likewise, that collected tradition and all the knowledge that it holds is opened like a treasure box whenever a skilled bard or skald performs.

In her cultural history of ballet, author Jennifer Homans discusses the tradition of classical ballet, which shares with ancient bards and skalds both intensive training and the physical as the vehicle of knowledge-transmission:

"Ballet, then, is an art of memory, not history…Memory is central to the art, and dancers are trained, as the ballerina Natalia Makarova once put it, to "eat" dances – to ingest them and make them part of who they are. These are physical memories; when dancers know a dance, they know it in their muscles and bones. Recall is sensual…and brings back not just the steps but also the gestures and feel of the movement…Thus ballet repertory is not recorded in books or libraries: it is held instead in the bodies of dancers." (Homans, p. xix).

It is much the same with the gifts of the Skald. Here, it is not only the physical and technical prowess of the 'tradition-performer' that comes into play, but also the willingness of the audience to listen and engage with and so become part of that process of cultural transmission. We who carry our ancestors in our bones: in our blood, marrow, skin, appearance, and DNA celebrate them and carry their stories forward through the physical process of listening and interacting with those who hold one of the keys to opening the doorway between then and now. Telling our stories, honoring our dead, celebrating through song and tales and music and dance…these are important parts of rebuilding a tradition. That restoration does not occur through clinging to the written word. The written word provides history. It is a thing to be studied. Memory however is something quite different. It provides for the future and it is a thing to be lived.

It's important that we remember the dead. It's important that we remember our ancestors, honor them, and call upon them regularly, helping them to remain part and parcel of our families and by extension communities. Honoring the dead benefits everyone. They provide strength, wisdom, guidance, and protection to their descendants. They lived, in many cases, the very traditions that we as Pagans and Heathens today are trying to restore. They can help root us in the origins of those traditions, origins that we have long forgotten. Their stories, their deeds – good and bad—formed us and the world we live in. Because of the latter, they too have an obligation to find, create, and maintain balance. They too share an obligation to restore right relationship between the living and the dead, between the living and the land, between the living and the Holy Powers, on all possible levels.

Our world is hopelessly out of balance. So many indigenous traditions, including our own as Heathens and Pagans, have been sundered. It's going to take both sides of that equation to return to some semblance of right relationship: it's going to take the living and the dead working in tandem. Bragi can help teach us how to do this.

Sometimes it can be very difficult to know where to start when it comes to honoring the ancestors. We don't have a conscious cultural tradition today of doing so. Most of us (in American culture at least) did not grow up in homes with active ancestor shrines. I believe remembering the dead is almost a genetic impulse, but we live today in cultures that try to sanitize everything, and sometimes even to pretend that death doesn't exist. Then there is so much abuse and damage so often perpetrated within families. It can be especially hard to move back past that to establish a working relationship with one's own ancestors. Sometimes doing so can take an awful lot of hard work and a very long time.

There's no shame in that. When honoring the dead, it's important, very important, to remember that we are not just the product of the past few generations of our line. We have a line of dead going back to the day the first primal critter pulled itself out of the primordial ooze to try a little land living. We have our tribal Mothers and Fathers, ancient ancestors and, very strong who watch over and protect the integrity of the line. We have friends and teachers, mentors, and those who inspire who may or may not be related to us by blood. They are ancestors too. If one is adopted, then one has adopted ancestral lines as well as biological. There is a rich and complex web of connections just waiting to be acknowledged and accessed. That it is difficult doesn't take away from its importance.

One can call on the dead to help forge this connection, but if that is too hard, going to the Gods can also help. Being in right relationship with our dead is part of what it means to live a healthy, whole, spiritually balanced life. This isn't something just for shamans or mystics, spiritworkers or priests to do, it's part and parcel of maintaining a stable household, in other words: something every man, woman, and child should be doing. This is our portion as responsible, hopefully pious human beings and adults.

That doesn't mean one can't call for a little help though. So if you are struggling in learning how to honor the dead, if you find it difficult to make or inhabit that connection, perhaps Bragi might be a good God to seek out for help. The very art and craft of which He is a God, rests on the shoulders of the dead after all. He too has a debt to them and what better way to discharge that debt than by helping us develop that ongoing contact? The skills of a Bard or Skald awaken dormant connections with our past, most especially with our ancestors. Call upon Bragi to help open those doors. Call upon Him joyously so that you might learn to sustain those ancestral threads. Call upon Him and maybe, just maybe, He can help.

Hail Bragi,
Skald of Asgard,
Walking amongst the Worlds,
Singer, Story teller, tale weaver
Speaker for the Dead.
Memory-Keeper
Memory's Teacher.
Hail, Bragi.

References

Homans, Jennifer, *Apollo's Angels: A History of Ballet*. NY: Random House Publishing, (2010).

(When you go to Bragi, it is good, as with any Deity, to go with gifts. I have found that a good and honorable way to honor Bragi, an appropriate offering, is to make a donation in support of musicians or dancers, or to your own community Bard or Skald. I've listed some useful organizations below to which folks might want to donate).

National Endowment for the Arts: *http://www.nea.gov/support/index.html*

Sphinx Organization: *http://www.sphinxmusic.org/index.html*

Tipitina's Foundation: *http://tipitinasfoundation.org/*

Music Therapy Charity: *http://www.musictherapy.org.uk/*

The Actor's Fund: *http://www.actorsfund.org/*

American Guild of Performing Artists: *http://www.musicalartists.org/AGMAReliefFund.html*

The Musicians Benevolent Fund: *http://www.helpmusicians.org.uk/*

Dancers' Career Development: *http://www.thedcd.org.uk/*

Elders of the Coven of the Catta: Lady Phoebe and Lord Merlin

By Gary Lee Hoke

This story of my elders is written at the request of Copper Cauldron Publishing and Christopher Penczak, who are collecting anthologies of elders of the craft. It is distilled from my two books *The History of Dr. Frederick LaMotte Santee and the Coven of the Catta* © 2010 and *Coven of the Catta – Elders and History, Unique Ritual Practices and Spells* © 2010 which contains the first book.

Contact with the Coven of the Catta

We arrived at the book house of the late Dr. Santee's in 1981. My witch girlfriend and I had seen an ad in *Circle Network News* about a coven located in Wapwallopen, about 100 miles northeast of where we resided outside of Harrisburg Pennsylvania. We arrived and were led into his 50,000 volume book house where we were greeted by three elder ladies, Janee the High Priestess, Jeannie and Judy sitting in rocking chairs around a roaring fireplace flanked by large iron cauldrons. It couldn't be more archetypal "witchy". They denied having placed that ad and were amazed at our arrival.

We arrived there one year after Dr. Santee's death and everything was in disarray. The temple was full of items salvaged from Santee's house and the book house had suffered a fire two years previously which left a hole in the roof. We asked for teaching and initiation and Janee A.K.A. Edna Jane Kishbaugh Williams A.K.A. Lady Phoebe Athene Nimue (acronym Lady PAN) accepted us. Their mood was somber as they had lost the center of their coven, Dr Frederick LaMotte Santee A.K.A. Lord Merlin, their High Priest. I will speak much more on them later.

History of the Coven of the Catta

The Coven of the Catta was formed around 1967 by Santee and Phoebe as I shall call them from here on. They both loved cats and supported the Humane Society and gave the coven the totem of the cat Bastet from Egypt. Santee had been familiar with many in the occult world including Sybil Leek. They met in NYC and she was invited to Wapwallopen. When Sybil arrived at the covenstead, according to Phoebe, she and the doctor's secretary-librarian asked her to teach and initiate them into witchcraft to form a coven. Sybil's lineage was from the Coven of the Horsa from the New Forest area SE of London England. She also hung out with and learned a lot from the Gypsies and their magickal ways. Before that the lineage came from Coven of the Red Dragon in Gorge de Loup (Wolf Gorge) in SE France. Santee himself, as I shall expand on later, carried a handful of witchcraft and occult lineages from Europe. The combination became the Coven of the Catta. At first they had their temple in the cellar of Santee's house.

Sometime in the 1970s Dr. Santee had a cinder block building built right next to his house and doctor's office. Over the years he amassed a library that contained 50,000 books on all manner of subjects, from the Greek and Latin classics he loved to history and religion, including a fairly large occult section. There was the main room with a fireplace and his large desk, another room with a round table for classes, a strong vault for the really old tomes dating back to the 17th century and, in the back, a room used for rituals. After the bookhouse was built, they moved their temple from the old to the new one in full ceremonial garb. From 1967 to 1980, the year of Santee's death, the coven flourished with mostly members from the local community. In fact the Coven and the Doctor are somewhat of an urban legend in the area now with rumors of Satanism and cat sacrifices! The fact is they were just practicing good ole white witchcraft from everything I can see. They also published a newsletter called *The Cat's Tale* in which various articles, spells and pictures were submitted by the main coven members.

In 1979 someone broke into the bookhouse to steal some of the doctor's 17th century books and gold and silver bars, and then set fire to the place to cover it up. The resident cat Bastet was killed in the fire but left this mark. The place never fully repaired and the doctor died the next year.

And that brings us up to 1981 when my Priestess Lady Iska Nuit Aradia and I arrived. Over the next few months we drove almost a hundred miles north, cleaned out the temple, re-painted the three circles as prescribed, and rituals began again with some people from that area and mostly witches who came up from the Harrisburg area 8 times a year for Sabbats. I drove up even more often to hand copy my own three Books of Shadows from Lady Phoebe's two books, which is over three hundred pages of material.

Unfortunately when she passed all her possessions, including these books, were just thrown into the dumpster. Most of the material is from the books on witchcraft available in the 1970s, and the rituals mostly from Lady Sheba's Books of Shadows. What Phoebe taught was what is called today "Old Guard Wicca". We were taught to do the rituals as they were written in the books with no additions or subtractions. I suppose it is similar to a Catholic doing the Mass over and over. It may sound boring but there is a certain comfort in this type of ritual. The rituals for the Sabbats were almost exactly alike except for short lines and ritual actions that were specific to the season. When it was time for our third degree initiation in which we were supposed to write our own ritual, Phoebe was not pleased with what we put together because it was too far off the original rituals. Away from the Sabbats we would often drive up and take Phoebe out into the woods at special places she loved. We would go up on Council Cup the nearby mountain and in the picture above she taught us how to call the winds by whistling for them. She felt close to her AmerIndian past life and would tell us stories about it. At one place where her father had helped build an old stone bridge, out in the woods, she showed us the white spirit snake that Sybil had passed on to her, and that spirit was passed on to me at my first degree and integrated into my magick. One thing about the COC system is that there is a lot of physical work between Probationership and the First degree and it does take a year and a day. In fact, that time period is between all the degrees. There are instruments to be made and found and consecrated. You can't just buy everything on the internet like nowadays. We got blisters and bleeding fingers cutting our wands and besoms. For 9 years (1981-1990) we led a coven of many members who came and went. We and a handful of other witches were initiated into our higher degrees over time.

From 1981-87 I was initiated into 1st degree as Shawnus, the 2nd degree as Merlin, and 3rd degree as Belarion. In 6/25/1988 Lady Phoebe Athene Nimue initiated me into the 3rd degree. Lady Iska Nuit Aradia also achieved her 3rd degree.

My Priestess and I eventually parted ways. Due to witch politics I eventually withdrew from being High Priest of the Coven and let things wane down, as they did. I had my fallings out with Lady Phoebe at times, but eventually was also reconciled with her a few years before her death. Phoebe lost possession of the doctor's house and bookhouse and the latter fell into a more dilapidated state. Sadly Lady Phoebe passed in 2005.

Biography of Lady Phoebe

Here is a short biographical note on Lady Phoebe. She was an amazing lady. Phoebe or Janee was the High Priestess of the remaining coven members and is the witch who taught and initiated me. She was born in Berwick Pennsylvania on 13 April 1921. She met Dr. Santee in 1956 and was his receptionist-secretary at the Santee Medical office and Santee Memorial Library in Wapwallopen, Pa. They both had married partners but they were each other's platonic soul mates. She had no children. She was afflicted with a degenerative arthritic disease which left her body twisted, one leg shorter than the other and her nose was replaced with an artificial one. Of course like all of Santee's girls she wore high heels even in her condition.

I obtained a lot of old photos from 1965 of Santee's girls and they were all in high heels, skirts just above the knee, faux fur coats and cat's eye glasses. Phoebe was an artist from a young age and she actually met Lady Alsace or Jeannie at a painting class. She drew a lot of the illustrations and wrote poetry and invocations for the Coven. Here is one of her drawings, and in the Addendum there are poems listed.

She wrote a column in the local newspaper called *The Witches Kettle*. She also wrote and edited the Coven's publication entitled *The Cat's Tale*. In 1967 she and Dr. Santee were initiated by Sybil Leek. Phoebe has said that she remembers previous lives, one of which was the wife of an Indian chief who lived along the Susquehanna River hundreds of years ago. She was a strong-willed Aries and we did not always agree on everything, but she was my mentor who taught me how to be a witch and a Priest.

She passed away on 5 December 2005 at the age of 84 and is buried in the Pine Grove Cemetery in Berwick, Pa. When I went to visit her grave a few years ago there was a small box built in front of it with rocks and flowers inside. On the edge of the box it said "I am watching" with some crescent moons around, almost warning people to not vandalize the site. I lit a red candle in remembrance but know she is not there. About a year ago I had a vivid dream that I was flying in a stormy night and to the left of me was Santee and Phoebe flying on brooms and they were both just staring intensely at me. So I know she is with her soul mate flying around and having a good ole witch time.

Lady Phoebe and Lord Merlin were definitely soul mates even though they were only platonically involved and she was happily married. Here are some poems they wrote to each other:

Invocation from Lord Merlin to Lady Phoebe

I AM HE.

Like a god I can wipe away the clouds from the sky if you want it blue. I will pull down the stars to light your room at night if you want me to. Tomorrow I will level off the mountains and drain the sea to make room for the palaces I have planned for you. Like a wall I stand between you and anything that might threaten your joy and peace. The kings and captains of the earth will wait outside to adore you on your new throne. While I live your will is law. The magic power I draw from you makes me invincible. There is nothing I cannot learn or do, no problem I cannot solve if you let me do it in your name and for your sake. The world has no existence for me apart from you. It has no meaning but what you give it. You are the cause and the purpose of all my deeds. If you leave me, my world will fall apart. Unless some other SHE comes quickly to the rescue, I shall die. To renew my strength, I have only to look upon you or touch you, and I go forth conquering in your name. What is it in you that revives and inspired me? I call it beauty. But this is only you creating and expressing yourself. For you are SHE.

Invocation from Lady Phoebe to Lord Merlin

I AM SHE.

I walk with you in the twilight that falls like fairy dust around us. My silvery robe and midnight blue cape swing in the gentle wind of the gods. No matter my gait, no matter whether I be slim or obese or my beauty be the beauty of 18 or 80, for I will always walk straight and tall, my slim legs twinkling under the cobweb silk of my robe. I am always willowy as the figure of SHE and my beauty is forever. I willingly allow you to be my wall between danger and myself. I willingly allow you to worship at my shrine. You have earned that privilege of adoring at my feet for I am SHE. You can do naught without me. The veiled Isis can be unveiled to you only if I am at your side. But I need you in order to be SHE. Without you I will be nothing as you are without me. With your strength and my beauty we will face and conquer the twilight of our world without fear, for you are HE.

A Biography of Dr. Frederick LaMotte Santee

At his point I will write all I know about Dr. Santee, which is from Phoebe's stories, some articles I found in the Santee Memorial Library and from the Harvard Yearbooks. I never met him, having arrived one year after his passing, but he was an amazing man, doctor, scholar and occultist.

He was born 17 September 1906 in Wapwallopen, Pa. He was born in a lineage of four generations of doctors who practiced medicine. His grandfather was a Civil War surgeon who helped runaway slaves. His father was Charles LaMotte Santee who held MD degrees from LaFayette and Jefferson colleges in 1901 and he passed away in 1963. His mother was Verna Caroline Lloyd Santee.

Santee showed signs of genius at an early age. By age 3 he would read both English and German. He learned Latin from his grandfather's grammar books. By age 8 he was translating Caesar's Gallic Wars from Latin into English and back again to check his grammar. He went to Wapwallopen High School and then on to Wilkes-Barre High School for his last year. He went to Central High School in Philadelphia for AB degree in Greek and had the highest score in the USA, and so went to Harvard.

At age 14 he was the youngest person to attend Harvard from 1924-26 where he graduated at age 16 with an AB Magna Cum Laude.

At Harvard he met EK Rand, the Latin scholar with whom he corresponded for years. When asked "Who interested you in the occult?" he cites Harvard teacher Professor Grandient who taught Medieval literature and old French, George L. Kitridge who taught English and TM Boura.

He went to the University of Oxford England where he graduated age 18 in 1928 with an AB and then his MA in 1929. While at Oxford he joined The Alpha et Omega Lodge of the Hermetic Order of the Golden Dawn where he met Aleister Crowley, HP Blavatsky, WB Yeats, Thomas Agee, Dion Fortune, AE Waite, and Israel Regarde. He also joined the Theosophical Society of England. At Oxford his main occult influence was from his philosophy teacher, a Professor Brabbart.

One source says he attended the University of Berlin in 1924-28 where he received his Ph.D. but this date does not seem to match the other records. He spent additional years in Rome, teaching positions at Harvard, Temple, Kenyon, Johns Hopkins, but held no tenure due to his socialist ideas. He was one of the 100 members of the Institute of Arts and Letters.

While at the University of Berlin he was initiated into witchcraft at a Coven 30 miles outside Berlin, the coven High Priest being an Arnold Reinman(d). In travels in the Middle East he met native adepts of the High Art in Egypt, learned from a German adept also in Egypt, and from a Sheik who was High Priest of a "coven" in North Africa.

Santee claims to have been a Homeopathic Doctor to Adolf Hitler but escaped Germany before the War. Santee also claims to have adopted into the USA the daughter of Hitler, named Tao, whom Hitler fathered to an English lady before the War.

In 1928 he married Edith Rundle from Allentown, Pa. In 1930 they either birthed or adopted a daughter named Ruth who died in 1938.

In 1930 he was a Sheldon Fellow and Fellow at the American Academy of Rome for 3 years. By then he could read Latin, Greek, German and some Sanskrit.

In the later 1930s he spent 6 years teaching in the USA at Lehigh, Vanderbilt, Harvard, Temple, and Kenyon colleges. As noted before he never achieved tenure at any of these institutions. During this time he jointed the America Rosicrucian Society and was initiated into the Illuminati degree.

In 1938 he graduated from John's Hopkins University in Baltimore Maryland with his MD degree.

From 1938-1942 he taught classical languages at Kenyon College in Ohio USA and was involved in the Humanistic Revival (see issues of the Kenyon Review). He opposed the US entrance into WWII since he was an avowed Socialist.

Also in 1942 he divorced Edith Rundle and married Betty Addis of Cumberland, Md. They adopted Tao. Betty died in 1966.

From 1943-45, he was drafted into the Navy, served in the South Pacific, but saw no action. Later stationed in Arkansas USA he was a Lieutenant in the Medical Corps. Also at that time he published *Sawdust and Tomatoes* (poems of his and his mother's).

The Harvard Yearbook of 1957 lists him as living in Baltimore practicing medicine there. From letters it appears he knew John Colhane the Irish writer, David McDowell at Kenyon and Random House, Father Flye from NYC, Clyde Pharr, and other famous classicists.

In 1956 Santee met Edna Jane Kishbaugh Williams aka Lady Phoebe Athene Nimue.

In 1963 on his father's death, he returns to Wapwallopen Pennsylvania to continue his medical practice. His home and office were the same at 5 River Street.

In the 1970s once the library was built next door he employed a total of 2 nurses and 4 secretaries and librarians. He wrote a newspaper column called: "The Country Doctor" and Janee wrote a column called "The Witches' Kettle". The locals say he was a kind and compassionate doctor, though a bit of an eccentric. He often treated the poor at no charge.

Santee was known to have rubbed shoulders with much of the northeastern occult community. He was also a scholar of the Faust novels and legend and wrote his own Faustian story entitled *The Devil's Wager* set in modern times. He had a leg and nylon fetish if I can say so based on the amount of slides of ladies legs he had. He required his nurses and librarians to wear skirts, nylons and high heels at all times. He loved cats and all animals and supported the Humane Society and money from his Will was donated to them. He was a regular to NYC and was known to frequent the Magickal Childe bookstore. He had met Sybil Leek at some time and invited her to his Covenstead. His ladies, foremost of which, Phoebe, encouraged him to get initiated by her and start a Coven. In 1967 that happened and they received their charter from her. They titled the Coven of the Catta after the cat totem as I have written before and that coven continues to this day with a short hiatus of rituals from 1979, the year of the bookhouse fire, through 1980, the year of his death. I wish I had arrived a few years earlier than I did to meet this intelligent, wonderful and weird man and magician.

Dr Frederick LaMotte Santee died on 11 April 1980 aged 72 after a long battle with liver failure. His body is buried at the Old River Church just north of Wapwallopen, Pa. His gravestone says "I shall return when Spring's shadow trails."

Here is a whimsical poem written about him:

How pleasant to know the good Doctor
Who writes all this horrible stuff; [1]
Some call him a scoundrel and rotter,
But a few think him pleasant enough.

His mind is abstract and fastidious,
His nose is remarkably big;
Were he only a little less hideous,
You would say he resembles a pig.

When he changes from far specs to near specs
The children are frightened and cry,
And their mothers shout, 'Hey! Don't you dare hex [2]
Poor Sam with your terrible eye!'

---

[1] Refers mainly to a newspaper column called the 'Country Doctor.'

[2] Actually he belongs to a coven of witches.

He has many friends, layman and clerical,
He sleeps every night with his cats,
His body is perfectly spherical,
His office girls never wear flats. [3]

His office is unsanitary
With pictures of girls on the wall,
Every week he drinks gallons of sherry,
But never gets tipsy at all.

He is silent with people who talk a lot,
He won't look at women in slacks,
His favorite flavor is chocolate,
He rails at inflation and tax.

He hides in the depths of the cellar
While his patients call down through the flue,
'Come out of that cellar, you yeller,
You yeller old lazy bones, you!'

He reads, but he cannot speak, Spanish,
He still prefers women to men;
Ere the days of your pilgrimage vanish,
He hopes you will see him again.

On rummaging through papers at the Library I also found a Master's Thesis that a visitor wrote about the Coven, containing the following bits of information I have copied verbatim:

> "This interest in occult subjects seemed to culminate in his activities in the 'Coven of the Moon' in 'Little Town', where he could teach this knowledge. Although he did not care to practice ceremonial magic, he considered himself a teacher and researcher in many occult fields. He conducted experiments with a fair degree of success, but this was not his emphasis."

---

[3] A psychologist sees a relation between his fetish for high heels and his love of cats.

The Coven formed in 1963 under urging of head nurse "J". On questioning individuals, he seems to have been pushed into High Priest position to please his girls, charter for coven in 1967. Although HPS should be leader, actually Santee was the leader, instructing approximately fifty people during his Priesthood.

He believed he was a witch, but didn't believe in spirits because he never saw any, held a belief in a Universal Force he presumed to be God, felt that explanations of the psychic were in the individual instead of from outside forces, believed the Magick of Wicca is centered in male/female polarity, he was both social and solitary, he kept his thoughts and feelings to himself, kept his anger hidden, owned another house on a mountaintop he'd retire to at times, his house/office in town being the center of activity in Wapwallopen, which was open to all as was the library also.

Uniqueness of the Coven of the Catta

Of course we are all what I like to call the bastards of Gardner and Valiente. I do know that our Books of Shadows are loosely based on Lady Sheba's *The Book of Shadows* and *The Grimoire of Lady Sheba*. Other rituals and spells are from other books published in the 1960s to 1970s. A comparison of passages from the *Grinoirium Verum* and the *Grand Grimoire* from Idries Shah's *The Secret Lore of Magic* shows many similarities to passages from rituals from the Books of Shadows of the Coven of the Catta. I can see in the rituals both the hands of Lady Phoebe and Lord Merlin. I think the more traditional practices she had copied from available books. I can see his hand in the parts which look and feel more like Golden Dawn material, a group he had been initiated into in England. But there are many practices which are quite unique from how we make our tools to how the rituals are performed. I am not going to go into these unique practices here but refer you to my second book.

The Coven of the Catta Today

A few years before Lady Phoebe's passing I started doing the rituals again in her presence with Lady Alsace Isa Brie, an early elder member of the coven, as my Priestess. She is an Australian, a gifted psychic and wonderful gardener. We did these rituals mostly outside a couple times a year on her hilltop property outside Berwick, Pennsylvania.

I also started having Lady Alsace down to my place north of Harrisburg to celebrate Sabbats, usually at All Hallows. I have a temple set up on the first floor and in the cellar for larger groups. Witches from other lineages are freely invited and do come to these rituals.

Over the decades there have been lots of stories told about the strange ole doctor and his coven. Some of these have taken on the style of what is called an urban legend. Some residents in the little town of Wapwallopen think he was a Satanist and his coven sacrificed cats. Reports of a supposed haunting in a house across the street from Santee's house and bookhouse brought in The Pennsylvania Paranormal Association and luckily I found out about this and gave my version of the story before it was filmed for the Animal Planet in a series called *The Haunted*. The story is called The Coven of the Cat and you can view it on Youtube.com

The Coven of the Catta and I also have listings at Witchvox.com

Over the years various people have lived in Santee's house while the bookhouse continued to deteriorate and be vandalized. The property has now been purchased and is being restored.

In the winter of 2008–2009 I took all my handwritten Books of Shadows and typed them into Microsoft Word documents. All of the rituals were already in that format. This took months to do and they are now on CD and flash drives for COC initiates. Since then the Books of Shadows have also been photographed page by page and are now in 3 PDF documents.

Now at age 57 I live with my two black cats in the mountains along a stream near Newport Pennsylvania. I still have my original Books of Shadows compiled from Lady PANs Books of Shadows, which I cherish. I occasionally do the COC rituals with Alsace, Phoenix and Adonis Merlin. Mostly I do the main rituals alone in my inside or outside temples. I have a good relationship with a handful of mostly 3rd degree witches in the local Black Forest Tradition.

I received permission from my elder Lady Alsace Isa Brie and the only other practicing 3rd* Lady Augur Nagi Astarte that it is time to share with the Black Forest Coven lineage of Silver Ravenwolf our rituals, formulas and spells, but not the initiation rituals or information only for a Probationer in the COC. This is based on what Lady Phoebe on her death bed told Lady Alsace when asked "what about the Coven?" her answer was "it's up to you". We can keep these seeds in a jar in the cellar, or sow them on the fertile ground of deserving, respectful, and initiated BFC High Priestesses and Priests.

As far as I know the following people are still practicing the COC system – Alsace, Pheonix, Augur, Adonis and myself, Shawnus. I do not take on Probationers but my student Adonis does. So as you can see the lineage of Dr. Frederick LaMotte Santee and Lady Phoebe Athene Nimue of the Coven of the Catta continues strong to this day, growing, changing and initiating those who are worthy of this honor.

Quotes:

Some quotes are from the Harvard Yearbook 50th anniversary of the class of 1924. The quoted notes from the master's thesis are from a document I found in the library, author unnamed.

THE LADY CIRCE

By Patricia (Bona Dea) DeSandro

She paused at the top of the curved staircase, an otherworldly vision in her ritual robe of white velvet and purple satin. Her long white hair, the trademark spider tattoo on her right cheek, her silver jewelry sparkling in the candlelight, and her piercing blue eyes identified her as the Lady Circe, but what I saw was the Goddess, backlit with radiating light like an ancient icon. In slow motion she descended the stairs, the edge of her velvet robe skimming each step. It took my breath away. Her bejeweled hands reached out to embrace me as her smile chimed in my heart. I was already a student of hers, but at that moment, I knew without a doubt I would serve her as priestess. I had found a home in her presence and she agreed to adopt me as her spiritual child. From then on, she was Mother Circe to me, as she was for several others.

She was a tough teacher, but we all loved her. A pat on the head with the words, "You poor, dumb child!" followed many a student's foolish statements or deeds as she guided generation after generation of young witches in the old ways.

Set in her small frame was the presence of great power and wisdom. She was about the same height as I, on the short side of average, but in my memories she is always much taller.

She had a talent for making grand entrances. She used her natural flair for the dramatic to her advantage. I never heard her boast, but people remembered their encounters with her and this was the core of many local legends.

A man in the medical community who did not know I knew the Lady, told me about a witch he and a college buddy had gone to see years ago. He said her name was Circe. They had been curious and were feeling particularly daring that day. He said she offered them tea. They asked for a reading. She made the teacup float in midair. He related this to me in hushed tones. He even glanced over his shoulder once or twice. He and I were the only ones in the room at the time. Was he afraid that by speaking of her she would suddenly appear?

When pressed by her students to share one of her adventures, she would pick one with an appropriate lesson for us. One of the stories she told us took place in the mid '70s. Circe had been arrested in Atlanta, Georgia, for fortune-telling. She was reading the Tarot as part of a consultation. She spent several hours in jail that day and the police were chagrined when, even after ten tries, they could not get her fingerprints to take. The story ultimately had a good outcome, having broken ground, so to speak, for eventual friendly relations with Atlanta law enforcement.

She opened a delightfully mysterious shop in Toledo, Ohio that went through several transformations, but catered to the Pagan/Wiccan community for many years. I remember it as the Boutique of the Unusual. One of the most memorable 'Circe legends' involves an incident that took place there.

A man came into her shop one day. He was being disrespectful and starting to make a scene. With her pointed gaze and gesture, she knocked him off his feet, propelled him through the air, out the door and onto the sidewalk. There were witnesses.

This is, perhaps, my favorite story. Here is what I saw in my mind's eye as she related the event:

She had gone to bed one evening and a housemate came to her room to tell her the ritual cauldron in the backyard was missing. Now this cauldron was quite large, maybe two and a half to three feet across. It was her sacred, ritual cauldron. She got up and ran outside in her nightgown. She had an idea of what might have happened to the cauldron. There she stood in the dark night, over the spot where the cauldron had been. The wind came up, fueled by her anger. It whipped her nightgown around her and blew her loose, white hair wildly around her face. She pounded the earth in front of her three times! Her voice boomed through the wind for the Many-Footed Walkers to rise up from the Abyss and hunt down those fools who had stolen her cauldron! Of course, her cauldron was returned.

Her home, the Elder House, was an amazing place. Set in Toledo's historical Old West End, it was a large Victorian, three story dwelling. The back yard was home to a spacious ritual circle, complete with a central, in-ground, white marble chip pentagram that glowed ghostly at night, in the firelight. In the center was the famed cauldron, where the ritual fires burned. Trees and vines lined the fences bordering the property, adding to the magical ambiance, especially at Hallows.

The interior of the Elder House, however, was the most magical. The foyer past the double set of doors was usually decorated. An elder, Lord Darkfel, who was also an artist, very successfully created the essence of the upcoming sabbat with his decorating. One entered the magical realm of the gods and faerie when walking through the doors. Lord Darkfel's artistry didn't stop in the foyer, he took it up the curved staircase from the foyer to the second floor, where some of the elders lived, including our beloved Lady Bast.

Circe's library, right off the entrance, was where she consulted with people. This small room was lined with books, floor to ceiling, and had an ancient, carved table right in the center. It was impossible not to speak in hushed tones when in this room; her wisdom was strongest here. It was in this room she read the Tarot for me, and where I waited in solitude for my Eldering.

The main parlor was where classes were held, and the kitchen and dining area were where nurturing took place.

Her altar was also in the dining room. Her ritual items on the altar were there to see, but not to be touched. The altar provided many impromptu lessons when new students wondered about the mysterious items. It was an honor to be asked by Circe to bring her an item from her altar. It gave one the feeling of having reached a level of spiritual accomplishment, Mother Circe's trust. Being able to hear the humming energy emanating from her altar marked for me the opening of Circe's door to the deeper mysteries. It appeared more than once as a portal in my dreams.

There were guardians in that place, of course. They were very protective, and those who weren't welcome, told tales of how dark, shadowy forms chased them out of the house. The Guardians wouldn't let anyone they didn't approve of get past the first landing on the stairs. There, they would hover like a dark curtain. I could see them, as could some of the others, but everyone could feel them. It was comforting to know we were safe. They were just members of the family with a job to do.

Lady Circe, whose mundane name was Jeffrey B. Cather, was born in Pennsylvania on September 8, 1921. Her roots were Scots-Irish. One day several of us were gathered around her dining room table. The ensuing discussion regarding ancestors led to her telling us about her first teacher.

Circe was born at home and there were complications with her birth. The doctor was not sure whether the mother or the child would live. As the doctor worked to save the mother, the great grandmother asked for the infant, who was not breathing, to be given to her. She left the room and breathed into the infant's mouth, restoring life. She returned to proclaim the child was indeed alive, and was now hers.

Circe's great-grandmother was her first teacher in the old ways. Circe slept in the same room with her each night and while she slept, many of the teachings were whispered into her ear. During the day, Circe learned the practical, everyday living side of the old religion, as exemplified by her great grandmother.

The tales of her experiences, both seemingly mundane and spiritual, were important and vivid teachings, usually shared around her dining room table. Blessed were those who were in the right place at the right time. Cleaning in and around the Elder House usually ensured this! An offer of a cup of coffee, a bowl of soup, or a piece of her well-known orange cake was most always accompanied by a story, a lesson, or a wise saying from her elders.

Some of the sayings she taught me that I still use today are:

"If I am right, help me to stay. If I am wrong, show me the other way."

"Witch power is NOW power. The Witches do not wait until the moon is in the correct sign. They are in the NOW and in their mind the moon is always in the correct sign."

"I am never broke (financially). I am merely between fortunes."

"If you would walk the Witch's way, observe with care a child at play."

"The weak witch is overtaken, the strong witch survives."

"Learn to keep your own counsel. But to do this, you must first know who you are."

"Let the spider run alive. Your business, then, is sure to thrive."

"There was an old owl who lived in an oak.
The more he heard, the less he spoke.
The less he spoke the more he heard.
We should try to be like that wise old bird."

My favorite is to be said when stepping on the grass or bare ground:

"Blessed be that which is under my feet,
for it is a living carpet that I walk upon."

Her name was whispered with both awe and fear, around the Toledo area as the Queen of the Witches. As the reach of her teachings grew, so did her reputation. Soon, people from all over the country, including a few from other countries, came seeking her wisdom. She spent some time living in California, Detroit, Michigan, and even a short time in Georgia, but she always returned to Toledo where she presided over the Alliance of the Old Religion, a group of covens nationwide, whose initiatory lineage traces back to her.

She carried on the family tradition as a fifth generation hereditary witch and blended in some modern occultism, Wicca, and other folk practices into what became the Circean line of the Romano-Celtic tradition of Witchcraft. She was dedicated to teaching those seeking the Craft of the Wise. She started a public school of the Craft in Toledo, Ohio, the Sisterhood and Brotherhood of the Old Religion (originally named the Sisterhood and Brotherhood of Wicca). She incorporated it as a church in 1971, making it the first state and federally recognized Wiccan religious organization in Toledo. Many covens were spawned there, including mine (Circle of the Sacred Grove), and the Lady Circe was our Queen Elder.

The Craft wasn't the Lady Circe's only focus during her very active life. She also had been a wife, a mother, a dancer, a registered nurse, and even spent time in the Women's Army Corps. Circe was an excellent cook and occasionally put on themed dinners for her many friends. She also was well known for the incense she made by hand and often had difficulty keeping up with the demand.

Much has been written about her, both positive and negative. Being in the public eye paints a target on oneself, especially if controversial. Circe was courageous and passionate enough to not let that stop her from what she was meant to do. She stated many times, "I fear nothing that comes from my lips."

The Lady Circe crossed through the veil into the Summerland, at the age of 82, on May 30, 2004. Her influence, love and teachings live on in the hearts of her many students, and even those whose lives she touched briefly.

What Circe wanted, I believe, above all else, was for the Craft to be taken seriously for what it is; a way of life that:

1. Honors the divinity in all things
2. Requires personal responsibility for thoughts and actions and knowing oneself
3. Honors our Ancestors, "those whose shoulders we stand upon"
4. Works within perfect love and perfect trust in all ways and with all living creatures.

My family was touched by Mother Circe. She knew my children and my grandchildren, providing for them a glimpse of the mysterious, and helping to guide some of them on the Path. She and my husband developed a friendship and he would build for her anything she asked.

Circe was the embodiment of the Goddess for me, but she was also human. She paid for her mistakes, as all of us do. This fact was a wonderful lesson for me. It taught me to just be who I am, to acknowledge my weak points, learn, and then move on. Good leaders need not be perfect, but they do need to have integrity. What she offered me as my teacher, guide and spiritual mother was acceptance and respect for who I was and who I would be. She nurtured an awareness of the Goddess force within me and helped me find my power.

In her words:

"We (witches) are to lead mankind back to the light to save them from themselves. We are the guardians of humanity."

All quotes are from Lady Circe as documented in my class notes.

George "Pat" Patterson

by Kurt Hunter

First off I'd like to acknowledge the contributions to my knowledge of Pat by my fellow elders of the Tradition: Queen Zanoni, Randy Weiser, Moondancer, Stephanie Henderson and Donna McLarty, and others I have neglected to mention. Like most of the Georgian initiates alive today, I never knew him personally. But the Craft continues to survive due to the efforts of those that did.

George "Pat" (as his friends and fellow coveners called him) Patterson established the Georgian Tradition in December, 1970 in Bakersfield, CA, with Ministerial credentials through the Universal Life Church for himself and his High Priestess, Zanoni Silverknife the following year. Along with another priestess acting as Maiden, Tanith, they worked together to form the initial core of the Georgian teachings. Their first student, Bobbie, joined them shortly thereafter. After that came Becky, and then subsequent others.

Patterson was 52 years of age at the time he formed the Georgian Tradition. This would make him a contemporary of Alex Sanders, who was only a couple years older than Patterson. He was born in 1928 and passed from this world in 1984. He left behind a large network of Georgian covens and practitioners from coast to coast. Many of the Elders of the Tradition continue to confer and keep each other up to date on a Georgian email listserv. There is one for Georgian Initiates, as well.

They decided on the name "Georgians", as it was felt "Pattersonians" was too bulky. He supplied the contacts, training materials, and guidance for the initial effort and, thus, he was the natural leader and founder of the Tradition. Since Georgian could not trace its lineage back to any coven in England it could not be considered "British Traditional". However, it drew upon many old coven sources and teachings from Britain, and in addition had a lineage-based structure. One could only be initiated into the Georgian Tradition by another Georgian in good standing. It takes a Georgian to make a Georgian, so to speak. The material of the

Georgian Book of Shadows is also Oathbound. In this way it can be considered British Traditional derived Wicca.

There were many teachers and resources that acted upon the new Georgian faith in those early days. Author Ed Fitch was prominent among these and much of his material. Initially, Patterson claimed to be trained from a Celtic coven in Boston, MA while in his teens. He had maintained a BOS and had tools for working the craft and was initiated into the Coven of the Four Winds in 1948. There was some disagreement as to whether the coven was a Family Tradition group or that it followed classical Greco-Roman and Norse traditions. Gerald Gardener never trained Patterson, nor was he ever initiated into the Gardernerian Tradition except near the end of his life, where he was cross-initiated into Silver Crescent coven, a Gardernerian line, by Lady Manon. In those days cross-initiations were much more commonplace than they are today.

Patterson fought in WWII and left his Craft tools behind. When he returned from overseas, all his tools and materials, including his BOS, had been destroyed and disposed of. Undaunted, Patterson continued to search for others who would help teach him and join him in his Craft training.

Georgian Wicca utilizes many practices reminiscent of British Traditional Wicca, as well as some Etruscan principles. As noted above, Ed Fitch's contribution to the Tradition is evident. Ed had written material in *The Pagan Way*, drawing upon the works of Franz Bardon and Willian Gray and making them more accessible. Lady Gwen of NECTW (New England Celtic Traditional Witches) and Doris and Sylvester Stuart (the Sylvestrians) of Essex, England were willing to share their knowledge and love of the Craft. This was greatly appreciated as was their friendship and guidance to the new coven.

The Georgian First Degree material was directly pulled from an LP by Alex Sanders *A Witch is Born*.

The Second Degree material came from the Slyvestrian's First Degree, and the Third is formed, in part, from the Sanders album with additional elements.

Many others helped influence the Georgian Tradition early on, including Leo Martello of New York (also a Stregheria priest), Tony Camisa from Georgia (Fam-Trad), Bonnie Sherlock of Utah, Kitty Lessing from Florida, Eddie Bucynski, Herman Slater, and many others. Patterson had a way of drawing support to himself and the Tradition.

The Georgian Tradition was a hodge-podge of various rituals and observances picked up and integrated into an overall body of eclectic work. It has a light-hearted approach and is celebratory of the life bestowed upon us, and yet the initiates are very serious in their approach to working for the aid and healing of others. "Let there be mirth and reverence..." One of Patterson's more well-known proverbs was "whatever works". Thus Georgians came to be known in some Pagan circles as a rather undisciplined but free-wheeling bunch. Arguably the dedication that the initial members had initially to the Georgian Tradition was no less serious than that of any other practicing Wiccan Tradition of the day. But there can be no doubt of the generosity shown by other Wiccan leaders towards the Georgian Tradition.

During his life Patterson edited the "Georgian Newsletter" from 1976 until his death in 1984. It provided a forum for one another and helped to build the Georgian community. Remember that there was no internet at this time. Following his death the newsletter continued for a few years, then went on a long hiatus, and has been re-started in recent years. It contains helpful hints, news of the Georgian Tradition including elevations and passings, events and historical perspectives. At present there are listserves for both elders and initiates to maintain close contact and share news quickly.

During the 70s and 80s Patterson also maintained long-distance communication through letters and tapes with many students, some as far away as Guam. Often they would study and learn the material through this correspondence and then come to Bakersfield for a period of time to practice and then be elevated by Patterson. This resulted in even more dissemination of the Georgian Tradition throughout North America, with known covens today being in British Columbia, California, Florida, Michigan, Oklahoma, Oregon,

Texas and Washington. All of which can trace their lineage back to George Patterson.

The impression I always received regarding Pat was that he was something of a character, charismatic yet demanding a lot of his students. The Tradition itself always seemed to be a work in progress, and continued to be fiddled with until his death. There are those persons referring to themselves as "Georgian Traditionalists" who are intent on preserving the values and BOS as written, and I believe this is a valuable resource and these guardians ought to be honored for their work. There are others who branch out from the BOS, using it as a springboard for other practices which they fuse onto the Tradition. My point of view is that, so long as you know where you came from and have mastered it, you are free to do "whatever works". There has been an upsurge of interest and initiations into the Georgian Tradition in recent years, and I believe that it will continue to serve a new community of young Witches looking for covens in which to belong and learn from. Today the Georgian Tradition is a fine example of the Craft as a growing, evolving entity and, Gods willing, it shall continue so in the years to come.

Pattalee Glass-Koentop "Lady Phoenix" (1943-2002)

By Virginia Villarreal

Pattalee Glass-Koentop was born on October 27, 1943 and crossed the veil on November 11, 2002. She was born in Dumas, Texas and throughout her life she gave her all for the advancement of the Wiccan Community. She lived her life to the max and was an inspiration to the Texas Pagan community. I did not personally know Pattalee, throughout the years that I have attended CROW (Counsel of Revolting Outrageous Women) and COW (Celebration of Womanhood)—two women's celebrations that she co-founded—Pattalee's memory has been kept alive so that women like me who didn't have the pleasure of meeting her could know what a wonderful person she was. Pattalee, I am told was a true founding daughter of the Craft and she would befriend all those who were seeking the way of the Goddess. She was born in the sign of Scorpio and she crossed the veil in the same sign of Scorpio which only goes to show that she lived her life the way a true Scorpio would do. She loved life, sex, and the magickal arts all of which are Scorpio traits. Pattalee was a High Priestess of Isis and she was the first to belong to two traditions at the same time, but in the end her heart and soul belonged to Isis.

Pattalee was a business woman and started the store, Flight of the Phoenix and another called Caravan. She was an accomplished writer whose published works include: *The Magic in Stones*, *Prosperity Magick*, *Whispers of Windsong*, and *Year of the Moons, Season of Trees*. There was nothing in the closet of the life of Lady Phoenix because she was usually the face of the Pagan community and was often interviewed by local newspapers, television and radio stations.

She was one of the founders of the Council of Magickal Arts, CMA, and many other celebrations after she founded Roundtree which included COWS. She was very public about her spirituality and even when Witchcraft was not as accepted as it is today, she would teach Wicca 101 to anyone who wanted to learn. Going against the stream did not phase Pattalee because she was a woman that walked her talk. She left behind a legacy that has sparked a flame of community in this fellow Scorpio. I wish I had gotten to know her in life as I am getting to know her in death. "Lady Phoenix" you are an inspiration to all the witches that have come and will come after you. "You opened the door so that we could walk in and celebrate the mysteries of the Goddess with more freedom and acceptance".

Through the accounts of all the women that have become my sisters, I have gotten to know Pattalee and all the wonderful accomplishments that this beautiful woman was able to fulfill in her lifetime for witches and witchcraft. She was loved and will forever live in the hearts of those who knew her and those who know of her.

TED MILLS (LORD THEO MILLS)

by Scott A. Sherter

I first met Ted Mills (who was also known as Lord Theo Mills in the Craft community) in my early twenties while I was still living in my home region of western Massachusetts. Ted was a very well-known and much loved local community elder during the late 1980s, particularly in the Earthspirit Community. Despite being confined to a wheelchair and to supplemental oxygen in his final years from COPD (Chronic Obstructive Pulmonary Disease), he still made an effort to attend local Pagan community festivals, even if his appearances were at best brief ones.

It was during the last remaining years of his life that I would first meet Ted. He not only became one of my very first Craft teachers when I was a very young man, but also someone who would eventually become one of my dearest friends, even like an uncle or a grandfather to me. My earliest memory of our first meeting was at a (now long defunct) Pagan shop called the Abyss in Easthampton, MA where he did a public lecture and workshop about the Craft. Even in his advanced years of ill health, he was still a very vivacious and personable man who commanded a powerful presence around himself. I was quite riveted by this man who wore a large ankh pendant and carried a beautiful walking staff with a silver pentacle carved into it. That one meeting with Lord Theo led to a close and wonderful friendship with him before his death only a few short years later in 1996.

Most of my time with Ted included fairly regular visits to his home in Florence, MA to spend time with him. Back then, my parents weren't accepting of my involvement with Wicca (particularly while I was still living under their roof), so my visits with Ted were a welcomed escape for me. Ted in turn enjoyed having visitors to his home, particularly from younger people whom he saw as the next generation and future of the Craft.

Some who read this essay might think that I learned the Craft from Ted through elaborate circle castings and rituals at his home. But that wasn't at all the case. My visits with Ted often involved sitting together with him in his living room, where he could easily spend hours telling countless stories about his past: his own childhood in western Massachusetts, and a chance meeting with a woman gathering herbs in the woods who told him "you have the Mark and one day you'll come to fully understand what that means." There were stories about his time in the military as a young man and his service in overseas countries, his life out west in Arizona, and then later in New Orleans and in different parts of the South. He not only spoke about his first spiritual vision and encounter with the goddess Isis (which not only later led him to Wicca, but also to a lifelong Craft priesthood to that same goddess), but most of all about his personal experiences in the Craft community and his own close friendships with such public Craft authors as Sybil Leek, Elizabeth Pepper, and Laurie Cabot. As with Leek, Pepper, and Cabot, Ted likewise walked the road of being quite public about his own Craft involvement, particularly during a time when it wasn't at all easy to do so.

Not only did Ted teach me knowledge, but also so many invaluable life lessons. Ted enjoyed showing me his personal Book of Shadows from time and time, reading me a few select parts in its otherwise unintelligible (to me) handwriting in Theban script. He also took joy in talking about his goddess Isis and his experiences with her, along with showing and sharing his personal letters and photographs from his correspondences with Leek, Pepper, Cabot, and other Craft friends of his over the years. But I think that Ted ultimately derived the most joy from mentoring younger people, whom he saw as the next generation of the Craft, and in them its continuing survival.

I was truly lucky at that young age to have had Ted as a mentor and a friend. I was able to share with him psychic and occult experiences that I didn't feel free to share with others and which I couldn't entirely understand. I had the resource of Ted's wisdom and experience to make sense of it all. He taught me several things about magic and how to manage my own psychic perceptions and abilities. But most of all, Ted taught me invaluable lessons about being true to one's own personal convictions and spiritual path, even if they go against the grain of mainstream expectations. Of all the knowledge and lessons that Ted gave me, that particular one was the biggest and most valuable one of all which he gifted to me while he was still living.

In many ways, Ted shaped me into the man and person and Witch I am today. Rest in the wings of Isis, my dear friend and first teacher.

MARGARET MAHER HOFFMAN HICKMAN

By Tish Owen

My grandmother, Margaret Maher Hoffman Hickman was born in 1874 to Irish immigrants. She was the second youngest of twelve children and one of two who were born in this country, the others had been born in Ireland. She was raised in Brooklyn, NY in a time that was not kind to Irish immigrants or their children. Her mother died when she was twelve and she took over the duties of the household so that everyone who was older could work. Her younger brother, Jimmy was ten and she took over the raising of him as well. One day when she was cleaning the house she opened the closet that was set under the stairs and her dead mother was standing there. Her mother smiled at her and then faded away. Years later when my grandmother told me this story I asked her why she thought her mother had appeared to her. "I think that she was proud of me, and she wanted me to know that. That is why she smiled at me, because she was pleased."

My grandmother came to live with my parents before I was born. My mother was pregnant with me during the Great Ice Storm of 1951. Nashville was shut down because of the weather. My parents got to work by riding a bus, the only vehicles that were on the roads besides emergency vehicles. As they left for work that fateful February morning, my grandmother reminded them that the trash needed to go out. The back stairs were steep and covered with ice. My parents both told her they would take care of it after work. She was a stubborn woman and decided to take the trash out herself and slipped, fell, broke a hip and lay in the snow for hours until the mail man discovered her. The fact that she did not die that day is a testimony of her strength. She claimed that she was protected by angels. Maybe she was. She was eighty years old.

She was in a wheel chair from that time on, so since I never saw her any other way, it was normal to sit in her lap in the chair so that she could read to me. From the beginning we had a special bond, we clicked, and when we were together there was no need for other people to share space with us.

My grandmother told me stories about Ireland, the conquests, the battles, the epic failures, the death, destruction, the fear and the magick. She believed that the English were not trying to conquer the land and the people, but were trying to stamp out the magick, which the English feared. Maybe she was correct. However the English did not succeed in stamping out the magick that lived in Ireland, it still exists there. Because the English exiled so many native sons and daughters to foreign shores, the magick lives in many other places as well. It has been distributed not destroyed. I still shudder a little when I see the color orange.

We had little people who lived in the back of our yard where the bushes and trees were thick just before the yard turned into woods. I saw them and reported them to my grandmother, who instructed me to feed them small amounts of honey and cream. Funny to think of it now, no one ever questioned why I went into the back yard with small bowls from my china set and came back empty handed. Quiet only children can get away with lots of stuff.

I knew things and saw things and heard things as a child. I would always go to her for confirmation. She would say to me, "And isn't it wonderful that you can do these things? Just remember that not everybody can." I was a pretty smart kid; I knew I was being told to be careful and keep my mouth shut.

My grandmother had an altar in her room, set up in a Hard Rock Maple secretary that sat across the room from her bed. There was a drop down shelf that exposed little nooks and crannies inside. Here was a wealth of treasures for a small child; rosaries, prayer cards with the faces of saints, prayer books, odd pieces of jewelry, little blessed metals with Jesus and Mary stamped into the surface, a bottle of holy water, salt, candles and rough stones. It was here that she prayed, and it was here that her prayers were answered. She allowed me to touch the collection of magickal items and I was intrigued with them. She, of course, never referred to these items as 'magickal'. They were just things that she liked.

She was able to cloak all of her magick under the cover of Catholic trappings. She bought the holy water at church and the candles and prayer cards. Actually my mother and father bought them for her since she never left the house after her accident. The other things she had owned for years and carried from home to home. She 'prayed' to the saints, especially the Blessed Mother. But when she prayed, she went into her room and shut the door behind her. No one, not even me, was allowed in her room when she prayed.

Once, my father was very late coming home from work. This was a man who was never late; my mother put dinner on the table at 6:00 because he would walk through the door at exactly that time. To make matters worse, it was storming badly. My mother was beside herself with worry, pacing the floor as the storm raged outside. Finally my grandmother excused herself to go to her room to pray. She returned about twenty minutes later to inform my mother that, "I saw Robbie, he is on his way home, he is safe, he will be here in about five minutes. Oh, and I saw Jesus and Mary watching over him." My mother can tell this story with a straight face never realizing that my Grandmother went to her room, dowsed for my father and found him.

My beloved grandmother died one Tuesday afternoon between lunch and dinner. She was in the kitchen and just slumped back into her chair. "Get your mother." She whispered to me. Before I could turn and run to my mother, my grandmother slumped further into her chair, her eyes closed. Then there was this outrushing of energy from her, and her spirit shot straight up out of her body like an arrow going heavenward. It was and still is the most amazing thing I have ever witnessed. She had her eyes on her target and she was gone.

Somehow in my very young self I knew that even though she was gone from her body I could still reach her. That night, she was laid out to rest in her own bed after she had been washed and dressed in her best clothes. I sat on the side of her bed for hours and talked to her. I do not remember anything that I said to her, I just remember sitting and talking. I felt like it was my last chance to ask questions and get answers from her. The house was full of people, I could hear them talking in the living room and kitchen, but I was alone with her as I needed and wanted to be.

Indeed I was right, it was many, many years before she showed up at a Samhain. But she did and she smiled at me, and I knew that she was proud of how I turned out.

In Memoriam: Fuensanta Arismendi Plaza (1950-2010)

By Galina Krasskova

I am writing this while sitting in a hotel room in Zurich, the same room that my adopted mother would take for the better part of twenty years on her twice-yearly visits to her homeland. This is the first time I have been to Switzerland since she died this past February and while I spent the past few weeks dreading the trip and the raw emotions it might unearth, and while indeed I have spent the better part of two days crying my eyes out, it has also been filled with unexpected blessings of memory, friendship, and support.

I never ask if miracles occur. I never ask any more if one can truly be blessed by the Gods. I know it's possible. Fuensanta Plaza was my blessing. She may not have given birth to me, and we may have had less than a decade together but she was my mom in all ways that truly mattered. She loved me as a mother loves a child and I loved her in return. She supported me....I'm writing this in English but the word for support is particularly lovely in German *unterstutzen* – to strengthen from beneath. She was my foundation, my sanctuary, the goodness in my life. She called me her miracle daughter but I was the one who had been given a miracle.

When she died, I was numb for weeks. A good friend stayed with me, and later my oath sister navigated me through the paperwork that had to be done, and then the setting up of an ancestral altar. It was the ancestral work that helped me hold onto the lessons my mom had taught me: how to do something more than survive. From the beginning, my mom treated me as a person of worth. She looked at me and saw beneath my rough exterior; she saw in me her pearl beyond price. No one else had ever seen me that way, not to that degree. I was barely holding on in my world, barely managing to pull myself through each day all but crippled with a back injury, slowly being worn down by poverty, drudgery, and the ongoing stress and disdain I had to wade through in my work. She changed all of that.

She tried to teach me to see myself through her eyes but I never quite could. What I could and did see, every day that I was blessed with her presence, was a woman of tremendous courage, integrity, devotion and strength. Words are weak when it comes to describing a character and hers was unbending. She loved me with a fierceness that even the Gods could not deny and I still have no idea how I ever managed to deserve it.

She said the happiest day of her life was the day we legally became mother and daughter. It was the happiest of mine too. What a journey that was. We had wanted for years to legalize our filial relationship, but neither of us thought it was possible for adults to do so. Then one day, on one of my many trips to see her, I found a Hallmark magazine while waiting in the airport, and bored, picked it up. In there, I read the story of two women who found each other after a long separation (one had been foster mother to the other when the latter was a teen, but they had been separated by the state agency and had lost touch for years) and in their thirties and fifties respectively went through a legal adoption. What a piece of blessed synchronicity. That magazine article changed my life and within months we were legally recognized as mother and daughter. I still just cannot believe how immensely blessed I have been to have this woman in my life. She, like Loki, took of my heart, ate of it, and somehow made it whole.

When she died it left in me an empty place that nothing could hope to fill. One would think being a spiritworker, priestess, and shaman that death would hold no charge for me. Oh, it did and only now do I understand the weight of grief that she would so often speak of when telling me of her own lost loves. She had been so weary, so worn down before she died. I was determined not to bother her with prayers or offerings until at least a month had passed. This is common in many traditions that honor their ancestors. She had a long journey ahead of her and I wanted to be sure I didn't distract her with my needs, even my need to honor her. It was so hard! My mom and I had talked multiple times a day, we exchanged reams of letters, and we traveled regularly together and saw each other as much as was humanly possible. To suddenly not be able to call her when I saw something she might like, or when something happened of interest, to not be able to share the small details of my day that only a mother would be interested in, to not be able to pick up the phone and hear her elegant Basel accent …that was just as bad as not having her by my side.

I was, however, able to prepare to honor her. I spent that month notifying friends, and fielding calls, but I also spent it finding the perfect photograph for her ancestral altar, slowly cleaning and setting up that altar, telling our story to friends who dropped by, and teaching other people how to honor their dead. More than once, I had an acquaintance come in on some errand and see the altar, ask what it was, receive my answer, and break down in tears suddenly being moved to tell me about their own beloved dead. I learned about true grief that month. I also learned what a powerful connection our loved ones can maintain. I felt my mother toward the end of the month. I felt her watching over me, checking in, fretting as she always fretted about my health, heart, and home.

I learned that for the sake of my dead, I had to own my grief, pick up and keep on going—otherwise I would cause her pain that she did not deserve. I learned that while she may not be here corporeally, she was there, a fiercely protective power standing at my back and giving me the dirty eyeball when I didn't clean my house. (It sounds silly but those who knew her will understand that she was an absolute *putzteufel* (neat-freak). Those who have seen my ancestral altar to her, and the picture I chose to use there will know the look I mean). I forged, through her, a closer connection to and better understanding of the importance of honoring our dead than I ever expected. Yes, it is true she is no longer here with me in the human world; that does not mean that she is not here and watching over me. She remains my mother and we continue to talk multiple times a day, she continues to fret, and I continue to pour out offerings in her name.

I think perhaps I had taken my connection to the ancestors, the necessity of honoring them, for granted. It wasn't until my Mom died, and took part of my heart with her, that I understood what a powerful and important thing honoring them truly is. She gave me, as her last corporeal gift, that understanding and blessing.

I hail Fuensanta Plaza,
I hail meine Mutti
Whom I love auf Zeit und Ewigkeit.
I honor you for all you were in life,
And for all you remain in death.
Your name will ever be held in my heart,
And its praises ever fall from my lips.
May the work of my hands,
The meandering contemplations and fierceness of my heart,
And every day of my life that remains,
Ever do you honor.
Hail, Fuensanta.

(This article first appeared at *http://krasskova.weebly.com/blog.html* and in a forthcoming anthology by Asphodel Press).

Denessa Smith (1965-2008) & Tempest Smith (1988-2001)

By Christopher Penczak

I must admit that while I knew Denessa, I didn't know her as well as I would have liked. I don't know her life story. I don't know the intimate details of her childhood or her magickal practice, but I feel it's important for me to write about her, to share what I did know from firsthand experience. It is important for our spirit kin to be loved and remembered and shared.

We shared only a few brief moments together, mostly in ritual and a few socially during festival gatherings. When we met, I had no idea of her story or her work. I just knew her name. I knew she ran a foundation. Our mutual friend Dorothy Morrison mentioned her in conversation a lot as if I already knew Denessa and later I understood why. After spending a little time with Denessa, I felt like I did know her. She affected me deeply as I know she did many others.

When we first met, we were both aiding in a public ritual together, in a warrior rite with teacher and author Kerr Cuhulain at ConVocation in Michigan. I had a fairly minor support role as a warder, and she had a major part as a priestess. After it was all said and done—and quite well done I might add—she confessed to me that she felt out of her depth and had never done something like that before. You'd never have known it. I didn't understand why she was there if it wasn't something she was comfortable doing, but then she shared with me her story, and Tempest's story. I was awed at her willingness to share so much, as I was a relative stranger she had just met.

Denessa's daughter, Tempest Smith committed suicide in February 2001 at the age of 12 due to the bullying she experienced. It started when she was in second grade and got continually worse as she got older. Tempest turned to Wicca in middle school, and while it brought her comfort, it also became the source of severe abuse from her fellow students. Classmates would sing "Jesus loves you" and call her a "Wiccan whore." She got the point where she could not take it anymore and ended her life.

Denessa's response to this tragedy was to make sure it would not happen again to another youth, Wiccan or not, and began a program of education and awareness and safety, founding the Tempest Smith Foundation in her daughter's honor with the help of the Pagan community that reached out to her in 2002. By 2004 the foundation was established. Denessa was a guest and presenter at many events in the Detroit area. Specifically in the Pagan community, she worked with the Witch's Ball, ConVocation, Metro Detroit Pagan Picnic and Detroit Pagan Pride Day. Her mission grew against stopping bullying specifically along with encouraging tolerance and education. With this exposure, the foundation grew. She raised funds to further her cause and got many different factions of the Pagan community to gather and support this important work.

We talked and I got to see Denessa in other settings during the festival, enjoying life and the people around her so much. I wondered if I were in her shoes, would I have been able to do the same? She was inspiring. And during the last few years when my own family has faced illness, mortality and death, Denessa sprang to my mind and inspired me more than once. I wish I had a chance to tell her that, though I have at the ancestor altar and during our ancestor rites. I think she knows.

After that first festival, our paths crossed a few more times, as I taught and she educated and raised awareness for the Tempest Smith Foundation. I've had the opportunity to watch her share with others as she did with me, and create a similar understanding of her mission, touching them, too. Our last real meaningful time together was when I called her to be a priestess again in a public ritual at ConVocation, aiding me this time in a ritual called the Sorcerer's Initiation. It was all about empowerment through direct inspiration. She not only came through, but helped me fill in the other parts of the ritual. Again, I saw a priestess through and through, and she didn't appear nervous at all though she later told me she was. I hadn't realized she came to all of this through Tempest. I would have thought she was always Wiccan and raised Tempest as such. Amazing how an immense tragedy and few years can transforms someone's spiritual path.

Afterwards, Denessa came to me to explain her experience from the ritual. She was moved by the journey, so much so that she took off her necklace with a metallic capsule on it, and put it around my neck. At first I didn't realize what it was, or what she was doing, but as she fastened it, she explained that she saw me carrying a light into the world, and wanted me to carry the light she carried as well, to carry some of that light in Tempest's name. She explained that the capsule had some of Tempest's ashes in it. I was both honored and a bit dumbfounded, but now I think of us all who are touched by Denessa, and through her, Tempest, whether we literally carry them with us or not. Even though I never met Tempest, I feel a bit of her presence with me in my work.

I later found that several of us were called to be ash bearers. Perhaps Denessa knew her time was short and on some level was preparing, through the foundation and through those that would help share her light in other ways. Perhaps she knew she would be soon reunited with Tempest as many Witches do have that inkling, even if they don't know it consciously when it's time.

During a gallbladder operation in 2008, Denessa unexpectedly died when the procedure went horribly wrong. I know I was stunned to hear the news. I was honored to be asked to send something to her service, as I couldn't attend in person due to my travel and teaching, but my heart was with those remembering Denessa.

The foundation's work continues with Denessa's partner and Tempest's other mom, Annette Crossman, aided by an enthusiastic board of directors. We are all called now to carry her mission, her light into the world, each doing a part to make it a bit brighter, stopping bullying and teen suicide for whatever reason. Denessa will be greatly missed by those whose lives she touched, yet her light will live on, always.

For those interesting in supporting the Tempest Smith Foundation, please visit *tempestsmithfoundation.org*. The Foundation's goals include promoting anti-bullying legislation; providing educational programs for schools and community organizations through its speakers bureau and "Tye Dye for Tolerance" events; offering scholarship opportunities to students who demonstrate a commitment to the foundation's goals; serving as a resource for information and tools to prevent bullying and discrimination; and providing networking opportunities through social events throughout the community.

(This entry is adapted from a tribute reading prepared for Denessa's memorial.)

Jane Y. Rojek
(1947-2011)

By Christine Moulton

My mother. We are here not to think of her in death but to celebrate her life. Though what I am about to share with you today may seem a bit lengthy it is the only way I can share with you the true essence of who she was as I saw her.

Things that she taught me:

- Be who you are, not who others want you to be.

- Everything happens for a reason, if things don't go as you want them to, it is because something better is coming.

- There is never enough time in a day, so don't waste it doing things that make you unhappy, just to please others.

- Love and make time for your family, they are the only people who have to love you no matter what.

- Stop looking for reasons to be offended.

- Give others a chance to say they are sorry; they may have just been having a bad day.

She was the most unselfish person I've ever known. As her daughter and friend, we had become great friends. I feel honored to have known her and proud to be her daughter.

I watched her evolution through this life. She struggled in her younger years with depression and anger for circumstances which she had no control over, but through the many teachings she studied later in life, she learned to live in the most giving of ways. She gave unselfishly of her time to the point that she took none for herself. She worked diligently to serve her community on the mail route she delivered, not only as a mail carrier, but as a friend. She even had many four-legged friends on her route.

I have read some of the Gnostic teachings of Jesus, and she was the closest person I knew to living those teachings. From my understanding, the belief in that religion is to love unconditionally and without judgment, which for humans is very difficult to do. In our daily lives we must be forgiving of each other's flaws as she was. Even when someone hurt her she forgave. She would hug people who had wronged her, because that was who she was. She lent money to absolute strangers with complete faith on many occasions. I know this because I spent the last thirteen years of my life working beside her five (and many times six) days a week. Some days we drove each other crazy!

Oh did she make us laugh though! She said the craziest things, things you couldn't believe she could come up with! She was also an avid hunter for years. I never understood this part, because of her love of animals, but her understanding was that as long as you made the shot precise and the death quick it was acceptable. Though I remember her telling me when she made her first kill, she had fallen asleep against a tree and woken up to a ten-point buck standing in front of her. He looked her straight in the eyes in shock when she shot him, and she cried. This woman would try to revive road-kill, yet she could shoot animals when hunting! She was a good hunter though, better than a lot of men she knew. I remember her coming down the stairs at the old Legion in her hunting gear, reeking of deer scent and carrying her gun and compass in all her glory! It was great!

Though she left us physically, she will remain with us here in spirit. She is no longer bogged down with this life, though she did everything of her own free will, it was all just too much for her, and she felt a lot of guilt for her past. I tried to tell her to slow down and take some time for herself, but she would have none of it. She has gone to a better place and now her spirit is free. I feel comforted that she is with her daughter, my sister Debbie, who left us a little over a year ago. Debbie was also a mail carrier.

I remember one day years ago when our boss Ed told us we were going to have a mail count at work and my mother went home the night before and did a "magical spell" to bring more mail to make our routes larger. When we came in the next day we had a huge excess of mail, more than we had ever had. Ed looked at us and said "damn Witches!" We all laughed about that for days! Being able to work side by side we were able to discuss so many things. She was involved with real estate which she did for years before the post office, she still loved it. One of us would see a house for sale and she would whip out her financial calculator and figure out the payment on that house in no time. We had big dreams! She had this crazy habit of falling asleep while driving. She would be out doing the route and fall asleep at a mailbox and wake up suddenly and say "Oh my God! How long have I been at this box?" (actually I think that runs in the family because Debbie and I have done that also!) But I think that explains why it took her so long to do the route. She once fell asleep on her motorcycle when riding with her friend Annette. They were going toward Wolfeboro and rounding the corner at Weston Auto Body she went straight and crashed!

    My mother studied the Wiccan path in her later years and had completed level 5 of a witchcraft series of classes with a teacher named Christopher Penczak. He has now, since we took these classes in his mother's basement, gone on to be world famous, and has written several books on the subject. I brought her to her very first class shortly after my grandmother died, as I was soul-searching myself, and had not found peace in the strict catholic beliefs taught to me as a child. Though I only completed Level 1 of these classes, my mother went on to complete all five and also learned the art of Reiki so that she could help to ease peoples physical pain. She became great friends with that teacher. I know that she found peace in this spiritual earth-based, feminine, religion as it has very few physical boundaries.

    She always referred to herself as a "recovering Catholic" she had never quite accepted the Patriarchal ways of the Catholic church. Her new found beliefs were a great distance from the restraints of the strict catholic upbringing she accepted as a child. I believe that she found peace in knowing that life can be beautiful, though she was very hard on herself for things she had lived through in the past. This gave her a way to forgive herself. She has thanked me many times for leading her to this path, as she has found some peace in this life through it.

    Our belief is that we chose our parents before we come into this life because we are here to learn from one another, as well as to teach each other. This is how we evolve in the human spirit and then, when we leave here, we take this knowledge with us into the next life and are more evolved because of it. She and I had found what we were here to teach and learn from one another. To me that was the greatest gift she could have given me. Most people go through this life looking straight ahead instead of all around. Most never realize why they are even here, but chose to question only "Why are these bad things happening to me?" never realizing that without suffering there can be no personal evolution.

This life, though it is good if we find the goodness in it, can pull us into despair if we allow it. She was a hard worker and also took care of her best friend who had cancer, and her friend Harold who had Alzheimer's. These things she did out of pure love and unselfishness because she wanted to. She also had tenants, as she was the landlord of a property in Berlin, NH. She took care of these people. One year she even brought their children Christmas gifts as they were very poor. She was constantly trying to give these people a better life through her generosity as they were all disabled or sick, (one with cancer), in one way or another.

She had also taken in two stray cats who had found their way to her doorstep. She fed all of the local wildlife that frequented her back yard, birds, foxes, raccoons (which occasionally came into the house through the cat door while she was at work to help themselves to whatever they could find) bears, etc. Animals loved her, and they flocked to her in droves. I remember when I started doing the mail-route as her substitute on her days off, one day as I was delivering the mail I noticed a rather large flock of ravens following me from box to box. I thought how weird is that? But when I asked her about it, she said that she throws all of the broken dog biscuits that she has left over from the bags of bones that she gives out to the dogs on her route to the ravens! I asked her why she didn't have internet service and she said she couldn't afford it. But when I went to her house she always had bags of dog food, bird food, etc. even though she didn't have a dog! She fed the animals and went without.

I am telling you all of these things because I want you to know who she truly was. She was happy doing all the things she did. I have come to understand that. She wasn't worried about what other people thought of her and she didn't get embarrassed by anything. She had evolved past that. I envy that, and hope that I can reach this point of evolution before I die.

My mother was and will always be the most wonderful person I have ever known. I only hope that I can grow to be as generous and loving throughout my life through what she has taught me.

My mother gave everything that she had to give and then she slipped away quietly into the night without a fight, peacefully into her dreams and let go of all the fears and worries of this life. She went to her true home where she will be forever free. She will wait there to welcome each of us when it is our time to leave here.

I hope that each person who knew or didn't know her, has come to know her through these words and takes something from the journey of her life that I have shared with you today, and hold that as your own personal piece of this wonderful spirit that she was in this life. Treasure it, because people like her come around only once in a lifetime and if you are lucky enough to get a chance to know them, you are lucky indeed!

I feel that through this journey that was her life, she became a "true Witch" in all of the senses, and as she reached "Crone" she was what I can honestly say a "true Witch" should be.

I love you mom, I will remember you in everything that I do.

I will meet you at the crossroads and we will journey to Avalon together.

Deborah King

By Christopher Penczak

Deb King was my friend, student and role model, though not necessarily in that order. When I first met her, she started out as my role model. She was the first out, proud and openly lesbian I knew. We met at a rented riverside beach house, at her younger daughter, Jessica's, birthday party. I was in college, barely twenty-one and not quite closeted but not quite out and proud. There she was with her then wife Linda and family. We didn't talk much. I'm sure she was a little suspect of her daughter's new heavy metal band friends. Dave, Jessica's boyfriend at the time, just joined our band, and she was lending her skill to our group by designing t-shirts and stickers for us in art class. When she invited us to her party, we thought why not? We were a little out of place, but Deb made a point to spend some time with us and I think that was the first time we talked about reading cards. She said she was into it but that was about it. She wasn't always comfortable talking about that side of her life.

But she was comfortable being out, even though it wasn't a topic for discussion. She just seemed so natural with that aspect of her identity. It didn't come up because it didn't need to. There wasn't a question. We didn't talk about it at all during the party, but I left very proud and impressed. I wanted to hold my own sense of self as well as Deb did. I hadn't really ever seen a happy, normal gay person before that day.

Jessica and I remained friends, even after her boyfriend quit the band and the eventual demise of the whole band. She attended the same college I did, and occasionally heard from or saw Deb over the years. For a short time, before she separated from her partner, they lived within a five minute walk of my parents and I would drive by the house often, though I didn't spend any time at their house. As I progressed into being more open about both my sexuality and my Witchcraft, I began doing more card readings for people professionally, reading at more psychic fairs. Deb requested a reading. I gave it to her and she heard the message she needed to hear. We talked quite a bit and over the years, she came to me for several readings and a little bit of a friendship grew. I had a greater appreciation of her life and her own struggle. She was closeted and married, raised two daughters and decided she needed to get out of a bad marriage and live her life more authentically. For a time she worked as an emergency medical technician on some very dangerous routes. She had seen anything and everything on her patrols. She dealt with a family member with a severe mental imbalance and then a diagnosis of cancer. She had been struggling with liver cancer for as long as I knew her, with periods of great difficulty and pain and other times of seemingly miraculous remission. While she often had the reaper's scythe hanging over her, being given an imminent death sentence, in some ways it seemed like she would never die. She always came back and kept miraculous humor and optimism through the process.

Her daughter was in the first Witchcraft class I ever taught, and soon a member of our coven. When I opened classes up to the public, it was not long after, that Deb asked to join. She took Witchcraft I and II in the Temple of Witchcraft program, long before we were ever calling it that. She bonded with her class mates. She particularly liked the sending light exercise and the scrying. She shared her love of some Native American traditions and stories of hauntings and ghosts she encountered. And of course, there was her experience with her cards. That was our first bond. I'm not sure if she was ever comfortable with the idea of being a Witch and doing spells, but she certainly was a magick woman, a medicine woman in her own way. Her daughter Jessica deepened the healing work of the family, studying both Witchcraft and Native American traditions.

We kept in touch over the years sporadically. We got together for coffee a few times and a few more readings. She moved further and further away, closer to the sea, but seemed distant. Some of her class mates that tried to keep in touch as the class progressed, mentioned difficulty in contacting her. Her illness progressed. We saw each other at some functions, like her daughter's wedding. Sadly I didn't see much of her in the last years, but I'll always remember Deb for showing me how to live a truly authentic and real life.

ROSALIE PENCZAK
(1944-2011)

By Christopher Penczak

I don't know if she ever realized it in life, but my Mother turned out to be the mother of the Temple of Witchcraft. Without her, I don't think our current community would have come together in such a meaningful way. While a very private Witch in her own practice, her home was always open to friends, neighbors and strangers alike, looking for a little bit of magick. Her willingness to mother everybody, particularly those who had no mother or were estranged from their family, and her sense of humor about it all made her more approachable than some Witches whom she found all too serious in their craft. I feel blessed to have her as my Mother and thankful for all her support in our community.

Rosalie lived quite a magickal life, an incredible adventure with stories that entertained and fascinated us all. It might not seem obviously magickal to some, but her life choices brought her to the winding and crooked road of the Witch, and a life she believed she had walked previously. Before it was ever fashionable to talk about such things, Rosalie would mention to those in her confidence about her belief in past lives, and her fleeting memories of Egypt and Italy. She attributed her phobias of water and enclosed spaces as originating in her past incarnations, having vivid memories of being entombed with her pharaoh as a servant and being murdered, stabbed in the back and left to drown in a river in Italy, possibly Venice. She would sometimes meet, somewhat awkwardly, people whom she associated with these past lives, and wasn't always shy about bringing it up, famously so at one particular Raytheon business party with her husband, my father, Ronald. It wasn't until years later that her belief and memories were truly validated in her training as a Witch and explored deeper.

Growing up in Lawrence, Massachusetts in an Italian American household, a lot of traditional folk beliefs survived in her family. While thoroughly Catholic, the Italian Catholics of her family were

Catholics of habit and community, not necessarily of theology and politics. I never heard them talk that much about Jesus, though they all had statues of Jesus, my mother included, in their bedroom. While some had the crucifix, they also had Christ the royal child, in a gold crown, white gown and scepter. If they did talk about Jesus, it was more about baby Jesus, not savior Jesus. Looking back on it, it was easy to see how she could transition to the Sun King Child of Witchcraft. She had already been working with him. Gold St. Christopher medals were popular among the men in her family, with the saint carrying baby Jesus across the river. My father wore one and for a long time I wore one, a gift for my first holy communion. It is now in my medicine bag. Interestingly, it was this popular saint who was the one who was de-emphasized by the Catholic Church for not being proven historically real. God seemed to be some nebulous force guiding us all from beyond, but Mother Mary was also emphasized. All the women also had a statue of Mother Mary somewhere. Rosalie, her mother Jenny and her aunt Mary all paid particular importance to Mary with baby Jesus. Mother Mary was not far from the image of the Goddess, with the Basque goddess Mari being one of the first we were "introduced to" in our magick, and the myths of Mother and Son deities continued to play a strong role in our own practice together.

Other Italian charms to protect against harm and the evil eye were worn by both the men and women. My mother talked about knowing the "witch" down the street. An old white longed-haired lady who lived down the street whom no one really talked to unless they needed help and then when they did, they didn't tell anyone about it. She was both a little scared of the Witch and afraid that she might be lonely, but she was primed in the belief that Witches are real and among us. Her Aunt read tea leaves for fun and seemed to know a few things about the cards, but didn't like to talk about it. Whenever it came up she'd say it was "only a game." Her godmother, Victoria, knew how to break the *Malocchio*, the Evil Eye, with oil, boiling water and a needle, and passed on the tradition to her on Christmas Eve, the customary time to learn it. It was particularly powerful when a baby experienced colic and nothing could cure it. She passed the teaching onto me in my adult life, also on Christmas Eve, through the eyes of a Witch, though also with the traditional prayer to Jesus and Mary. So magick was alive around her, though they never called it that.

Her childhood was one of a poor second generation immigrant family, with her mother working in the mills and her father, Alfred D'Angelo, was often out of work. He originally had planned to be an opera singer in New York City, making the chorus of an opera house. He was kicked out for playing a practical joke on the female star, and eventually made his way north to Lawrence looking for work. He met the Salvucci family, and the three daughters Jenny, Mary and Josephine, marrying Jenny. Rosalie was an unexpected baby coming late in life, but welcomed with joy by the whole family. Mary, without children of her own, took a special interest in her niece, having four other nephews from Josephine.

Rosalie was denied schooling to the local Italian Catholic private school due to her age. Her mother wanted her in school as quickly as possible so she could go back to work full time for the family, so Jenny enrolled her instead in the Polish Catholic school, Holy Trinity, and Rosalie eventually learned to speak a bit, and sing, in Polish, along with Italian at home and English. While she forgot conversational Polish as an adult, she still remembered her hymns in Polish. From grammar school she went to St. Mary's Academy, an all-girls school and sister school to Central Catholic's all boys high school.

She met her future husband Ron "Ronnie" Penczak at a young age, at a carnival. All her friends refused to go on the carousel of daubie horses, feeling they were too old, but it was still her favorite ride. Ron went with her and they kept in touch through mutual friends and social contacts. Her parents were very strict and didn't allow her to date, and Ronnie, a student in public school, was a little more wild and carefree. Alfred died from complications due to surgery when she was sixteen. Being an avid smoker, he had a lung removed successfully, but developed pneumonia in the hospital and never recovered. From then on it was Rosalie, her mother and her aunt living together, and Mary taught her how to drive as Jenny never learned and always took public transportation. Other than vacations at Hampton beach, occasional visits to Boston with Mary and a family outing by train to visit cousins in New York State, Rosalie did not leave her local area.

Photos from her young adult life were reminiscent of Marlo Thomas, "That Girl" as she attended Macintosh Business School and then worked first for an attorney's office in Lawrence, Trombly and Sullivan, and then later as an executive secretary at the American Mutual Insurance Company of Boston. Not having much experience dating in High School, she had both awkward and entertaining experiences in the dating scene, and would tell stories about potential suitors. One in particular that I remember was most likely gay as he wore more make up, and reapplied it on the date, than she did! She would say that she would know pretty immediately that she could not envision anything serious with her date and would break it off fairly quickly to not lead anyone on.

During this time, Ronald Penczak had joined the Marines and gone overseas to Korea. Every year, he would return to visit family and friends, and would make a special date to visit Rosalie. Every time he did, he would propose to her. Each time, she would politely decline, saying he was not ready. At age twenty-four after three proposals, she agreed, stunning him. Ronnie had already decided this was the last time he was asking, and had fully expected her to say no. He explained to her that marriage would require her to move, to live overseas in Asia, specifically South Korea. She knew and agreed. He soon left engaged and she planned for the wedding with their families.

While her mother, aunt and Ron's father Michael were all supportive, Ron's mother, Ann, was not. After threatening Rosalie and her family to make Ron call off the wedding, Rosalie called her bluff and Ron smoothed over things by siding with his bride-to-be and continuing plans for the wedding. Sadly we don't think Ann ever forgave Rosalie for that, and their life long relationship was somewhat fractious despite Rosalie's best effort. The two were wed on May 4, 1969 among family and friends, a day before her own birthday. They soon left for a honeymoon in San Francisco and their new life together on a military base in South Korea. While Ronnie was no longer enlisted in the Marines, but working for the Raytheon Service Company, their housing was still in the military base. Rosalie had never been on a plane before, let alone another coast or country. Their adventure began, and no sooner had they arrived then Ronnie was shipped out for several weeks to Vietnam, during the war, not as a soldier, but a technical radar specialist for Raytheon. She was alone in Korea, with the other business and military wives. Thankfully he returned safely, but she was immersed in a new world of sights, sounds, foods and politics.

She made friends with several wives whose husbands worked with Ron, including a fellow American named Edie. The two had many adventures exploring Korea. One of their shopping trips seemingly resulted in the purchase of a Korean national treasure, an image of Quan Yin which was shipped back to the US before either the authorities, or members of the local black market posing as the authorities, caught up with her. Since they dropped interest in it once it was in the US, the family always doubted if it was someone lawful pursuing her and the painting. Her overseas shopping resulted in several Quan Yin images returning to the U.S. Quan Yin is the goddess of compassion and forgiveness, particularly the patron of women and children. Much of our house was decorated with finds from Korea, often from the black market.

Rosalie also made friends with a woman named Maria who was also part of the social circles with her husband Jim. Jim, Maria, Rosalie and Ron all returned to New England, eventually all settling in New Hampshire roughly at the same time to raise families. Ron and Rosalie reconnected with Maria after Jim's death, while Rosalie was struggling with her own illness. Before they returned, Rosalie got to see Japan and Hong Kong and got quite a worldly education meeting people from many different countries through their relationships in Raytheon.

Upon returning, due to illness with his own father, Ronnie quit Raytheon and worked at Michael's Television Repair Shop in Metheun, Massachusetts, his father's shop. Rosalie was soon pregnant with me and Michael decided to close the business rather than give it to his son. Ron went back to work for Raytheon, moving from engineer and radar systems into management, and pursuing higher education to further his career. He and Rosalie soon bought their first house in Salem, New Hampshire, where they spent the majority of their life. After both working in the repair shop, Rosalie chose to stay at home to raise her son, giving birth to me on May 10, 1973. May became an important month in our lives, with their anniversary, her birthday, my birthday, Mother's day and later Beltane and her own passing.

We had a fun suburban upper middle class life. My father's travels for work afforded us many frequent flyer vacations so we got to see much of the country as a family, with trips to Florida, New York City, California, Texas, Arizona, Las Vegas, Montreal and Hawaii, as well as all of New England through driving trips and even a later visit to Hong Kong. Our house became the "hang out" for many of my friends, and my mom took a particular delight in cooking for us all and hosting sleep overs and various parties. Both of my parents were very supportive of my own dreams, at various times ranging wildly from art to chemistry to music and playing in a band.

While close to both of my parents, my dad traveled a lot for work, and the bond between my mother and I grew especially close. She shared, or at least pretended to share, my love of comic books, and later glam metal. While it might have been a point of bonding, she could name on sight all of Spider-man's villains and knew most of the words to Bon Jovi's *Slippery When Wet*, Cinderella's *Night Songs* and Guns N Roses' *Appetite for Destruction*. In turn, she shared with me her love of Italian opera and Broadway music and I learned all the words to *Phantom of the Opera* and *Les Miserables*. We both followed the career of Michael Crawford, first Phantom, and the three of us got to see him in a Broadway review, along with many other plays and concerts. Both of my parents visited me often when I was playing in various biker bars and heavy metal dives with my college band, Doctor Soulshine, and hosted many a rehearsal of my various high school bands. We also shared a love of Ann Rice's vampire novels, having a special understanding of the main character, Lestat, and his mother Gabrielle, and their unique relationship roaming the world together before their eventual parting.

Much of Rosalie's own time was spent taking care of her elderly mother and aunt, and while Ronnie traveled, his parents as well. Michael was prone to unexpected hospital visits and emergency procedures as he slowly deteriorated. After an experimental brain surgery procedure to save his life sometime in the 1970s, he never fully recovered his sense of self or personality. It seemingly unlocked a lot of his own repressed emotions and thoughts, and his marriage with Ann and his relationship with the family suffered tremendously for it. He tried to cope through his art and was an amateur portrait and landscape painter. Her aunt passed 1989 due to cancer and Jenny lost the will to live, but continued onward ailing in body and mind, moving in with the family in Salem until her passing in 1993. Michael passed in 1991 and soon after Ann in 1998. Despite their original difficulties, at the end of her life Rosalie was the one who spent the most time caring for and giving support to her mother-in-law.

Our relationship really deepened, and our family changed in many ways, while I was in college. Going to an all-boys Catholic school, Central Catholic, and realizing I was gay yet still closeted, made me question the wisdom of an all loving and forgiving god who did not accept homosexuals. So after my mandatory religious education, I began to explore. My studies brought me to all sorts of interesting, but for various reasons, impractical, looks into Shinto, Taoism, Buddhism and Hinduism. All had a certain intellectual appeal, but none set me on the path. I looked into some Jungian psychology in terms of understanding myself. That was slightly closer. I was starting school, taking a one-eighty from chemical engineering and into music performance and sound engineering. My previous interests in alchemy were thwarted by the prevailing myth that alchemy was not real but rather, it was a spiritual science, a superstition that thankfully led to chemistry. Then a fateful older family friend introduced me, and eventually my Mom, to Witchcraft.

Though I didn't know it at the time, my new interest in Witchcraft and the occult gravely concerned my Mother. She didn't know what to think other than the misconceptions on television and movies at the time. She envisioned a group in black robes sacrificing goats, or worse yet, babies! But she knew me well enough that if she forbid me, she would most likely lose my attention, so she feigned interest to see what I was getting involved with. Unknowingly proving the old adage "fake it till you make it" she did fake it, attending circles with this friend and mentor and mostly deeming it harmless and sometimes interesting. She liked the crystals and the cards. She loved gazing at the Moon and calling it down to her. She loved the incense and candles because it reminded her of all the things she liked about Church, but she loved Witchcraft as there was no sin, just responsibility, and no politics, at least in terms of the oppression of women. Eventually she committed to it when she decided that she could be her own priestess and didn't have to answer to a man.

She remained somewhat opened minded until the mentor was ready to pass me to her own teacher, a famous and controversial Witch in Salem, Massachusetts, holding the title of "official witch" Laurie Cabot. All she saw was this serious Witch, ready to teach her baby. So she decided to also tag along with me and our family friend and soon to be Witch Sister, Laura, for Witchcraft One: Witchcraft As A Science. She kept her concerns hidden from me, and didn't mention it until years later what her motivation was, but in the meantime, by the end of Witchcraft Two: Witchcraft As An Art and Science, she had given up on Catholicism and formed our first coven with me and Laura. We celebrated the Full Moons doing spells together, making potions and celebrated the eight sabbats. The psychic healing work was very empowering and quite honestly mind blowing, changing the three of us, as we all believed we couldn't do it. Rosalie also had a very personal healing experience in a counseling session with Laurie, at our graduation night in Witchcraft II in Laurie's home.

Soon after, we got brave, and invited friends who were interested. Our friend Christina joined us regularly in circle and to do magick. Ronnie, first fearing his family had lost their mind to become Witches, became a little more open minded when our spells for him worked better than he could have hoped. We soon started a tradition of hosting an invitation only Samhain celebration for friends, family and the curious but respectful. I would organize the ritual proceedings, while Rosalie would host the party, and cooked for the entire crew. The first circle started with around twenty people, and by the last open Samhain, twelve years later, we had over seventy people in the back yard of their second house, well into the period of my own writing and teaching career.

These Samhain gatherings formed the nucleus of people coming together who would eventually form the Temple of Witchcraft. She even hunted down High Priestess Alix Wright, her former neighbor at our first house, because of her pagan bumper sticker, and invited her to classes and events, not knowing she would be one of the strongest foundations for the Temple.

From that first Samhain our little group of regulars grew somewhat. When we formed a larger, formal coven, Rosalie withdrew from the group, but continued to host rituals, parties, esoteric book club dinners, and various circles for when needs arose. She practiced her psychic readings on friends and neighbors who were curious, sometimes using cards, but more often using her lead crystal ball or simply holding their hand and letting the reading flow out of her. She explained Witchcraft to others who asked in a very informal and down to Earth way, often over coffee or tea and cake in the dining room or porch if the weather was nice. As I came out of the closet, dated and married Steve Kenson, she and Ronnie welcomed him with open arms into the family. When we later welcomed Adam Sartwell into our marriage, although unorthodox and a little confusing for her and my father at first, they both welcomed Adam into our family as well.

She supported all our work in the Temple of Witchcraft, often being the test case for a lot of new material and discussing new ideas for classes and events. She was my first proof reader and editor for my early books, offering some critical suggestions and advice to improve them. Both parents created space in our first home, and then later when building a new home, for an office-class room for me, rather than renting a space at a metaphysical center. With that support, I was able to begin and flourish my writing and teaching career. All of this laid a foundation for our current community and without them, I'm not sure where we would be.

Rosalie's own practice took her from the Cabot Tradition of Witchcraft into Stregheria, the Italian form of Witchcraft. A favorite author was Raven Grimassi, one of the few writing about her own magickal heritage. In his work, she could see connections between Italian folk customs and began her own adoration of the Queen of the Wise through the image of Diana, a Roman goddess of the Moon,

Witches and Faeries. While never initiated as a Strega in a formal lineage, she identified with the word, and used material from *Aradia, Or The Gospel of the Witches*, in her own rituals. The book is believed by some to be a grimoire of Strega magick and lore involving Diana, her brother-lover Lucifer and their daughter, Aradia, who came to Italy in 1313 to teach the peasants the ways of Witchcraft and to overthrow the Catholic Church's power. Rosalie had a mural of Diana at Lake Nemi commissioned by a local American-Italian artist in the foyer of their second home, and displayed her massive crystal ball collection to the side of the mural. She took a special delight in the Aradia material and her practice involved food magick.

Not only did my mother love to feed people, but also the animals of her home, making a nightly ritual and altar space in the back yard to them. Their suburban yard tended to attract all manner of creatures, from crows and hawks to foxes and deer. She saw them all as manifestations of spirit, children of the Goddess. She decided against having further household pets after the death of our German Shepard, Apollo, after a very long, emotional and expensive time with a variety of rare illnesses and conditions.

As her path continued to unfold, she explored a variety of other healing modalities, including Reiki with my Dad, studying Reiki I with my own teacher, Joanna Pinney-Buel, and then taking Reiki II with me after I received my mastership. She also received crystal healing, flower essences and transformational breath work at various times. Later she became part of the Tong-Ren healing community in Haverhill, receiving weekly treatments in their group setting, and visiting with their founder, Tom Tam, for private sessions.

Rosalie was diagnosed with pancreatic cancer in 2007 and, despite all the doctor's predictions of a life span measured in months, she underwent surgery and continued with her family and friends for another four years, passing just before her anniversary on May 3, 2011, just short of 42 years together with Ron. While the surgery was successful, complications due to her following chemotherapy and radiation treatment ultimately proved to be the cause of death. She left behind a beloved husband and son, two sons-in-law, her adopted daughters Laura and Christina, her adopted grandkids, Rowan and Olivia and an amazing community of Witches building upon the foundation she helped create. It was never so evident than at her wake and funeral.

In true Witch style, she was buried in her cloak, with gold pentacle and in the Osiris position, arms crossed over her heart, wand in one hand, blade in the other. A selection of Broadway, opera, pagan chants and her favorite "I'll Be Seeing You" by Tony Bennet cycling in the background. Her funeral circle occurred in the back yard she so loved, lit with torches and candles, decorated with flowers and fire. The day was preceded by sun, wind, hail, rain, then a light mist throughout the service. The gathering was followed by her house filled with people and an Italian feast cooked with love and magick, just as Rosalie would have wanted.

Her body was cremated and her ashes scattered on Maui, Hawaii, in the Valley of the Kings and Queens.

Epilogue: What is Remembered, Lives...

The following is a list of modern ancestors compiled by pagan elder and author Oberon Zell Ravenheart. It included a wide range of teachers and leaders, some famous and some fairly unknown, but nonetheless important in their local communities, where their teaching and magick ripples out to us all in ways unknown and unseen. This list was circulated when compiling this anthology, as Oberon was working on a similar project, and is reproduced with permission from Oberon.

Departed Pagan Pioneers, Founders and Elders

Since records began Samhain has been considered a night of occult power, when the veil between the unseen world and ours is at its thinnest, a night when the spirits of our departed are free to roam. As such, Samhain has always been considered the best time to honour our ancestors and other departed souls. Oberon Zell-Ravenheart, George Knowles, Angie Buchanan, and many others in the Pagan community have been working together to construct a list of contemporary departed "Pagan Founders, Pioneers and Elders," those who have died over the past 100 years. These are the people whose dedication and inspiration has helped shape the foundations of our beliefs to-date. Please all light a candle on Samhain and let us remember them:

Died 1900-1940

Charles Godfrey Leland (8/15/1824-3/20/1903)

Old George Pickingill (5/26/1816-1909)

S.L. MacGregor-Mathers (1/8/1854-11/20/1918)

Died in 1940s

Arthur Edward Waite (10/2/1857-5/19/1942)

Dion Fortune (Violet Mary Firth Evans) (12/6/1890-1/8/1946)

Adriana Porter ("Rede of the Wiccae") (c. 1850-1946)

Aleister Crowley (10/12/1875-12/1/1947)

Rosamund Sabine (probable matriarch of group into which Gardner was initiated) (2/5/1865-5/6/1948)

Died in 1950s

Old Dorothy Clutterbuck (1/19/1880–1/12/1951)

Pamela Colman-Smith (Pixie) (2/16/1878-9/18/1951)

Jack Parsons (10/2/19146/17/1952)

Lydia Becket (Aradian Temple of Diana; Lawrence Museum of Magic & Witchcraft) (5/31/1871-12/21/1953)

Austin Osman Spare (12/30/1886-5/15/1956)

Franz Bardon (12/1/1909-7/10/1958)

Died in 1960s

Donna Gardner (1895-1960)

Katherine Oldmeadow (best friend of Dorothy Clutterbuck and probably a member of the group who initiated Gardner) (6/10/1878-7/8/1963)

Margaret Alice Murray (God of the Witches) (7/13/1863-11/13/1963)

Gerald Brousseau Gardner (6/13/1884-2/12/1964)

Robert Cochrane/Roy Bowers (1734 Tradition) (1/26/1931-7/3/1966)

Ciarriadhe (Kerry Harvey) (Daughters of the Triple Goddess, Framingham, MA) (6/21/1899-6/21/1969)

Norman Lindsay (Australian Pagan artist) (2/22/1879-11/21/1969)

Gleb Evgenievich Botkin (Church of Aphrodite—1930s) (7/29/1900-12/27/1969)

Died in 1970s

Barbara Vickers (Gerald Gardner's first initiate) (7/13/1922-1973)

Arnold Crowther (10/7/1909-5/1/1974)

Edith Woodford-Grimes (Dafo) (12/18/1887-10/28/1975)

Phillip Peter Ross Nichols (6/28/1902-4/30/1975)

Charles Cardell (Rex Nemorensis / The Fish) (1892-1977)

Bonnie Sherlock (Delphic Coven, Lander, WY) (d. late '70s)

Walter Ernest Butler (British occultist and esoteric author) (1898-1978)

Ernie Mason (hereditary Witch in the group who initiated Gardner) (9/1/1885-2/26/1979)

Susie Mason (hereditary Witch in group who initiated Gardner, sister of Ernie Mason) (8/22/1882-3/30/1979)

Monica English (traditional Witch from East Anglia and member of Bricket Wood coven) (1/8/1920-9/30/1979)

Rosaleen Miriam Norton (Australia) (10/2/1917-12/5/1979)

John Score (8/1914-12/30/1979)

Died in 1980s

Jack Bracelin (member of Bricket Wood coven, ran Fiveacres naturist club, co-author of biography *Gerald Gardner Witch*) (6/2/1926-7/28/1981)

Bill Mohs (the Mohsian Tradition) (??-1981)

Sybil Leek (Diary of a Witch) (2/22/1917-10/26/1982)

Monique Campbell Wilson (Olwen) (1923-1982)

Gwydion Pendderwen (the Faerie Shaman) (5/21/1946-11/9/1982)

Jane Roberts (Witches USA) (5/8/1929-9/5/1984)

George "Pat" Patterson (Georgian Wicca, Bakersfield, CA) (d. 1984)

Mary Cardell (1912-1984)

Francis Israel Regardie (11/17/1907-3/10/1985)

Grady Louis McMurtry (OTO, San Francisco) (10/18/1918-7/12/1985)

Lady Gwen Thomson (NECTW) (9/16/1928-5/22/1986)

"Grandmaster Eli" (Barney C. Taylor) (Druidic Craft of the Wise) (1/30/1916-1/24/1983)

Alex Sanders (Orrell Alexander Carter) (King of the Alexandrian Witches) (6/6/1926-4/30/1988)

Edmund "Eddie" Buczynski (Lord Hermes) (Minoan Brotherhood, NYC) (1/28/1947-3/16/1989)

Died in 1990s

Simon Goodman (9/16/1951-9/23/1991)

Herman Slater (Govannon) (The Magickal Childe, NYC) (2/1/1938-7/9/1002)

William G. Gray (1913-1992)

Scott Cunningham (6/27/1956-3/28/1993)

Marija Gimbutas (1/23/1921-2/2/1994)

Robert Joseph Shea (co-author with Robert Anton Wilson of the *Illuminatus!* trilogy) (2/14/1933-3/10/1994)

Lawrence Durdin-Robertson (Co-Founder of Fellowship of Isis, Ireland) (5/6/1920-8/4/1994)

Margaret St Clair (Sign of the Labrys) (2/17/1911-11/22/1995)

Adam Walks-Between-Worlds Rostoker (CAW Bard) (??-2/20/1996)

Lord Theodore Parker Mills, Jr. (Craft Elder, Pagan veteran) (11/19/24-2/21/96)

W. Holman Keith (Neo-Dianic Faith) (6/11/1900-1996)

Lord Theodore Mills (d. 1996)

John Patrick McClimans (Priest No. 3 of CAW) (11/19/1947-11/10/1996)

Vivian Godfrey (Melita Denning) (Grand Master of the Order of Aurum Solis) (6/16/1905-3/23/1997)

Kerry Wendell Thornley (Omar Khayyam Ravenhurst) (Principia Discordia) (4/17/1938-11/28/1998)

Ayeisha (KAM, Baltimore-DC area) (d. 1998)

Annette Hinshaw (PEN, ESBAT, WPPA) (d. 2/22/1999)

Emmon M. Bodfish (Founder of the independent RDNA newsletter, the DRUID MISSAL-ANY) (4/20/1943-6/30/1999)

Sandy Kopf (Covenant of the Goddess) (d. 7/11/1999)

Doreen Valiente (Ameth) (1/4/1922-9/1/1999)

Marion Zimmer Bradley (The Mists of Avalon) (6/3/1930-9/25/1999)

Grechon Leigh (founder of SageTree in Michigan) (d. 7/18/1999)

Cecil Hugh Williamson (9/18/1909-12/9/1999)

Died in 2000s

Stewart Farrar (Alexandrian Wicca, Ireland) (6/28/1916-2/7/2000)

Leo Louis Martello (Sicilian Strega, NYC) (9/26/1030-6/29/2000)

Gregory Hill (Malaclypse the Younger) (Principia Discordia) (5/21/1941-7/20/2000)

Judy Foster (Calypso Iris) (11/2/1932-10/8/2000)

Joyce Rasmussen (Lady Tara) (High Tor Gardnerian Lineage) (??-3/21/2001

Victor Henry Anderson (Feri) (5/21/1917-9/20/2001)

Eleanor Ray Bone (Artemis) (12/15/1911-9/21/2001)

Pauline Campanelli (1/25 1943-11/29/2001)

Marilee (Starwhite) Lewis (Minister CAW, Gold Mountain Nest, Berkeley) (7/27/1938-1/6/2002)

Jessie Wicker Bell (Lady Sheba) (7/18/1920-3/20/2002)

Charles Clark (4/26/1930-8/17/2002)

Kay Gardner (Pagan feminist musician) (2/8/1940-8/28/2002)

Baba Raul Canizares (Oba, Santerían priest, author, artist, musician and professor of religion who founded the Orisha Consciousness Movement) (9/24/1955-12/28/2002)

Jeffrey John Koslow (longtime member of Circle Sanctuary and Pagan Spirit Gathering) (8/31/1947-6/18/2003)

Tim Maroney (Gnostic Priest; initiate of the Ordo Templi Orientis, Neo-Pagan Witchcraft, Golden Dawn. Author, *The Book of Dzyan*) (10/28/1961-7/3/2003)

Nelson White (The White Light) (10/29/1938-8/23/2003)

Ellen Cannon Reed (3/21/1943-10/7/2003)

Patalee Glass-Koetep (Lady Phoenix) (10/27/1943-11/11/2003)

Evan John Jones (1936-2003)

Harry McBride (Belenus) (founding board member Fellowship of the Spiral Path) (3/7/1941-12/27/2003)

Donald D. Harrison (Church of Eternal Source) (5/31/1931-1/7/2004)

Andrew Chumbley (past Magister of Cultus Sabbati) (9/15/1967-1/15/2004)

Donna Cole Schultz (Pagan Way, Chicago, IL) (5/15/1937-3/31/2004)

Lady Circe (Alliance of the Old Religion) (9/8/1921-5/29/2004)

Alison Harlow (Covenant of the Goddess) (8/29/1934-6/13/2004)

Joseph "Bearwalker" Wilson (brought 1734 Tradition to U.S.) (12/11/1942-8/4/2004)

Robert Larson (co-founder and Arch-Druid of Berkeley Grove of RDNA) (9/31/1943-8/6/2004)

Judy Carusone (Isian, HP of Lady of the Sacred Flame) (d. 9/21/2004)

Albert N. Webb (aka Ur) (West Coast Eclectic Elder) (1/8/1947-1/7/2005)

Elizabeth Pepper Da Costa (The Witch's Almanac) (12/7/1923-7/14/2005)

Lady Galadriel (Jodi Monogue) (High Priestess Grove of the Unicorn, Atlanta, GA) (1956-2/8/2006)

Leigh Ann Hussey "motogrrl" (musician, Annwfn; Elder Priestess NROOGD & OTO) (7/31/1961-5/16/2006)

Robert Anton Wilson (Illuminatus!) (1/18/1932-1/11/2007)

Lady Ariadne (High Priestess Unicorn Grove Chattanooga TN) (8/16/1940-6/21/2007)

Shekhinah Mountainwater (10/24/1939-8/11/2007)

Susan Grace Falkenrath (aka: Susan North, Susan Green, Susan Wolf, Susan Oak) (long-time member of the Reclaiming community) (7/4/1954-1/12/2008)

Lady Phoenix (Mimi Rohwer) (HPs & Nat'l Director 1st Celtic Wiccan Church, Inc.) (6/21/1932-1/21/2008)

Cora Anderson (wife of Victor) (Feri) (1/26/1915-5/1/2008)

Frederick MacLaren Adams (Feraferia) (2/4/1928-8/9/2008)

Christopher Hyatt (Founder of Extreme Individual Institute (EII); president New Falcon Publications) 7/12/1943-2/9/2008)

Phoenix (Tom Kneitel) (Long Island Gardnerian Coven in 1970s; husband of Theos) (?/?/1933-8/22/2008)

John Lyon Burnside III (Founder of Radical Faeries) (11/2/1916 to 9/14/2008)

Tara Webster (founder of the Death Crones coven, inspiration of "Death Crones" comic strip; wife of Sam Webster) (??-10/9/2008)

Sequoia Greenfield (Dianic, Earth First!) (9/12/1944-10/10/2008)

Gloria Gonzales Villanueva (Circle Sanctuary priestess, curandera) (3/26/48-12/25/08)

Eric Erickson (founding member of the Order of the Pentacle) (11/27/1956-2/27/2009)

Joel D. Gainer (Wolfhawk) (founding member of the Order of the Pentacle) (12/26/1948-3/25/2009)

Laura Thompson (Rasmussen—daughter of Joyce & Quentin) (High Tor Gardnerian Lineage) (4/4/2009)

Marion Weinstein (author of *Positive Magic and Earth Magic*) (5/19/1939-7/1/2009)

Ted Andrews (author of *Animal Speak*) (7/16/1952-10/24/2009)

Norman Nelson (Reformed Druids of North America) (d. 4/2009)

Shay Lee (SCPN, Santa Rosa, CA) (3/24/1945-10/16/2009)

Thomas Eddie Hufford (aka Balu, Lord Patrick O'Reilly the Tall) (HP of Wes Tran Alpha Coven, Wash., DC; SCA) (12/21/1947 to 11/29/2009)

Died in the 2010s

Pam Kolozsy (Illinois. Co-Founder, PSG Crone Temple of Wisdom) (1948-1/31/2010)

Roy 'Cuchulainn' Moorman (11/18/1957-3/1/2010)

Susan Leigh Star (d. 3/24/2010)

Hummy Byron (1947-4/24/2010)

T.J. Collins (Ohio. LGBTQ activist; Co-Director, PSG Rainbow Center) (12/4/1978-4/26/2010)

Robin Goodfellow (Stephen Richard Edwards) (3/11/1945-5/1/2010)

Alexei Kondratiev (High Priest, Coven Mnemosynides, Queens, NY) (2/15/1949-5/28/2010)

Svetlana Butyrin (wife of Fred Adams) (Feraferia) (11/2/1934-5/6/2010)

Bruce Kirk Parsons (Wisconsin. Wiccan priest & teacher) (5/10/1947-6/15/2010)

Harold Moss (Church of Eternal Source) (1/30/1937-7/15/2010)

Phillip Emmons Isaac Bonewits (ADF) (10/1/1949-8/12/2010)

Lady Sintana (Candace Lehrman White) (House of Ravenwood, Atlanta, GA) (1937-9/17/2010)

Len Rosenberg (Black Lotus) (partner of Alexei Kondratiev) (1951-10/15/2010)

Richard Lance Christie (co-founder of ATL, Church of All Worlds, Earth First!) (4/7/1944-10/28/2010)

Jehanah Wedgwood (OBOD groves: Manannan Mac Lir, House of Danu) (1/28/1941-11/15/2010)

Trudy Herring (Mama Dragon) (co-founder of Summerland Grove, Memphis, TN) (??-12/18/2010)

Ardath Elizabeth "Beth" Saunders Stanford (Bone Blossom) (co-founder of Reclaiming Tradition Craft) (12/21/1948-2/10/2011)

Sharon Mitchell (Lady Bastet) (HPs Our Lady at the Shoreline, Gardnerian Witch Queen) (3/1/1947-1/12/2011)

Kenneth Grant (Head of the Typhonian Order, operator of New Isis Lodge during the 1950s, and spiritual heir to Aleister Crowley) (5/23/1924-1/15/2011)

Tammy Breckenridge (Tzaddia Morningstar) (Summerland Grove minster) (7/4/1971-1/20/2011)

Merlin Stone (When God was a Woman) (9/27/1931-2/23/2011)

Steve Collins (Lord Senthor) (Elder of Ravenwood Church, Atlanta, GA; headed Pagan band "Moonstruck") (1956-3/14/2011)

DenaJoy Peacemaker (Texas CMA, CAW Fred Nest) (1/24/1967-3/9/2011)

Bronwen Forbes (co-founder, Free Spirit Alliance) (?/?/1963-4/10/2011)

Gary Ball (Between the Worlds, Mendocino Environmental Center, Rocky Mountain Peace & Justice Center) (12/14/1948-5/8/2011)

Lady Amythyst Avalon (Bobbie Osley) (Avalon Isle, Highlands of Tennessee Samhain Gathering) (2/2/1932-7/2/2011)

George Moyer (Dragonfest, Hole in the Stone) (8/23/1952-8/25/2011)

Tania Levy (Greenfield Ranch pioneer) (1/7/1946-9/1/2011)

Lord Merlin (Elder High Priest of the House of Ravenwood, and numerous covens) (7/12/1935-9/23/2011)

Lady Judith Brownlee (Fortress Temple, Denver CO. In *Who's Who of Religious Studies*) (4/28/1942-10/1/2011)

Carl Henry Dietz (Los Angeles, CAW Live the Dream) (1/9/1937-10/2/2011)

Joyce Siegrist (Lady Genevieve) (Rosegate Coven, Witches' Anti-Defamation League, Rhode Island) (2/5/1943-10/3/2011)

Lady Morganna (Co-founder of KAM (Keepers of the Ancient Mysteries) in the Baltimore area in the 1970s) (??-12/27/2011)

Bran Starbuck (Greenfield Rancher, Mohsian Craft) (11/30/1940-1/22/2012)

DeAnna Alba (Wendy White) (priestess, singer, author of *The Cauldron of Change*). (3/31/52-1/24/2012)

Gordon Pepin (Circle Sanctuary, Pagan Spirit Gathering Community) (9/20/51-2/10/2012)

Lord Athanor (John Mongue) (High Priest of the Grove of the Unicorn, Atlanta, GA) (11/25/1956-2/13/2012)

Grey Cat (NorthWind Tradition of American Wicca, Tennessee) (6/16/1940-3/30/2012)

Julie Ann Wichman (Circle Sanctuary) (12/27/1963-8/22/2012)

Anne Ross (Celtic historian, author of *Pagan Celtic Britain* and other influential books) (1925 – 8/29/2012)

Mike Gleason (Alexandrian High Priest, New England) (3/14/51-8/30/2012)

Richard Joel Ravish (Magister Azaradel Coven of Akhelarre, Temple of Nine Wells-ATC, Founder White Light Pentacles/Sacred Spirit Products Inc./Nu Aeon, Salem, MA) (12/26/1952-9/15/2012)

Lady Amber (Amber Maeve Szymanski) (High Priestess, Winged Scarab/Unicorn Tradition, Acworth, GA) (1/5/1946-10/3/2012)

Patricia Monaghan (*Book of Goddesses & Heroines*) (2/15/1946-11/11/2012)

Herbert John DeGrasse (Fellowship of the Spiral Path) (9/22/1941-11/9/2012)

Thomas T. Clauser (Radagast the Bard) (2/18/1944-1/20/2013)

Deena Celesta Butta (Fellowship of Isis priestess) (6/1/1950-1/27/2013)

Captain Dennis Presser (Circle Sanctuary environmentalist, foundering member Order of the Pentacle) (11/10/58-2/16/13)

Kyril Oakwind (CAW Priestess) (1951-3/9/2013)

Quentin Rasmussen (High Tor Gardnerian Lineage & various other Covens) 3/30/2013)

Bronwynn Forrest Torgerson (author of *One Witch's Way*) (5/1/1953-4/12/2013)

Stuart Wilde (author of over 20 books on Spirituality & Personal Development; considered one of the greatest metaphysicians who ever lived; founder of the Taos metaphysical tradition) (9/24/1946-5/1/2013)

Laura Jansdaughter (ArchPriestess, Temple of Isis Pelagia) (??-5/25/2013)

Dal Burns (Gypsy Stargiver) (Gwydion's partner on Annwfn 1980-'82) (7/2/1951-6/5/2013)

Craig Pierce (Elder, Iron Web Coven of Austin, TX) (1957-6/20/2013)

Tom Davis (Elder, Gaia Tradition of Austin, TX) (7/18/1945-6/27/2013)

Demian Allan Moonbloode (NROOGD, OTO) 1/6/1947-9/14/2013

Stephany Lyn Rasmussen (Joyce & Quentin Rasmussen's last child; all were instrumental in the 1970s working and teaching with Gardnerian covens & groups) (4/10/1960-10/10/2013)

Deborah Bourbon (Pathways New Age Books Music & Gifts, St Louis; Oberon Zell's first Craft teacher) (8/26/1949-10/20/2013)

Dawn Decker (Feri Trad; major Annwfn supporter) (12/12/1940-10/24/2013)

Layne Redmond (author of *When the Drummers Were Women*) (1951-10/28/2013)

Olivia Durdin-Robertson (Founder of the Fellowship of Isis) (4/13/1917–11/14/2013)

And so many others we have known whose lives and works made our Pagan world what it is today. But what is remembered, lives...

CONTRIBUTOR BIOGRAPHIES

Christine Ashworth

Christine Ashworth is a native of Southern California. The daughter of a writer and a psych major, she fell asleep to the sound of her father's Royal manual typewriter for years. In a very real way, being a writer is in her blood—her father sold his first novel before he turned forty, and he is still writing and selling novels. At the tender age of seventeen, Christine fell in love with a man she met while dancing with California Ballet Company in San Diego. She married the brilliant actor/dancer/painter /music man, and they now have two tall sons who are as intelligent and witty as their parents, which keeps the dinner conversation lively. Christine's two dogs rule the outside, defending her vegetable garden from the squirrels, while a huge polydactyl rescue cat holds court inside the house. Everything else is in a state of flux, leaving her home life a cross between an improv class, a musician's jam session, and a think-tank for the defense of humans against zombies and demons. Christine's first novel, a paranormal romance called *Demon Soul*, was released in March 2011; her second novel, *Demon Hunt*, released on July 15, 2012 from Crescent Moon Press. Follow her at *www.christine-ashworth.com* .

Patricia (Bona Dea) DeSandro

Patricia (Bona Dea) DeSandro is a seer and works within the Wisewoman/Shamanic and Romano-Celtic traditions as an Elder and High Priestess. She founded the Circle of the Sacred Grove Temple of the Old Religion in 1999. She is also a Certified Hypnotherapist. Patricia has been presenting public rituals and workshops nationally since 1989 and has authored guided meditation CD's, available on Amazon.com, Rhapsody, and iTunes. For more information, visit *www.kenningstone.com* and *www.circleofthesacredgrove.org*.

Jimahl di Fiosa

Jimahl di Fiosa is a respected Elder and High Priest of Alexandrian Witchcraft. His interest in the occult spans many years. In 1999 he caused a big splash in the pagan publishing world when he penned his first book, *A Voice in the Forest, Spirit Conversations with Alex Sanders*. The book became an overnight success with critics and readers alike and is now considered to be a classic of pagan literature. In 2010 he completed work on *All the King's Children, the Human Legacy of Alex Sanders,* which in two short weeks after release had literally swept the world and was being read as far away as Japan and India. In December 2010, Jimahl released a long awaited new biography of Alex Sanders entitled *A Coin for the Ferryman, the Death and Life of Alex Sanders,* which he considers the third book in what he refers to as "The Alex Trilogy." Jimahl makes his home in New England with his husband Karagan. To learn more about Jimahl, please visit his website at *www.jimahldifiosa.com*.

Bill Duvendack

Rev. Bill Duvendack is an ordained independent Spiritualist minster who can legally perform spiritual ceremonies of all kinds. He has been working with the Western Esoteric Tradition for 25 years, and has extensive knowledge and experience in many of those different traditions, as well as familiarity with Eastern Traditions. He is also an internationally known professional astrologer and published author. For more information, please visit *www.418ascendant.com*.

Storm Faerywolf

Storm Faerywolf is an artist, writer, poet, teacher, and initiate of the F(a)eri(e) tradition of witchcraft. He has been practicing the Craft for over 25 years and teaching for more than 15. He has lead open circles, given lectures, and taught classes in the San Francisco Bay Area and across the U.S. He holds the Black Wand, an honor bestowed by Feri Grandmaster Cora Anderson. He has studied diverse practices from various branches of the tradition which he incorporates into his own line of Feri, BlueRose. He is the author of *The Stars Within the Earth*, the editor of *WitchEye: A Journal of Feri Uprising* and an owner of The Mystic Dream, a spiritual supply store in the San Francisco East Bay. For more information about his classes or his art visit his website at *www.faerywolf.com* .

Daniel Fox

Daniel Fox is a High Priest in the Temple of Witchcraft. He is also a software engineer with 23 years of experience in, as he calls it, puzzle-solving. In 2009, he took a three-year hiatus from software engineering to write a novel, which is currently being professionally edited. Having witchcraft affect a balance of engineering and writing is an ideal that Daniel strives for.

Raven Grimassi

Raven Grimassi is a published author of many titles on witchcraft and Wicca, including *Italian Witchcraft, Hereditary Witchcraft, The Cauldron of Memory*, and *Old World Witchcraft*. He is Co-Directing Elder of the Ash, Birch, and Willow Tradition, a system reflecting the commonality of European rooted traditions of Witchcraft. Raven is also Co-Director of the Fellowship of the Pentacle. He maintains a website at *www.ravengrimassi.net*

Elizabeth Guerra

Elizabeth Guerra discovered Wicca in 1989 and was initiated into both a traditional group and an eclectic group. In 2000, she received her Third Degree Initiation from Janet Farrar and Gavin Bone. Over the years, she has written articles in local periodicals, has appeared on radio, a local news program, and has been interviewed in two documentaries. For many years, she studied the ancient sites of Ireland and conducts tours each year *www.sacredsitetour.com*. Today her spiritual journey has taken her on a different path and she no longer practices any one religion, considering herself to be simply "spiritual". Professionally, Ms. Guerra holds a degree in Human Services from Springfield College and is certified in addiction counseling. She currently resides in New England. *Stewart Farrar: Writer On A Broomstick* is Ms. Guerra's first major book.

Gary Lee Hoke

Gary Lee Hoke is the author of *The History of Dr. Frederick LaMotte Santee and the Coven of the Catta* © 2010 and *Coven of the Catta – Elders and History, Unique Ritual Practices and Spells* © 2010.

Kurt Hunter

Kurt Hunter, CADC, is a Georgian Elder and NROOGD red cord living in Portland, OR. He was initiated into coven-based Wicca in 1990 and continues to work within former Traditions while presently studying as an honored member of the Temple of Witchcraft. Kurt works as a professional counselor and clinical supervisor and is an avid stone collector, photographer and cat whisperer.

Steve Kenson

Steve Kenson began his esoteric journey with Western Ceremonial Magick, leading him to the works of the Chaos Magick current. His current practice can be described as a mixture of Chaos Magick, ecstatic Witchcraft, and New Orleans Voodoo. He is a co-founder of the Temple of Witchcraft and its Gemini lead minister. A professional author and game designer in tabletop roleplaying games since 1995, Steve is also managing partner of Copper Cauldron Publishing. He maintains a website and blog at *www.stevekenson.com* and lives in Salem, NH, with his partners Adam and Christopher.

Galina Krasskova

Galina Krasskova has been a devotee of the Norse Gods for twenty years. A Northern Tradition shaman and ancestor worker, Galina is also a fairly prolific author. Her books include *Neolithic Shamanism* (with Raven Kaldera), *Exploring the Northern Tradition,* and the first devotional to Odin in modern Heathenry, *The Whisperings of Woden.* She holds a Masters degree in Religious Studies, a diploma in interfaith ministry, and is currently pursuing a PhD in Classics. She maintains a regular blog at *http://krasskova.weebly.com* where she can often be found causing trouble.

Deborah Lipp

Deborah Lipp is the author of six books, including *The Elements of Ritual* and *The Way of Four.* Her memoir, *Merry Meet Again: Lessons, Life & Love on the Path of a Wiccan High Priestess,* is available from Llewellyn Publications.

In no particular order, Deborah is a Gardnerian High Priestess, a blogger, a movie buff, a crazy cat lady, and a mother. Find her at *www.deborahlipp.com*.

Leanne Marrama

Salem Witch Leanne Marrama has been with Festival of the Dead since October of 2004. She currently hosts famous Messages for the Spirit World in Shawn's honor, helping to reunite the living and the dead. Leanne also is proud to host The Mourning Tea, a grand Victorian tradition honoring our dearly departed. Leanne has appeared on TLC's What Not to Wear and currently teaches Glamor and Sex Magic Classes at Omen in Salem in Salem Mass. Leanne Marrama is a reverend and minister in Our Lord and Lady of the Trinacrian Rose Church. She is still a High Priestess and Elder in the coven Raven Moon, the coven Shawn Poirier founded 15 years ago.

Michael Lloyd

Michael Lloyd is a chemical engineer and writer. He is the author of *Bull of Heaven*, the biography of Eddie Buczynski, and is the co-founder and co-facilitator of the Between the Worlds Men's Gathering, an annual spiritual retreat for men who love men. He lives in Columbus, Ohio.

Shea Morgan

Shea Morgan is a founding member of her coven and a priestess of the Morrighan. Shea is a presenter at the annual St. Louis Pagan Picnic, and has contributed essays to *The Green Lovers: A Compilation of Plant Spirit Magic* and *The Waters and Fires of Avalon*. She is a co-founder of Spirit's Edge: A Seeker's Salon, a spiritual community of connection, instruction and spiritual wisdom, offering rituals and workshops (*www.spiritsedge.org*). Shea has been a student of all things spiritual throughout her life, has a particular love of shamanism, and has been on the path of a Witch since 2001. She lives in St. Louis, MO, and enjoys gardening, antiquing, and visiting the family "Century" farm.

Christine Moulton

My name is Christine Moulton, memories of my mother will live with me always as I continue on my own journey through this life on the path of Witchcraft. I believe, as I have said, that this path is not only the most peaceful, but also that embracing the Divine through it, we are better able to establish and accept diversity. While other paths try to "force" the masses to be "like-minded" and molded to specific patterns, Witchcraft opens its arms and embraces all who come to it with an open mind and heart in complete acceptance without "judgment". This to me is the only true way to give oneself completely without looking back with regret, as I have many times in the past when involved with organized religions.

Shani Oates

Shani Oates, a devoted practitioner of "Mysteries" proper, fulfills her Path of Wyrd within the County of Derbyshire (UK) where, true to those tenets intrinsic to her work, she is fully engaged as a mystic, a pilgrim, author, and artist. Though formerly a professional photographer, her lifelong studies and research of theology, philosophy and anthropology eventually coalesced, becoming concrete in her status as the Maid of the Clan of Tubal Cain (see *www.clanoftubalcain.org.uk*). Her published works are included within *Genuine Witchcraft is Revealed* by John of Monmouth (Capal Bann): *The Wanton Green* by various authors (Mandrake of Oxford); *Hecate: Her Sacred Fires* by various authors (Avalonia Press) in addition to many articles appearing in various popular pagan, folklore, and occult publications for over a decade. The second 2011 edition of *Abraxas Occult Journal* features her most recent contribution on the Mysteries. Her debut book *Tubelo's Green Fire* was launched through Mandrake of Oxford in April 2010, followed by *The Arcane Veil* in 2011 and Volume 1 of *The Star Crossed Serpent* in January 2012 & Volume II in June 2012. She is currently working on the third volume that explores and explains further the deeper aspects and histories of her Craft. She has also recently self- published *The People of Goda* on CreateSpace.

Tish Owen

Tish Owen is a woman of abundance. She resides in Nashville, Tennessee with her husband Patrick, two cats who boss everyone, and an African Gray parrot who is much smarter than most humans in the room. She loves her life and is grateful for more things than there is room to list here. Tish is a daughter, a mother, a grandmother, a wife, a friend, owner of The Goddess and the Moon shop in Nashville since 1991, a published author, a seamstress, a sailor, and a brewer. She's written *Spell It Correctly* and *Chasing the Rainbow*, through Willow Tree Press. Long recognized as an authority in the area of psychic phenomena and occult activity, she has lent her expertise to occult crime investigations. Tish is a media staple, appearing on numerous radio, television and print venues. She is the coordinator of the Pagan Unity Festival, the largest festival in the Mid-South. For more information, visit *www.goddessandthemoon.com* and *www.paganunityfestival.org*.

Gede Parma

Gede Parma Akheron is a Wild Witch, Pagan Mystic, initiated Priest and award-winning author of books on Witchcraft and Paganism. He is an initiate and teacher of the WildWood Tradition of Witchcraft and the Anderean Thread of Old Craft; a hereditary healer and seer with Balinese-Anglo-Irish ancestry. He is the lover of and married with nine gorgeous and ever-deep Potencies – Persephone, Aphrodite, Hekate, Hermes, the Blue God, the Weaver, the Green Man, the Crescent-Crowned Goddess and the Horned-Cloaked God. Kali Maa is one of hir most beloved Names and Images of God. Ze is an Anderson Faery Witch (not formally initiated) and a Reclaiming Witch and teacher and is the creator, director and main mentor of a Shamanic Craft Apprenticeship. He is a vessel, a diviner, a spell-caster and spirit-worker who adores the Mysterious Craft. Gede has devoted his life to communities striving for 'excellence and elegance', and that in Love, Truth, and Wisdom commit to walking through the Gates of Paradise and opening to Beauty. He likes to laugh, play, cry, eat, dance, sing, wyrd-out, pray, and make ceremony with other Cunning Folk and Bright Spirits and is earnest in his love of 'dreaming big' and daring to enact those dreams for our Holy-Whole Cosmos. Gede is a poet and priestess of the Black, Wild Heart and endlessly hopes to help others realise the Divine. Gede has an Erotic Relationship with God and would love to see more of this in the World.

Ruby Sara

Poet, essayist and performance artist, Ruby Sara is the author of the blog, "Pagan Godspell," a member of the performance collective Terra Mysterium, and former editor-in-chief for *The Temple Bell*, official newsletter of the Temple of Witchcraft. She lives in Chicago with her intrepid spouse and their demon-monkey-cat, Pinky.

Adam Sartwell

Adam Sartwell began having psychic experiences and studying Witchcraft in his teens. He is a Reiki Master, co-founder, and Virgo lead minister of the Temple of Witchcraft, where he puts his healing and crafting skills to work making incense, candles, potions, and herbal preparations for the community. Adam lives in Salem, NH, with his partners (and Temple co-founders) Steve Kenson and Christopher Penczak.

Matthew Sawicki

Matthew Sawicki hails from Pennsylvania and has been interested in the magical arts since he was a boy, having been introduced to them by the spirit of the mountains where he grew up and the famous witches in the Disney movies he saw as a child. He is living out his dream of making potions and working magic as a professional psychic reader and Witch with many happy clients all over the world.

Matthew is currently an initiate of the Clan of Tubal Cain under the tutelage of Shani Oates and also works in the Hoodoo and Rootwork traditions of the American South. He still honors his Gardnerian lineage and continues to take on Craft students very selectively.

Matthew can be contacted via his website *www.witchandfamous.com*

Scott A. Sherter

Scott A. Sherter is a western Massachusetts native, whose childhood love of the outdoors along with strong psychic experiences led him to first discovering Wicca in his teenage years. He is a priest of the Norse god Freyr and currently resides in Colorado.

SilverMoone

SilverMoone is a Shamanic Buddhist Witch, Clinical Hypnotherapist, priestess, teacher, healer, writer, seeker…Her spiritual journey has taken her to the deepest layers of Self, where she finds the heart of her personal practice is devotion. Her vocation has led her to embracing the teachings of Womyn's Empowerment and Mysteries and facilitating the journey of re-birthing into Spirit.

Andrew Theitic

Theitic, publisher of *The Witches' Almanac* and the *Olympian Press*, was born in 1956 in Rhode Island. A longtime friend of Elizabeth Pepper, he began his extensive witchcraft studies in 1969, founding the Center for Exoteric Research and Esoteric Studies (C.E.R.E.S.) in 1975. Theitic was initiated into the N.E.C.T.W. (New England Covens of Traditionalist Witches) in 1976. Theitic serves as historian for the N.E.C.T.W. He also works with a Ceremonial Magic tradition and has been initiated into Palo Mayombé, Santeria, traditional Nigerian spiritual practices, and the Alexandrian Tradition. Theitic owned The Flaming Cauldron, a metaphysical and occult store in Rhode Island and is the co-author (with Robert Mathiesen) of *The Rede of the Wiccae* (Olympian Press). A 32nd degree Freemason, Theitic is executive director of Acts of Kindness (*www.a-o-k.org*); Sacred Ground (*www.sacred-ground.org*), and the Society of the Evening Star (S.O.T.E.S.) (*www.sotes.org*). He resides in Providence with his partner Thor and their beloved dog, Dana.

Timothy Titus

Tim Titus is a psychology teacher and Pagan blogger from southern California. He specializes in analyzing live theater from a Pagan perspective. His work appears in *The Juggler,* a blog within the

Pagan Newswire Collective. He also is a regular contributor to *Modern Witch Magazine* and the new *Modern Witch Online*.

Kala Trobe

Kala Trobe is an author and artist whose published books include *A Witch's Guide to Life, Magick of Qabalah,* and several works of esoterically-inclined literary fiction. She is currently studying for a PhD in Literature and completing a trilogy of novels. She lives in Glastonbury, UK, with her husband Jonny and kitties, Pesky and Bluff.

Virginia Villarreal

Virginia Villarreal is currently a 4th year student of the Temple of Witchcraft. She is also very open in her spirituality and wants to be of service to the Pagan Community. She is a local coordinator of Houston Pagan Pride Day as well as the co-coordinator of CROWs and coordinator of GLBT Pagan Pride.

Rich Wandel

Rich Wandel, is the High Priest and co-leader of Polyhymnia, a Gardnerian Coven in New York City. Archivist, historian, and storyteller, he is nationally known as an advocate for community history and is the founding archivist of the New York LGBT Community Center's National History Archive.

Paul Weston

Paul lives in Glastonbury, the mystical capital of Britain. He is the author of *Avalonian Aeon, Aleister Crowley and the Aeon of Horus*, and *Mysterium Artorius*. With a background in Reiki, Psychic Questing, the Fellowship of Isis, Druidry, and a wide variety of western and eastern paths, his frequent lectures cover extensive and often unique ground.

About the Editor

Christopher Penczak is a teacher and co-founder of the Temple of Witchcraft and the author of numerous books, including the *Three Rays of Witchcraft, Plant Spirit Familiar, The Gates of Witchcraft, Feast of the Morrighan, The Might Dead,* and *Buddha, Christ, Merlin.* For more information, visit his website at *www.christopherpenczak.com.*

The Temple of Witchcraft
MYSTERY SCHOOL AND SEMINARY

Witchcraft is a tradition of experience, and the best way to experience the path of the Witch is to actively train in its magickal and spiritual lessons. The Temple of Witchcraft provides a complete system of training and tradition, with four degrees found in the Mystery School for personal and magickal development and a fifth degree in the Seminary for the training of High Priestesses and High Priests interested in serving the gods, spirits, and community as ministers. Teachings are divided by degree into the Oracular, Fertility, Ecstatic, Gnostic, and Resurrection Mysteries. Training emphasizes the ability to look within, awaken your own gifts and abilities, and perform both lesser and greater magicks for your own evolution and the betterment of the world around you. The Temple of Witchcraft offers both in-person and online courses with direct teaching and mentorship. Classes use the *Temple of Witchcraft* series of books and CD Companions as primary texts, supplemented monthly with information from the Temple's Book of Shadows, MP3 recordings of lectures and meditations from our founders, social support through group discussion with classmates, and direct individual feedback from a mentor.

For more information and current schedules, please visit: *www.templeofwitchcraft.org*.

www.ingramcontent.com/pod-product-compliance
Lightning Source LLC
Chambersburg PA
CBHW060106170426
43198CB00010B/782